Francis Frith's
Villages of Sussex

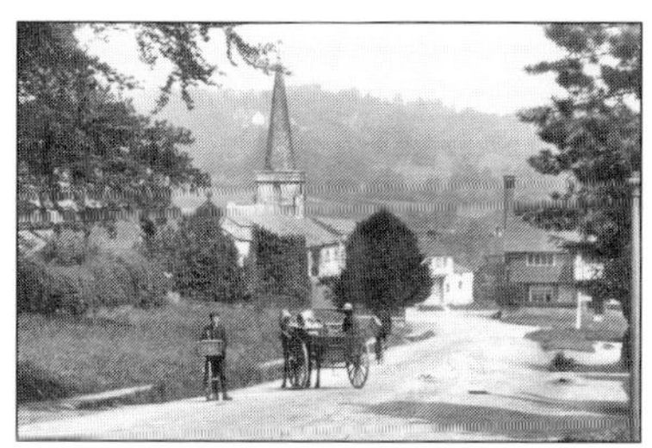

Photographic Memories

Francis Frith's
Villages of Sussex

Anthony Bryan

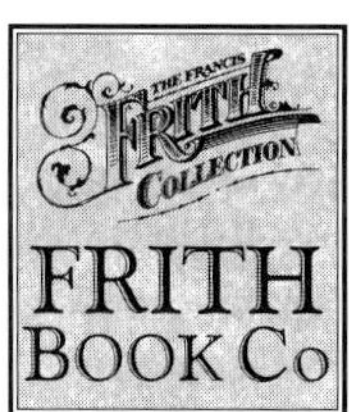

FRITH
BOOK Co

First published in the United Kingdom in 2001 by
Frith Book Company Ltd

Paperback Edition 2001
ISBN 1-85937-295-3

Hardback Edition 2001
ISBN 1-85937-446-8

British Library Cataloguing in Publication Data

Francis Frith's Villages of Sussex
Anthony Bryan

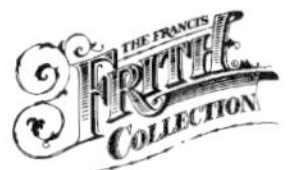

Frith Book Company Ltd
Frith's Barn, Teffont,
Salisbury, Wiltshire SP3 5QP
Tel: +44 (0) 1722 716 376
Email: info@francisfrith.co.uk
www.francisfrith.co.uk

Printed and bound in Great Britain

Front Cover: Billingshurst, Church Causeway 1912 64881

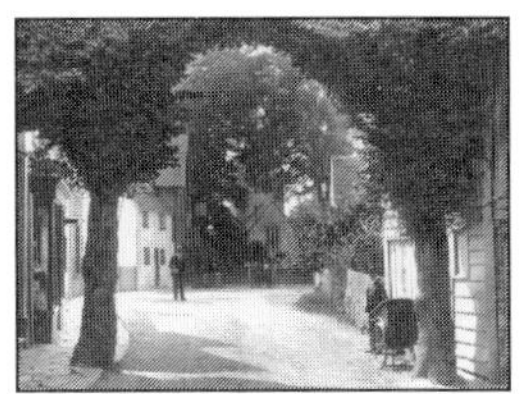

Contents

Francis Frith: *Victorian Pioneer*

FRANCIS FRITH, Victorian founder of the world-famous photographic archive, was a complex and multi-talented man. A devout Quaker and a highly successful Victorian businessman, he was both philosophic by nature and pioneering in outlook.

By 1855 Francis Frith had already established a wholesale grocery business in Liverpool, and sold it for the astonishing sum of £200,000, which is the equivalent today of over £15,000,000. Now a multi-millionaire, he was able to indulge his passion for travel. As a child he had pored over travel books written by early explorers, and his fancy and imagination had been stirred by family holidays to the sublime mountain regions of Wales and Scotland. 'What a land of spirit-stirring and enriching scenes and places!' he had written. He was to return to these scenes of grandeur in later years to 'recapture the thousands of vivid and tender memories', but with a different purpose. Now in his thirties, and captivated by the new science of photography, Frith set out on a series of pioneering journeys to the Nile regions that occupied him from 1856 until 1860.

Intrigue and Adventure

He took with him on his travels a specially-designed wicker carriage that acted as both dark-room and sleeping chamber. These far-flung journeys were packed with intrigue and adventure. In his life story, written when he was sixty-three, Frith tells of being held captive by bandits, and of fighting 'an awful midnight battle to the very point of surrender with a deadly pack of hungry, wild dogs'. Sporting flowing Arab costume, Frith arrived at Akaba by camel seventy years before Lawrence, where he encountered 'desert princes and rival sheikhs, blazing with jewel-hilted swords'.

During these extraordinary adventures he was assiduously exploring the desert regions bordering the Nile and patiently recording the antiquities and peoples with his camera. He was the first photographer to venture beyond the sixth cataract. Africa was still the mysterious 'Dark Continent', and Stanley and Livingstone's historic meeting was a decade into the future. The conditions for picture taking confound belief. He laboured for hours in his wicker dark-room in the sweltering heat of the desert, while the volatile chemicals fizzed dangerously in their trays. Often he was forced to work in remote tombs and caves where conditions were cooler. Back in London he exhibited his photographs and was 'rapturously cheered' by members of the Royal Society. His reputation as a photographer was made overnight. An eminent modern historian has likened their impact on the population of the time to that on our own generation of the first photographs taken on the surface of the moon.

Venture of a Life-Time

Characteristically, Frith quickly spotted the opportunity to create a new business as a specialist publisher of photographs. He lived in an era of immense and sometimes violent change. For the poor in the early part of Victoria's reign work was a drudge and the hours long, and people had precious little free time to enjoy themselves. Most had no transport other than a cart or gig at their disposal, and had not travelled far beyond the boundaries of their own town or village. However, by the 1870s, the railways had threaded their way across the country, and Bank Holidays and half-day Saturdays had been made obligatory by Act of Parliament. All of a sudden the ordinary working man and his family were able to enjoy days out and see a little more of the world.

With characteristic business acumen, Francis Frith foresaw that these new tourists would enjoy having souvenirs to commemorate their days out. In 1860 he married Mary Ann Rosling and set out with the intention of photographing every city, town and village in Britain. For the next thirty years he travelled the country by train and by pony and trap, producing fine photographs of seaside resorts and beauty spots that were keenly bought by millions of Victorians. These prints were painstakingly pasted into family albums and pored over during the dark nights of winter, rekindling precious memories of summer excursions.

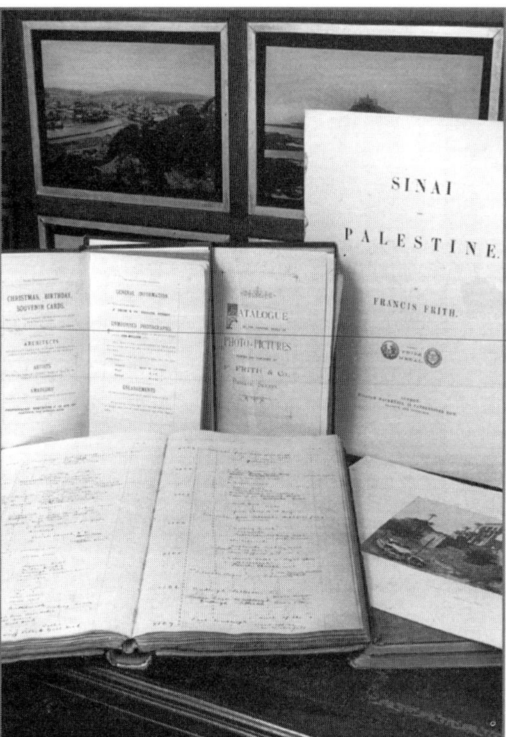

The Rise of Frith & Co

Frith's studio was soon supplying retail shops all over the country. To meet the demand he gathered about him a small team of photographers, and published the work of independent artist-photographers of the calibre of Roger Fenton and Francis Bedford. In order to gain some understanding of the scale of Frith's business one only has to look at the catalogue issued by Frith & Co in 1886: it runs to some 670 pages, listing not only many thousands of views of the British Isles but also many photographs of most European countries, and China, Japan, the USA and Canada — note the sample page shown above from the hand-written *Frith & Co* ledgers detailing pictures taken. By 1890 Frith had created the greatest specialist photographic publishing company in the world,

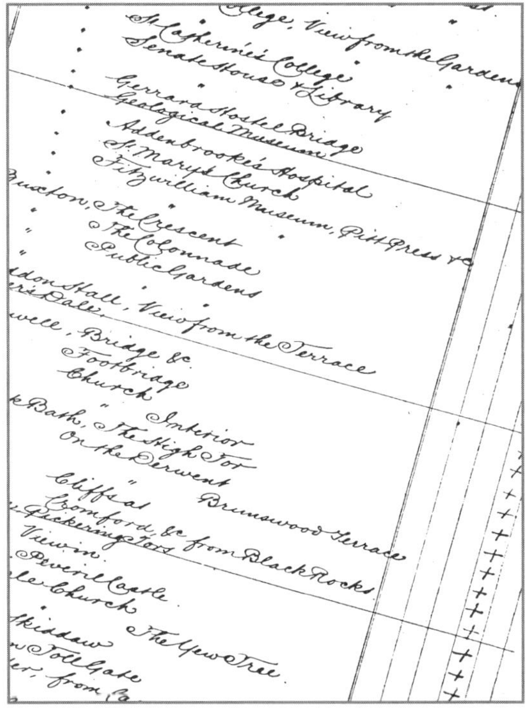

with over 2,000 outlets – more than the combined number that Boots and WH Smith have today! The picture on the right shows the *Frith & Co* display board at Ingleton in the Yorkshire Dales. Beautifully constructed with mahogany frame and gilt inserts, it could display up to a dozen local scenes.

Postcard Bonanza

The ever-popular holiday postcard we know today took many years to develop. In 1870 the Post Office issued the first plain cards, with a pre-printed stamp on one face. In 1894 they allowed other publishers' cards to be sent through the mail with an attached adhesive halfpenny stamp. Demand grew rapidly, and in 1895 a new size of postcard was permitted called the court card, but there was little room for illustration. In 1899, a year after

Frith's death, a new card measuring 5.5 x 3.5 inches became the standard format, but it was not until 1902 that the divided back came into being, with address and message on one face and a full-size illustration on the other. *Frith & Co* were in the vanguard of postcard development, and Frith's sons Eustace and Cyril continued their father's monumental task, expanding the number of views offered to the public and recording more and more places in Britain, as the coasts and countryside were opened up to mass travel.

Francis Frith died in 1898 at his villa in Cannes, his great project still growing. The archive he created continued in business for another seventy years. By 1970 it contained over a third of a million pictures of 7,000 cities, towns and villages. The massive photographic record Frith has left to us stands as a living monument to a special and very remarkable man.

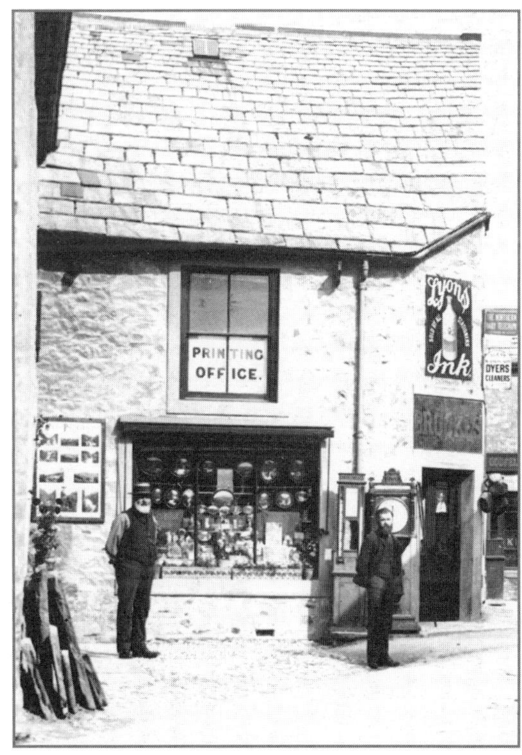

Frith's Archive: *A Unique Legacy*

FRANCIS FRITH'S legacy to us today is of immense significance and value, for the magnificent archive of evocative photographs he created provides a unique record of change in 7,000 cities, towns and villages throughout Britain over a century and more. Frith and his fellow studio photographers revisited locations many times down the years to update their views, compiling for us an enthralling and colourful pageant of British life and character.

We tend to think of Frith's sepia views of Britain as nostalgic, for most of us use them to conjure up memories of places in our own lives with which we have family associations. It often makes us forget that to Francis Frith they were records of daily life as it was actually being lived in the cities, towns and villages of his day. The Victorian age was one of great and often bewildering change for ordinary people, and though the pictures evoke an impression of slower times, life was as busy and hectic as it is today.

We are fortunate that Frith was a photographer of the people, dedicated to recording the minutiae of everyday life. For it is this sheer wealth of visual data, the painstaking chronicle of changes in dress, transport, street layouts, buildings, housing, engineering and landscape that captivates us so much today. His remarkable images offer us a powerful link with the past and with the lives of our ancestors.

Today's Technology

Computers have now made it possible for Frith's many thousands of images to be accessed almost instantly. In the Frith archive today, each photograph is carefully 'digitised' then stored on a CD Rom. Frith archivists can locate a single photograph amongst thousands within seconds. Views can be catalogued and sorted under a variety of categories of place and content to the immediate benefit of researchers.

Inexpensive reference prints can be created for them at the touch of a mouse button, and a wide range of books and other printed materials assembled and published for a wider, more general readership - in the next twelve months over a hundred Frith local history titles will be published! The day-to-day workings of the archive are very different from how they were in Francis Frith's time: imagine the herculean task of sorting through eleven tons of glass negatives as Frith had to do to locate a particular sequence of pictures! Yet

See Frith at www. frithbook.co.uk

the archive still prides itself on maintaining the same high standards of excellence laid down by Francis Frith, including the painstaking cataloguing and indexing of every view.

It is curious to reflect on how the internet now allows researchers in America and elsewhere greater instant access to the archive than Frith himself ever enjoyed. Many thousands of individual views can be called up on screen within seconds on one of the Frith internet sites, enabling people living continents away to revisit the streets of their ancestral home town, or view places in Britain where they have enjoyed holidays. Many overseas researchers welcome the chance to view special theme selections, such as transport, sports, costume and ancient monuments.

We are certain that Francis Frith would have heartily approved of these modern developments in imaging techniques, for he himself was always working at the very limits of Victorian photographic technology.

The Value of the Archive Today

Because of the benefits brought by the computer, Frith's images are increasingly studied by social historians, by researchers into genealogy and ancestory, by architects, town planners, and by teachers and schoolchildren involved in local history projects.

In addition, the archive offers every one of us an opportunity to examine the places where we and our families have lived and worked down the years. Highly successful in Frith's own era, the archive is now, a century and more on, entering a new phase of popularity.

The Past in Tune with the Future

Historians consider the Francis Frith Collection to be of prime national importance. It is the only archive of its kind remaining in private ownership and has been valued at a million pounds. However, this figure is now rapidly increasing as digital technology enables more and more people around the world to enjoy its benefits.

Francis Frith's archive is now housed in an historic timber barn in the beautiful village of Teffont in Wiltshire. Its founder would not recognize the archive office as it is today. In place of the many thousands of dusty boxes containing glass plate negatives and an all-pervading odour of photographic chemicals, there are now ranks of computer screens. He would be amazed to watch his images travelling round the world at unimaginable speeds through network and internet lines.

The archive's future is both bright and exciting. Francis Frith, with his unshakeable belief in making photographs available to the greatest number of people, would undoubtedly approve of what is being done today with his lifetime's work. His photographs, depicting our shared past, are now bringing pleasure and enlightenment to millions around the world a century and more after his death.

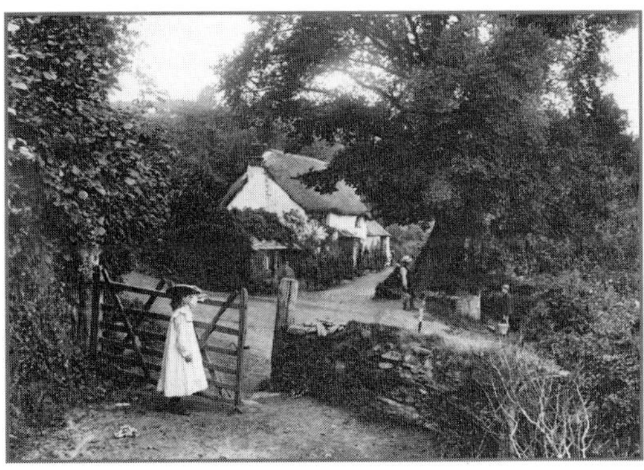

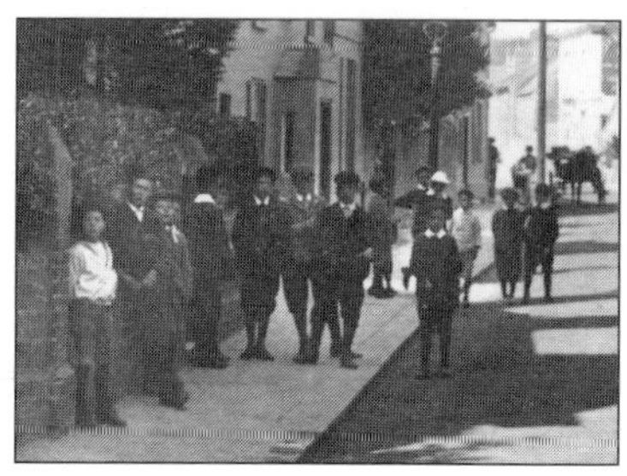

Villages of Sussex - *An Introduction*

Sussex is a county of great landscape variations and contrasts, from smooth green hills down to flat marshland, all within quite small distances. The coastline has huge chalk cliffs leading down to shingle beaches; there are also sandy beaches near river estuaries and in the eastern and western extremities. The type of settlement and buildings vary with the local conditions. The pictures in this book are arranged in four sections, Forest, Weald, Downs and Coast - these sections correspond to the differing topography and underlying geology.

Forest

The forest ridge is the high ground at the northern border of Sussex; from it the land gradually slopes down southwards towards the Weald. It is an area of smaller villages and panoramic views from hilltops. It is forested with mixed woodland that forms an important timber resource. In the past, the forests fuelled a nationally-important iron industry that pre-dated the smelting of iron by using coal. The fuel used was charcoal: this was made from wood as a renewable resource obtained by coppicing managed woodlands. Iron ore was also mined in the forests. Artificial ponds provided water power.

Weald

The Weald is a flattish region of heavy land situated between the forest ridge and the scarp edge of the South Downs. It is an agricultural region of arable land with fairly small fields and mixed

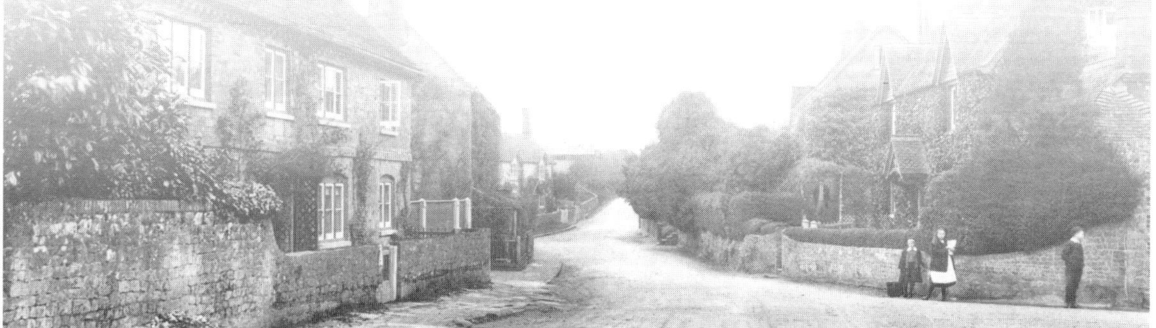

farming. The famous Sussex oak trees can be seen in the woods, hedgerows and fields; the oak trees produced strong timber for shipbuilding and for the framing of half-timbered houses. Large and ever-expanding villages extend along the main roads. Bricks and tiles are made from local mineral deposits, and are used a lot in local building construction. A ridge of sandstone, the Hastings beds, extends from the centre of the Weald south-eastwards and ends in substantial cliffs on the coast at Hastings, near the Conqueror's Castle. Sandstone was used as a building material.

Downs

The South Downs are a range of chalk hills extending from Salisbury Plain across Hampshire to the Sussex border, and then south-eastwards across Sussex to Beachy Head. Here, they terminate in slowly eroding cliff faces. The Downs are smooth in contour and mainly grassed over; they are used for sheep and cattle grazing, and sometimes for cornfields. Walking on the South Downs Way is a popular activity - from it there are panoramic views. Downland villages are often small and hilly, with the settlements following natural land contours. Chalk and flint provides building materials, and also lime for improving the land.

Coast

The English Channel forms the southern boundary of Sussex. The South Downs smoothly slope downwards towards the sea, and these lands contain the larger coastal towns. Ports on the coast have brought trade and invaders, and the fishermen who lived in the coastal villages provided fresh food. The beaches were a vast source of flint pebbles, which were widely used as walling for buildings and land enclosure.

A lot of the smaller villages have now been absorbed into nearby towns. Villages with harbours have been conserved, and retain a lot of their old-world charm, and coastal hamlets survive, some at the top of high cliffs, with great coastal views. Shingle beaches are a feature of the central part of the coastline, while sandy beaches are found near the river estuaries and the flat areas to the eastern and western extremities of the coastline and in the sandstone cliff area near Hastings.

Village Life

Village life was centred on the shop, public house, church, village hall, school, telephone kiosk and bus stop and shelter, and all were bound together by the availability of local employment. Examples of these are seen in the pictures. The postal service is important to village life. Most villages have a Post Office: many are pictured in this book, together with posting boxes and stamp vending machines.

Modes of travel have progressed from the time when local workers walked to their workplace, and when wealthy people used horse-drawn carriages

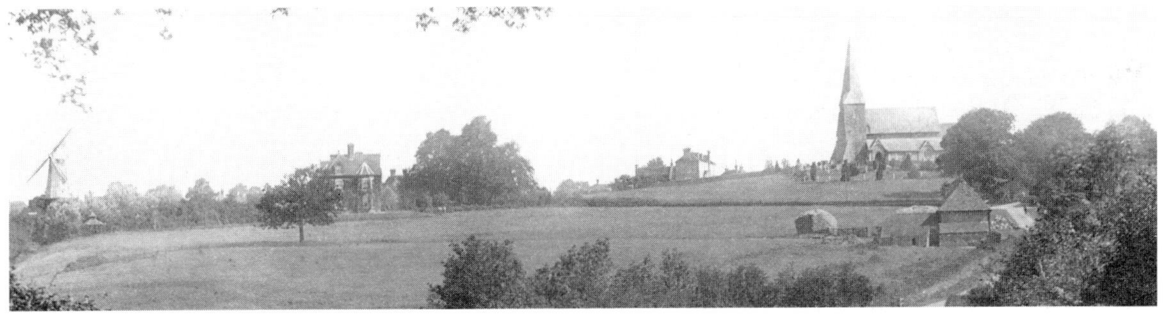

and stagecoaches for local and trunk travel. When the stone-chip roads were smooth enough, the bicycle was useful for local personal travel. Motor transport came along with smoother roads, and enabled more journeys to the towns. Railways provided some villages with reliable travel to anywhere in the country. In recent years, the construction of international railways and airports has made journeys to anywhere in the world quickly accessible from anywhere in Sussex.

Sussex has many large country estates; in private ownership, they were a complete and very self-sufficient entity. Their main business was agricultural and horticultural production, together with pleasure activities. The very large estates had their own timberyards, brickworks and blacksmiths, and they also retained their own building tradesmen. Some villages were created solely to service the needs of a country estate. Many country estates have now been dispersed by being sold in separate lots.

Changes in village life from 1900 to 1950 were greatly accelerated by two world wars. Government control of agriculture in both world wars caused big changes in country life, which were mainly brought about by enforced mechanisation. Agricultural workers who could be spared were called up into the armed services; this caused wartime shortages of male workers, which led to a much greater use of female workers on farms and in rural industries. By the end of both wars, fewer manual workers were needed in agriculture, and draught animals were progressively phased out. Village war memorials are seen in several of our photographs. Also, many country estates did not survive the two wars intact. This was partly owing to shortages of labour and materials. Many large country houses were requisitioned by the government for wartime purposes, and did not return to family domestic use. Labour costs rose after the Second World War, so estate workers were kept to a minimum. Several Sussex country houses were war-damaged, but this was often owing to unfortunate accidents rather than enemy action.

The changes in village life since 1950 happened in a sequence that is still progressing. Personal transport was a catalyst of change - the bicycle, the motor cycle and then the car. The motor car caused the really big change, which was from about 1960 onwards. At first, the car was used as family transport, for shopping and for exploration on trips and holidays. From 1980 onwards, the car became personal transport, so that several members of a family could work, socialise and shop in different places. The increasing use of road transport in villages is recorded in our photographs. The effect of family and personal transport on village life was that the profitability of the local shop was greatly reduced, and so was the viability of rural bus routes. The shops became run-down, and many closed because they could not compete on price and variety of goods with the new supermarkets in the

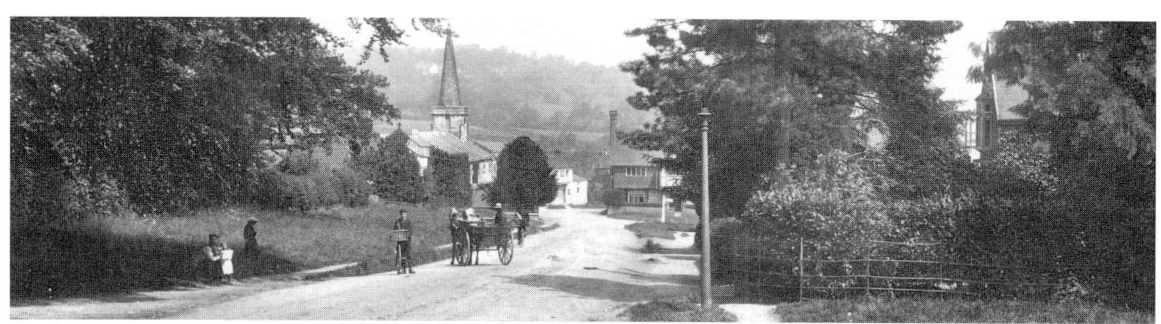

towns. Bus routes were cut back, and smaller vehicles operated a reduced service to fewer destinations.

Very recent changes affecting village life are the mobile telephone and high fuel and car ownership costs. The mobile phone has brought personal communication to all, wherever they may be, so public telephone kiosks are little-used and non-viable. High fuel costs make energy-efficient homes desirable. High transport costs reduce the profitability of commuting, so working from home is attractive. The telecommunications service providers will need to be able to offer fast data circuits in rural areas, so that those villagers working from home can communicate with their customers. High fuel costs may help village shops to survive as convenience stores, for it is not economic to travel far to a shop by car to collect small orders. We can see many examples of small village shops in the photographs in this book.

The existence of large international airports in the region affects village life considerably, even where aircraft noise is not a problem. Airports employ thousands of shift workers who need personal transport to get to work, so they prefer to live in the countryside. Also, regular airline customers find it convenient to live in the countryside near an airport. Aircraft components are sometimes serviced in specialised workshop facilities in converted farm buildings. This all brings life, employment and prosperity to an up-to-date village. New developments of large modern family homes in and around villages have brought an influx of new residents, and the conversion of older houses and agricultural buildings into dwellings has become very popular. Village public houses (we can see many pubs pictured in this book) have survived, because many now offer restaurant facilities which suit a modern lifestyle.

The Future

The conservation of villages and areas of outstanding natural beauty will proceed apace, and there will be a greatly increased rural residential population. In recent years, Sussex has been practically divided into two halves, east and west, by trunk road and rail routes between London and Brighton; further expansion of road and rail routes is inevitable, and some closed rail routes are likely be re-instated. The Channel Tunnel road terminal near Folkestone and the international railway station at Ashford, both not far over the Kent-Sussex border, have started to bring international tourism to the eastern end of Sussex.

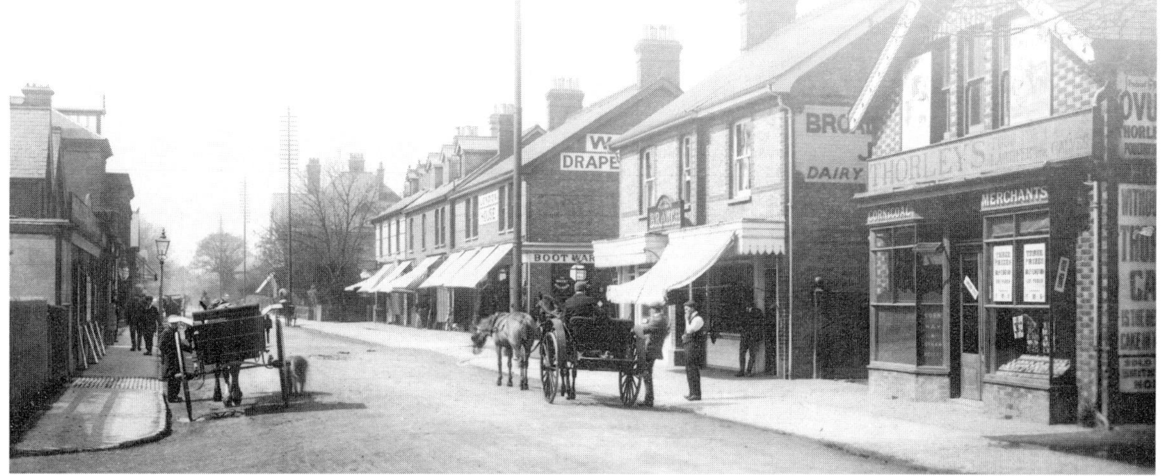

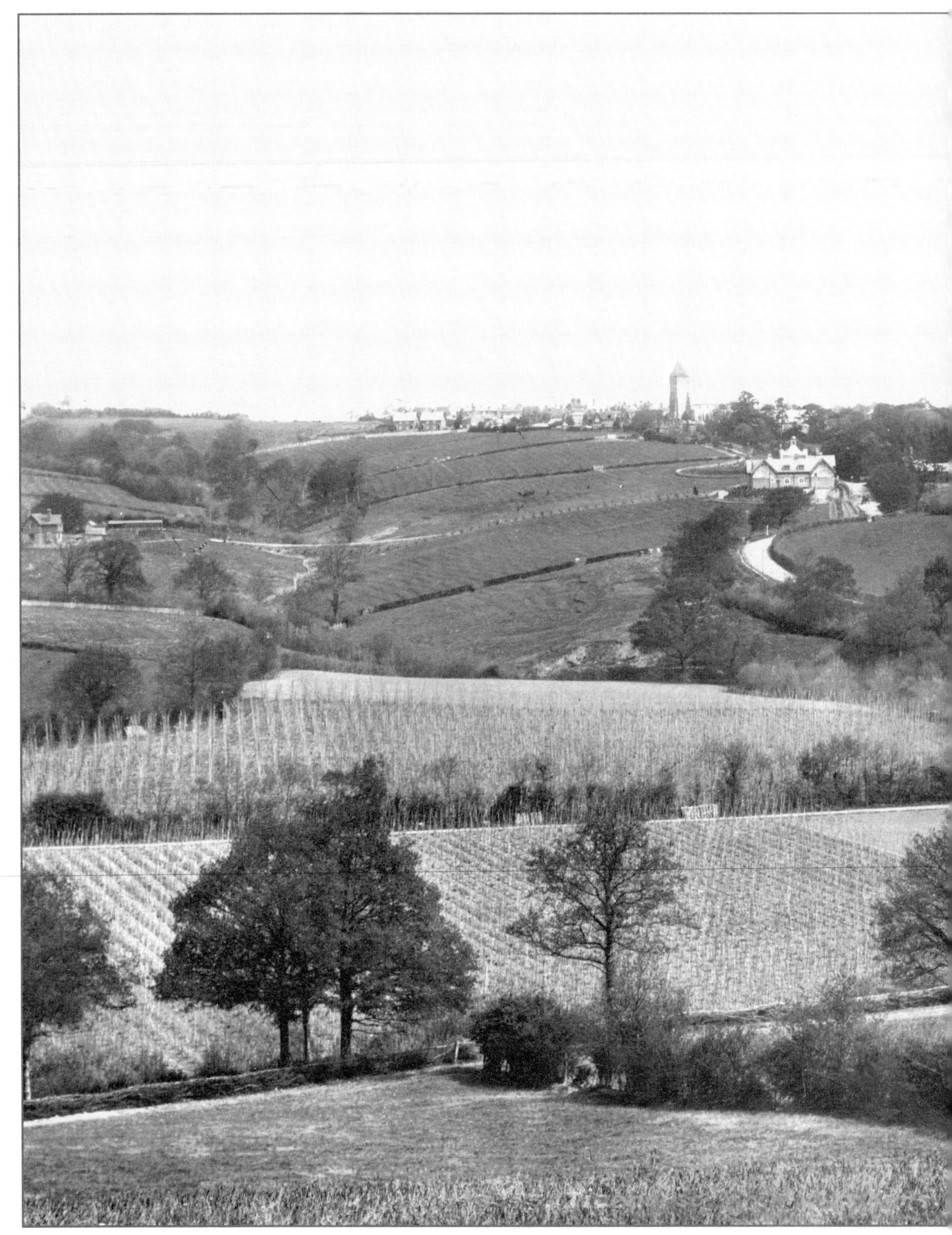

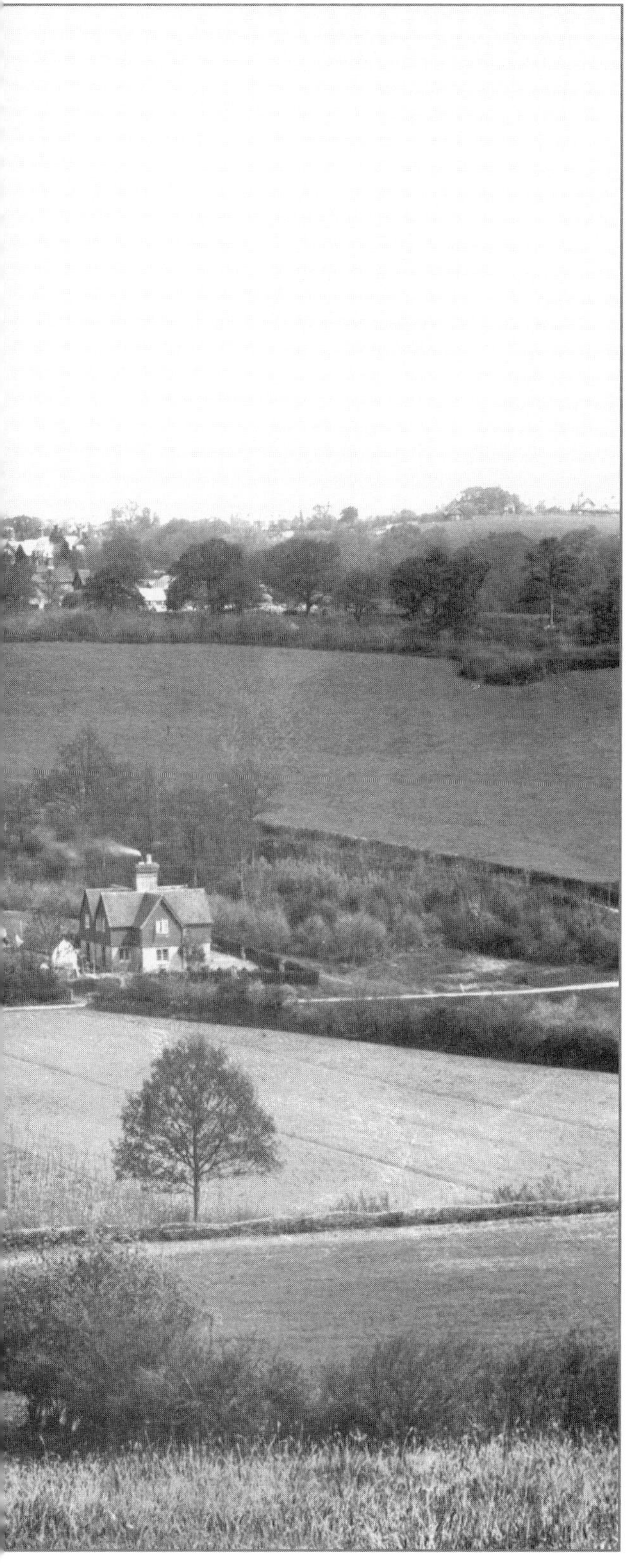

The Forest

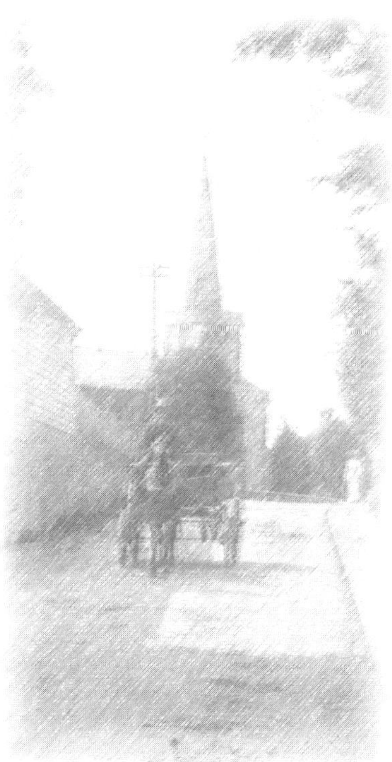

Ticehurst, From Myskyns 1903 49345
Ticehurst is an old Roman habitation near the Kent border. Situated on a hilltop in rolling countryside among hopfields, it has fine views. St Mary's 14th-century church has a conspicuous broach spire and some 15th-century painted glass. Nearby, Pashley is a 17th-century manor house with beautiful gardens.

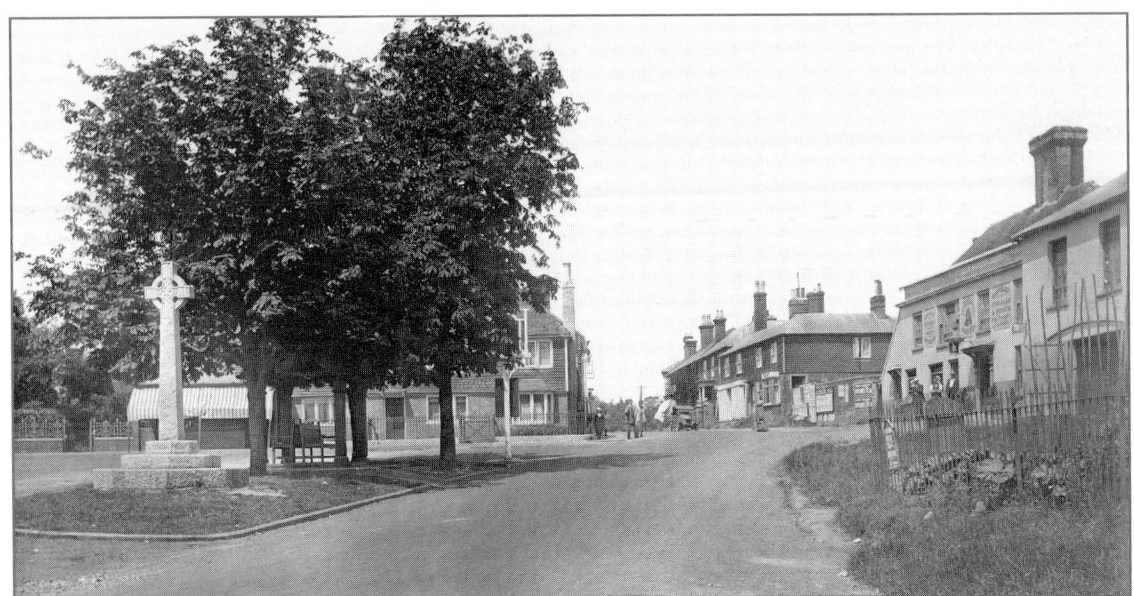

Ticehurst, The Square 1925 76997

The rendered façade of the Bell Inn, a 14th-century coaching inn, has now been removed, exposing a fine timber-framed building with a conserved interior. The Duke of York Inn is on the left-hand side of the square, and the church is nearby. Whiligh is a 16th-century house; timbers for Westminster Hall in London were cut from trees felled on the estate in the late 14th century. Dunster's Mill House was a 15th-century semi-aisled hall house with an associated watermill; it has now been moved because the old site is inundated by the new Bewl Water reservoir.

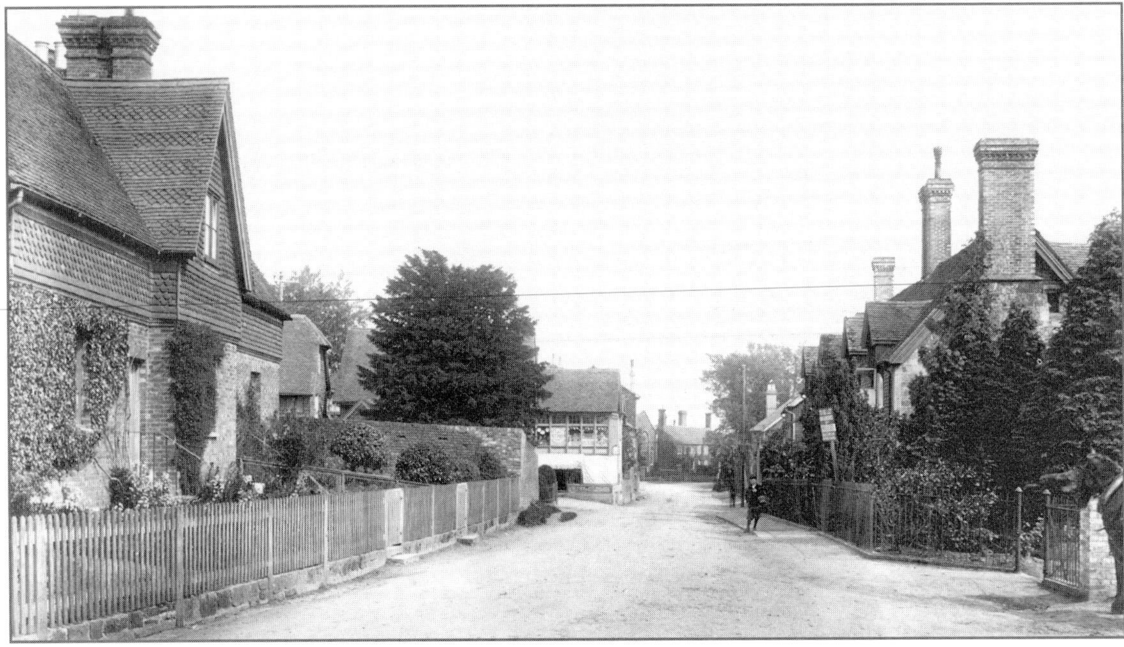

Wadhurst, High Street 1903 49367

The quiet street scene gives no hint of an industrial past. All we can see in this photograph are cottages and the village shop. It had a weekly market from 1253 until it was closed in 1982. The last bare-fisted boxing match was held in Wadhurst in 1863. The street is now very busy with traffic and people.

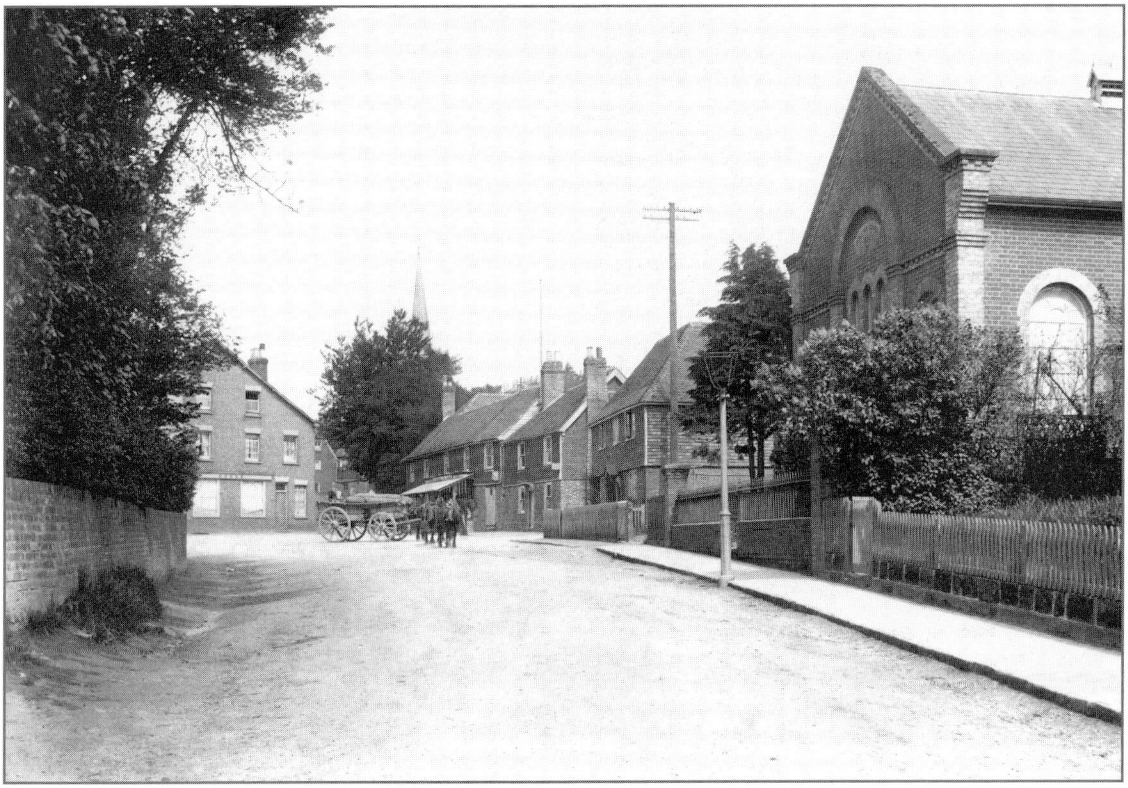

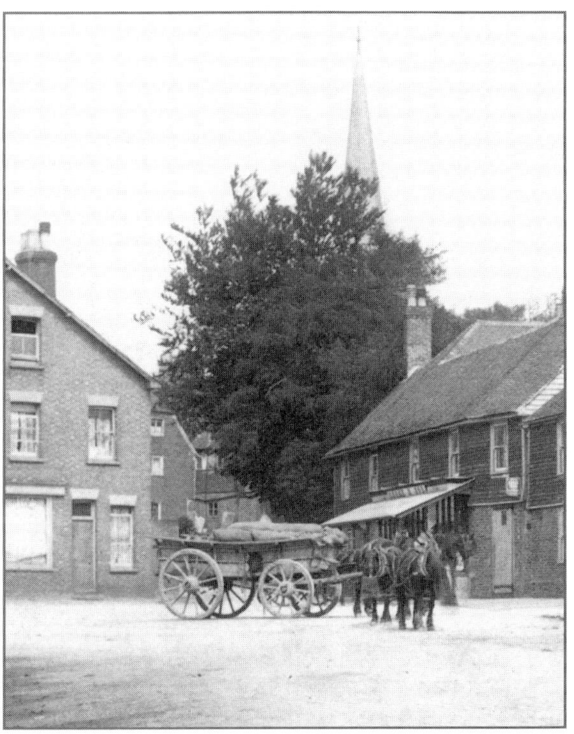

Wadhurst, High Street 1903 49366
Wadhurst is high up in the forest ridge and was noted for its market and iron industry.
The church of St Peter and St Paul has many cast iron graveslabs in the floor. They are mainly of the Barham family who were ironmasters and landowners in the era of the Sussex iron industry 1617-1799 - the last iron-smelting furnace closed in 1808. In the picture, the spire of the church is visible above the trees on the hilltop.

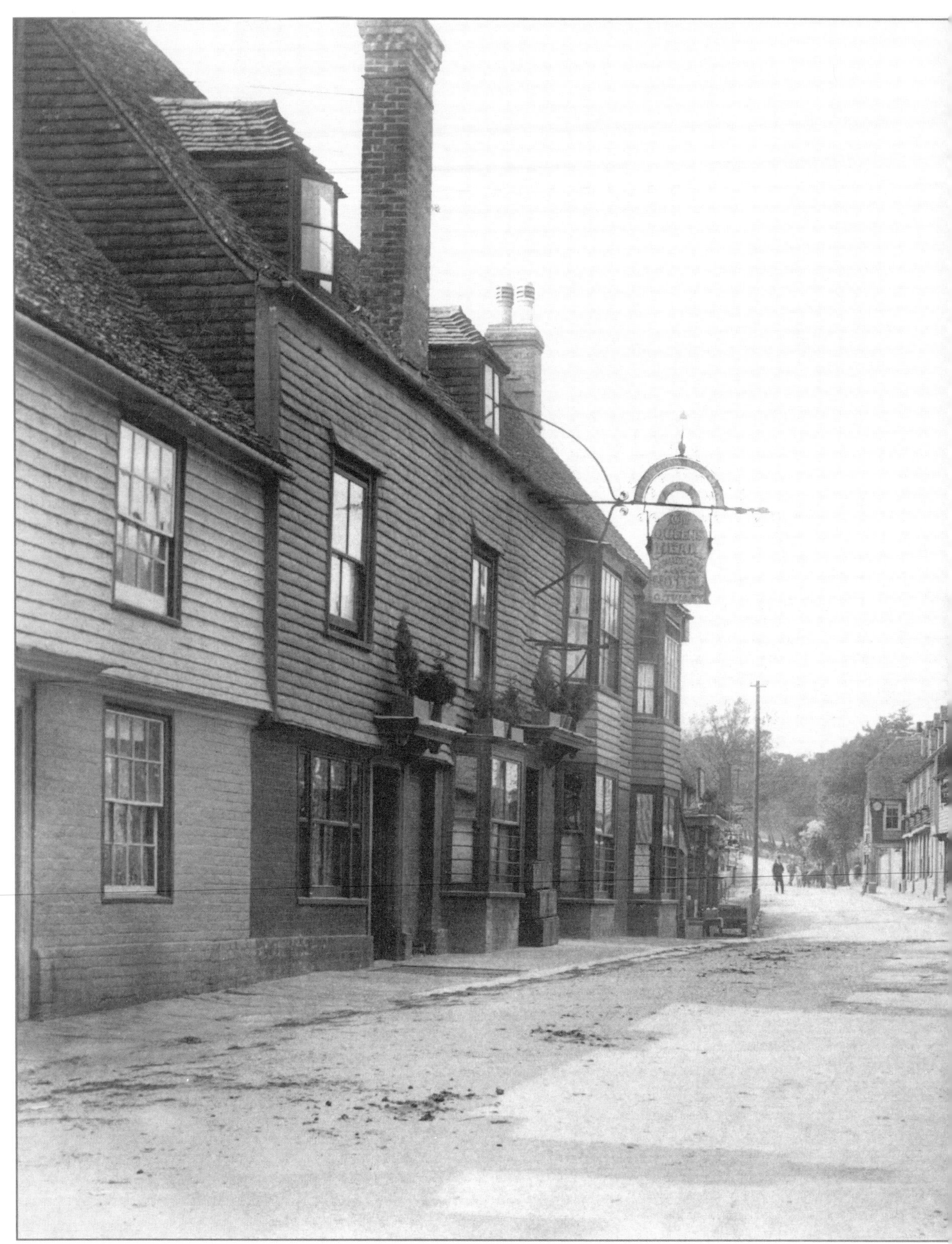

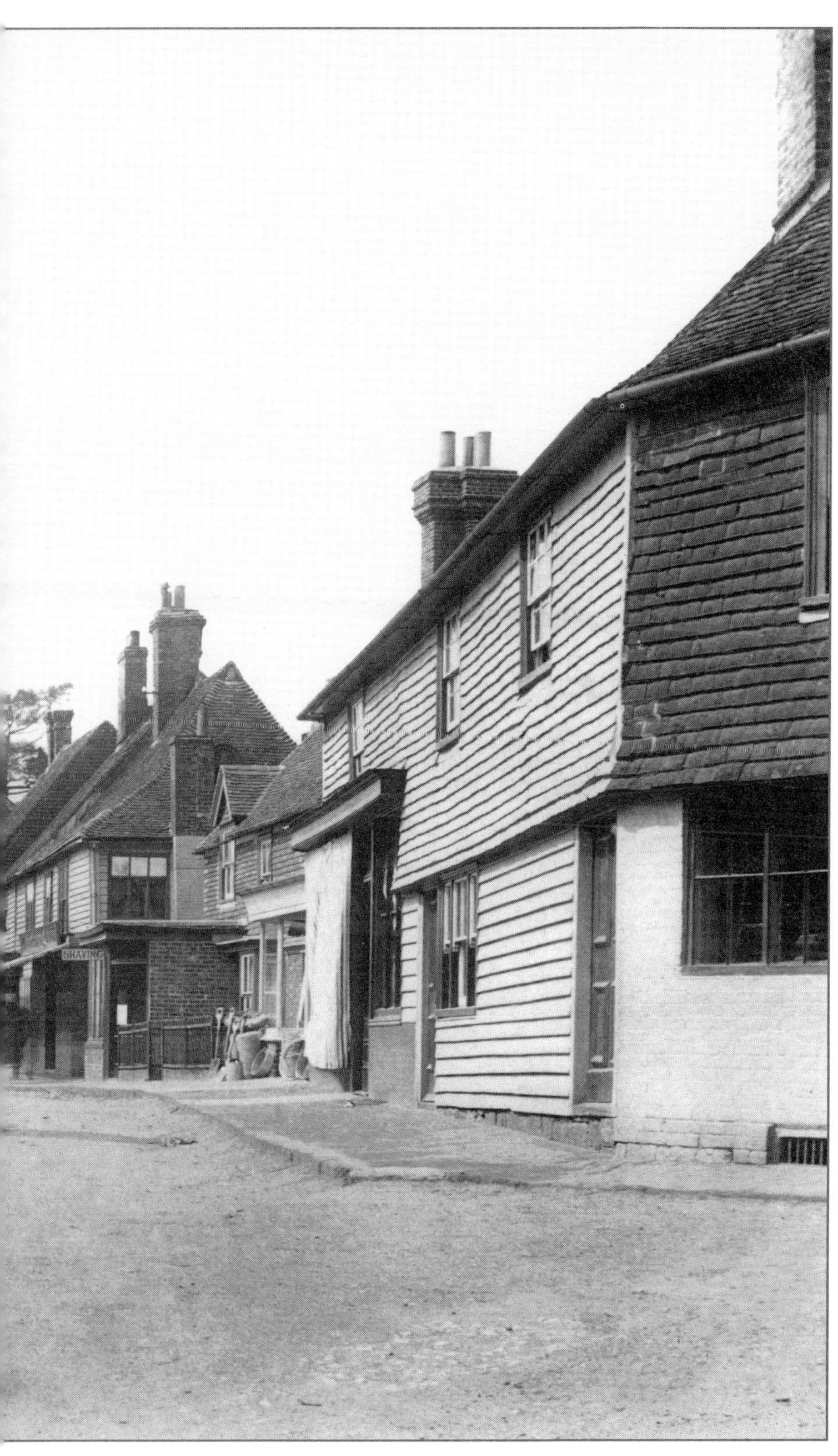

Wadhurst, High Street 1903 W4501
A sign outside the old barber's shop offers 'Shaving', while tools and hardware stand outside another shop. A fine sign overhangs the road - it reads 'The Queen's Head Commercial Hotel, C Tulley proprietor'. High Street was devastated in 1956 by an air accident involving a Meteor jet fighter aircraft. Many buildings were destroyed, including The Queens Head Hotel, and have been replaced by modern shop units.

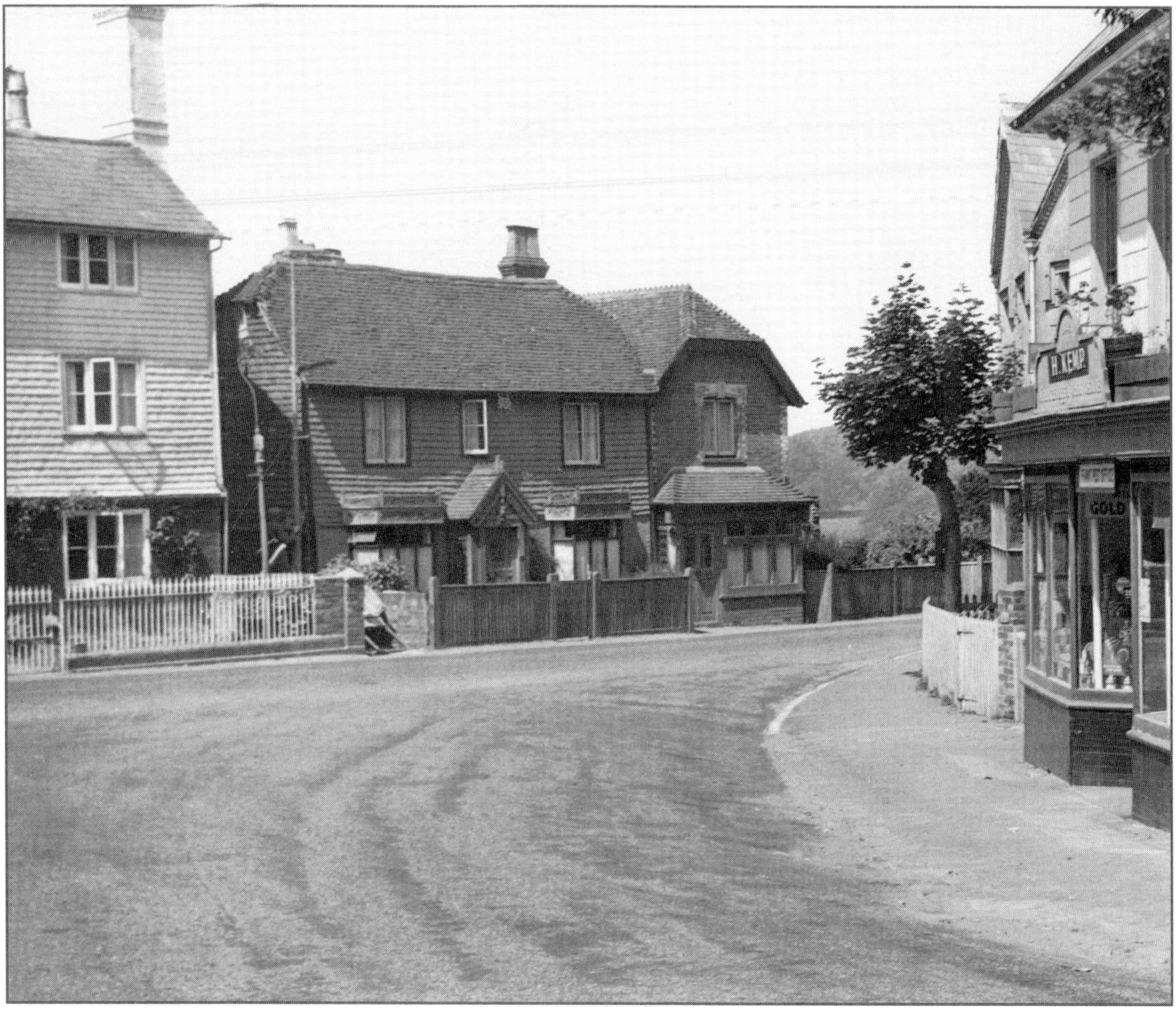

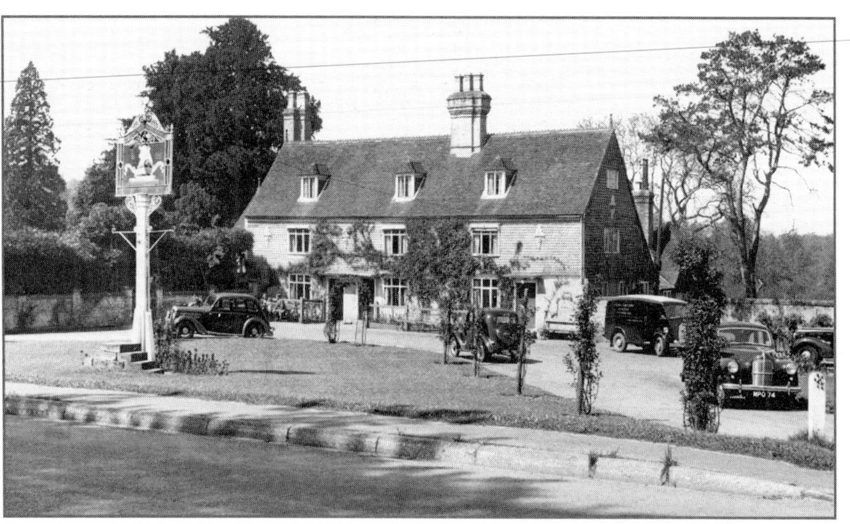

Eridge Green, The Nevill Crest and Gun c1950

E214008

This inn is named after the Earl of Warwick, Richard Nevill. He was known as the Kingmaker and lived in Eridge Castle, the ancestral seat of the Marquis of Abergavenny. The lands of Eridge have been in the hands of the Nevill family in a direct male line from 1450. The scene is much the same today, with business continuing beside the busy main road.

Frant, The Post Office c1955 F173002

Frant is 600 feet above sea level and has extensive views. Most of the houses are positioned around the large green where there were once old archery butts. In the 12th century King John had a hunting lodge in the area. The 15th-century church of St Alban was rebuilt in 1822. Iron smelting and gunfounding brought prosperity to the area in the 16th century. Eridge Old Park is a deer park with a large lake; there is also an observatory tower on Saxonbury Hill on the site of an Iron Age hill-fort. Shernfold Park is a Victorian house of 1853. Just off the main through road, H Kemp, Stores and Post Office, is still trading.

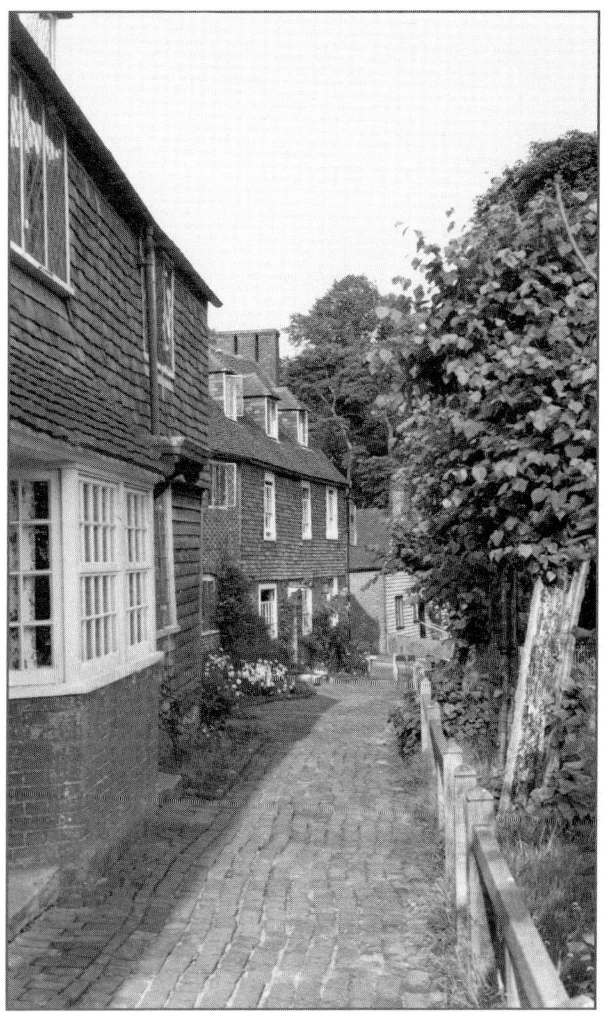

Groombridge, The Walks, Old Town c1960 G203053

Groombridge straddles the Kent border on the River Medway. Strictly speaking, the old part is just in Kent. The Walks face onto The Green, and at the end of the row is The Crown Inn - originally a tollhouse. Groombridge Place is a late 17th-century moated house attributed to Sir Christopher Wren. In 1415 it was owned by Richard Waller who imprisoned Charles, Duke of Orléans for 25 years, because a ransom could not be paid. Nearby, the family of the great Quaker, William Penn, owned Penn's in the Rocks house from 1672 to 1762.

Hartfield, The Village 1906 56691

We are on the upper River Medway north of the Ashdown Forest, near the Kent border. The 13th-century church of St Mary is on a knoll in the centre of the village. The Lychgate, c1520, is a half-timbered cottage by the churchyard with an upper floor extending above. Bolebrooke was a 16th-century brick mansion, once the home of the Dalyngrigge and Sackville families; only fragments survive.

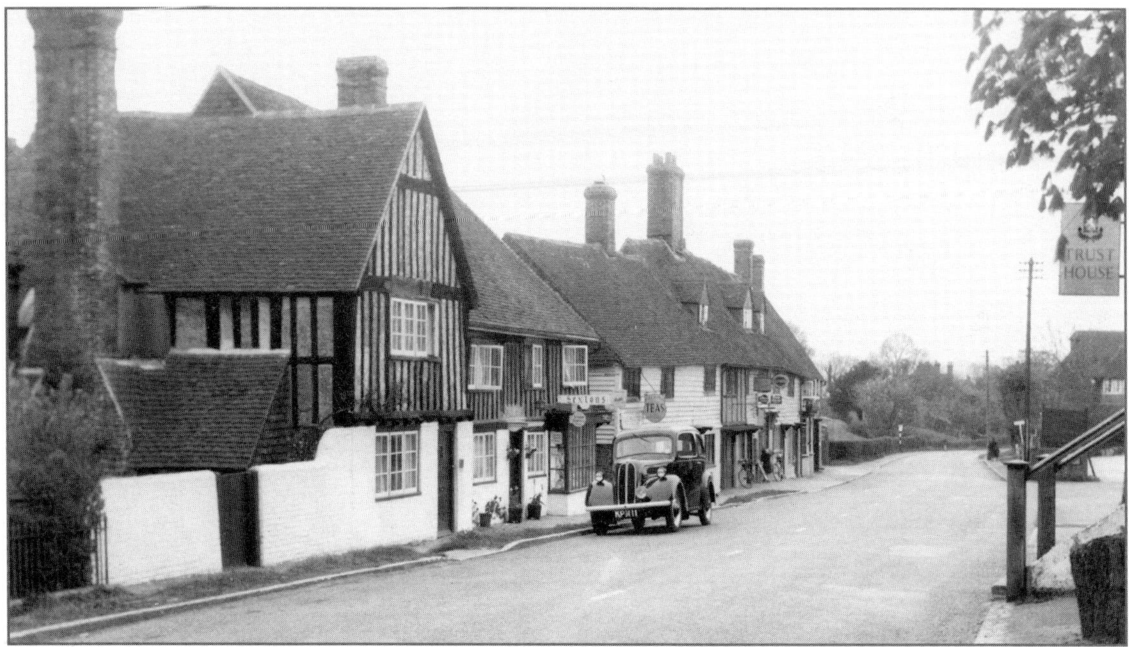

Hartfield, High Street c1950 H28016
Hartfield is at the heart of 'Winnie the Pooh' country - conceived by the author A A Milne. 'Pooh Corner' is in the High Street and all the 'Enchanted Places' are in the parish. In the picture there are close-studded timber-framed houses on the left, including Sexton's shop. The Hay Wagon Inn is just visible on the right, with a temporary sign.

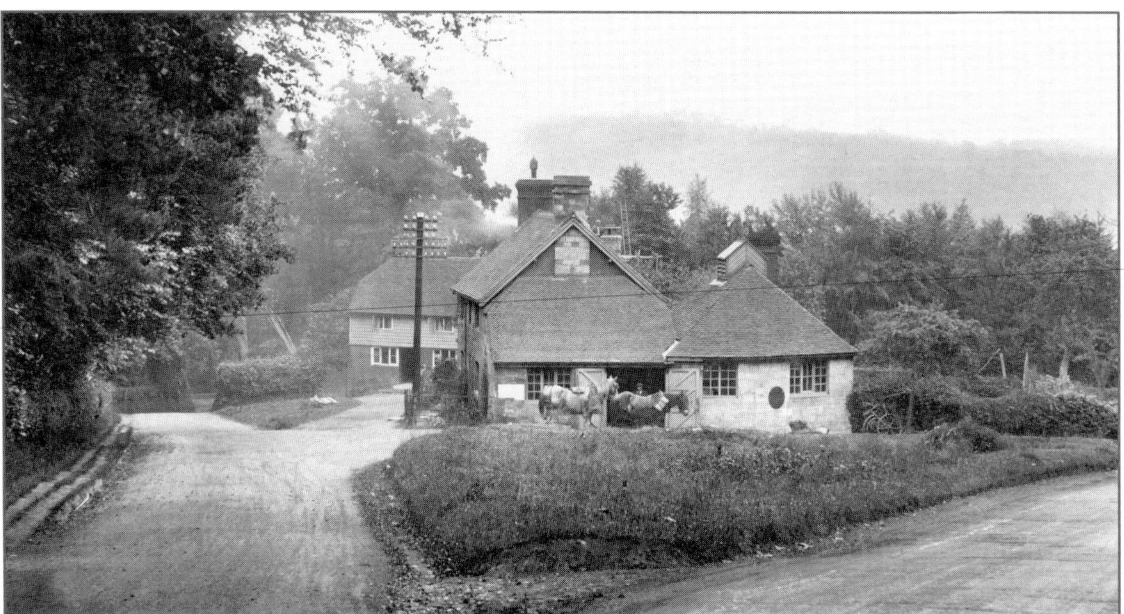

Colemans Hatch, The Hatch Inn 1927 79599
A small village on the edge of the Ashdown Forest, east of Forest Row. Holy Trinity church was built towards the end of the last century and features a copy of an Italian Pieta by Francesco Francia. Nearby Hollyhill is a large house with a Jacobean façade built in 1885. In the picture, heavy horses wait patiently by the stable while they are prepared for work. On the roofline a builder stands on a scaffolding platform repairing a chimneystack.

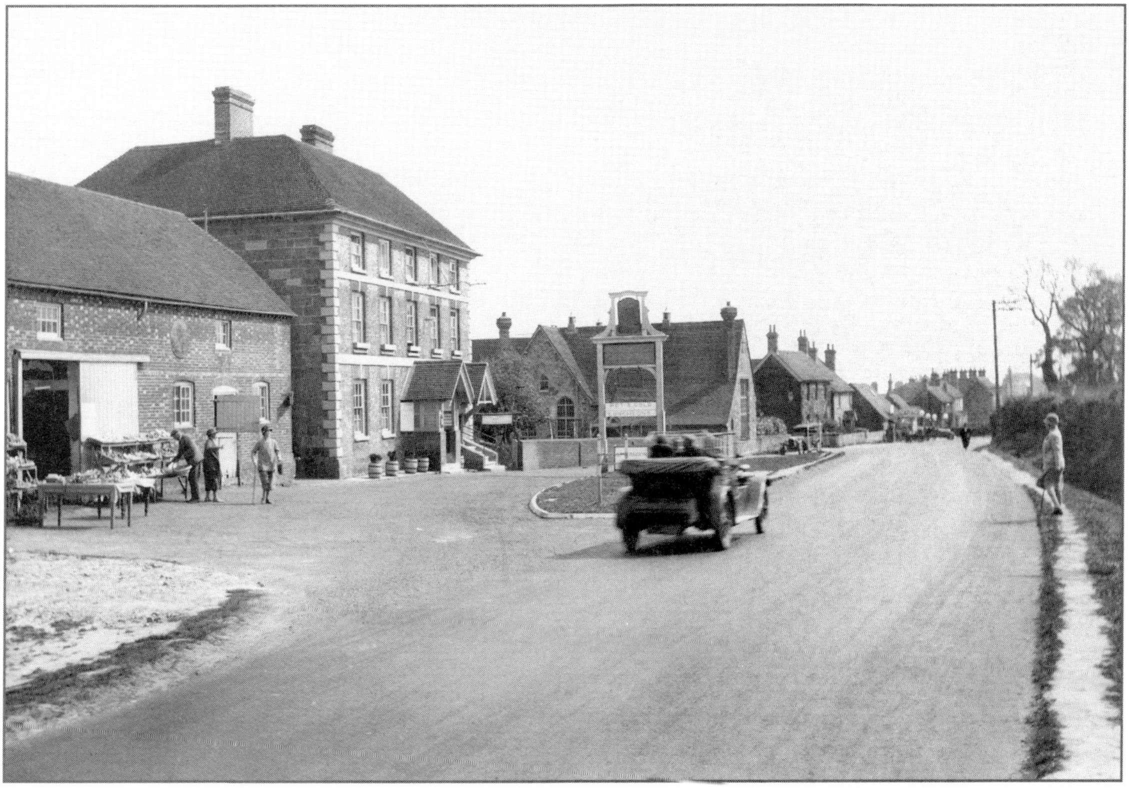

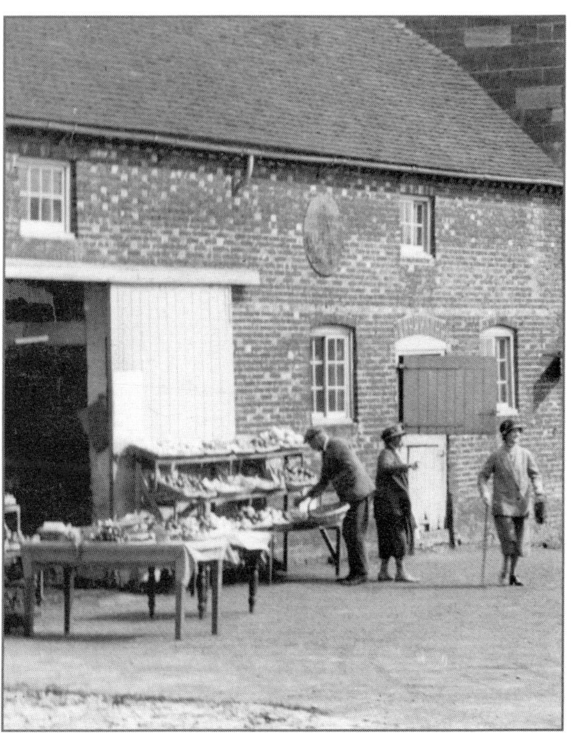

Nutley
The Hotel 1928 80744

We are on the Eastbourne to London main road. Outside the stables of the Shelley Arms Hotel, a large 18th century coaching inn, produce stalls display items for sale. A car speeds past - the event was recorded on slow film, so the image is blurred. Nearby is Nutley windmill, an open trestle post mill that has been restored to full working order and is open to visitors.

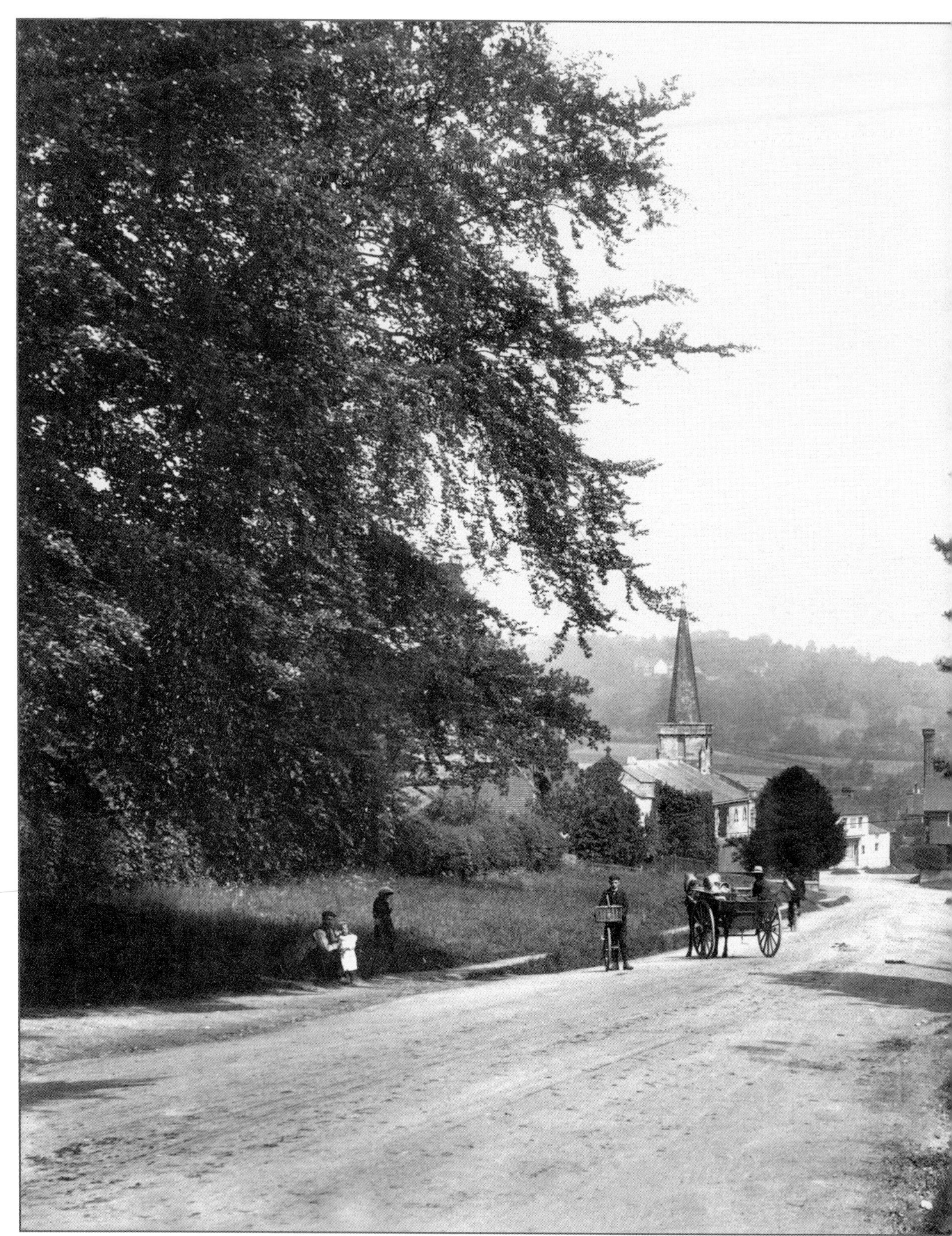

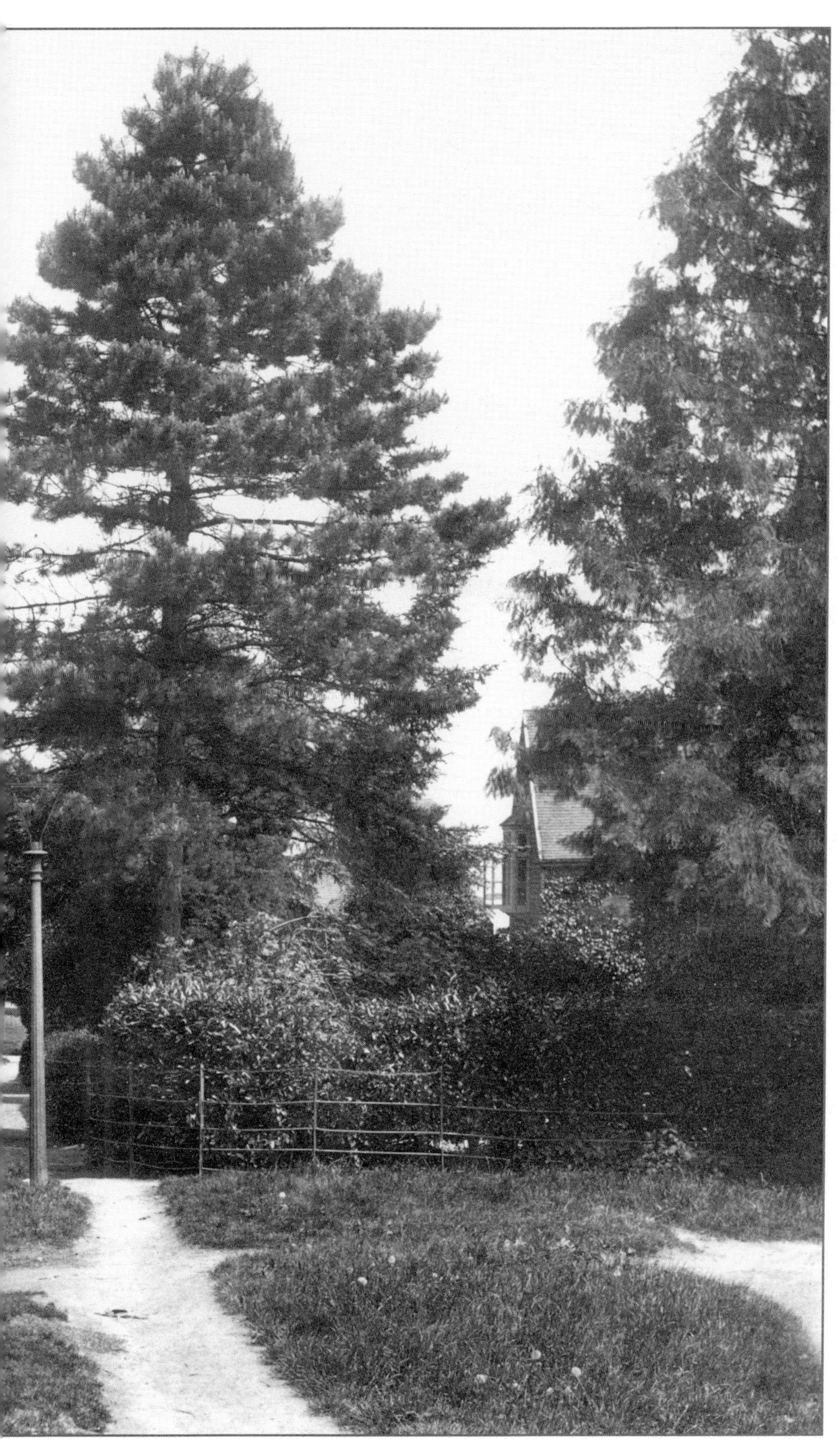

**Forest Row
The Village 1909**

61439

A large village on the northern edge of the Ashdown Forest, Forest Row was a popular place in the 14th century when the King and his Lords used it as a base for hunting. Brambletye was the first mansion in the area; it was built in 1631 and destroyed by 1680. The ruins are extant. A new Brambletye was built nearby in 1919. The main road leads down past Holy Trinity church, which was built in 1836. The scene is similar today but the road is very busy with motor traffic.

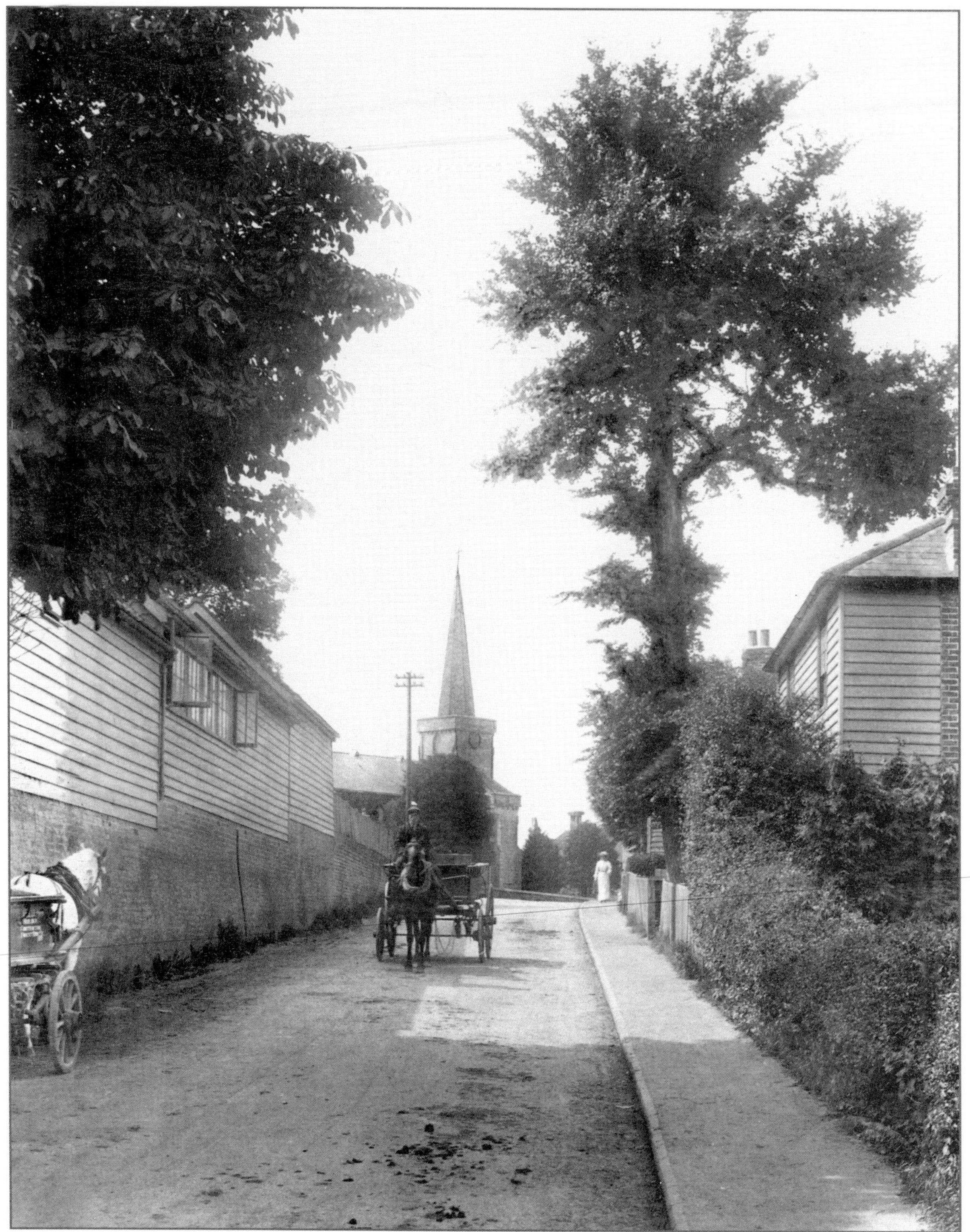

Forest Row, Hartfield Road 1907 57959
This photograph was taken further down the road and two years earlier than No 61439. Buildings clad in white weatherboarding line the road, which is quite steep for horse-drawn transport. Holy Trinity church is seen in the distance.

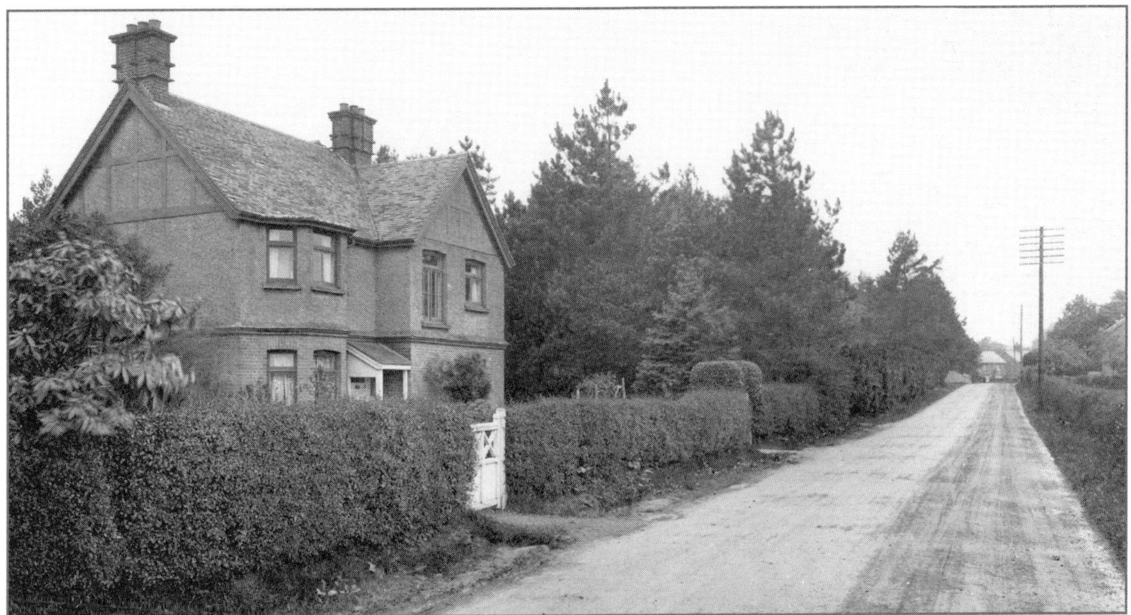

Chelwood Gate, Beaconsfield Road 1928 80736B
We are at the eastern edge of the Ashdown Forest. Not far away are Chelwood Vachery, a re-created hall-house
originally called Trimmer's Pond, and Kidbrooke Park, a much altered and decorated house with gardens laid out
by Repton. Charles Abbot lived and died here; he was speaker of the House of Commons at the time of the Battle
of Waterloo. Sun House is in modern style, built in 1931

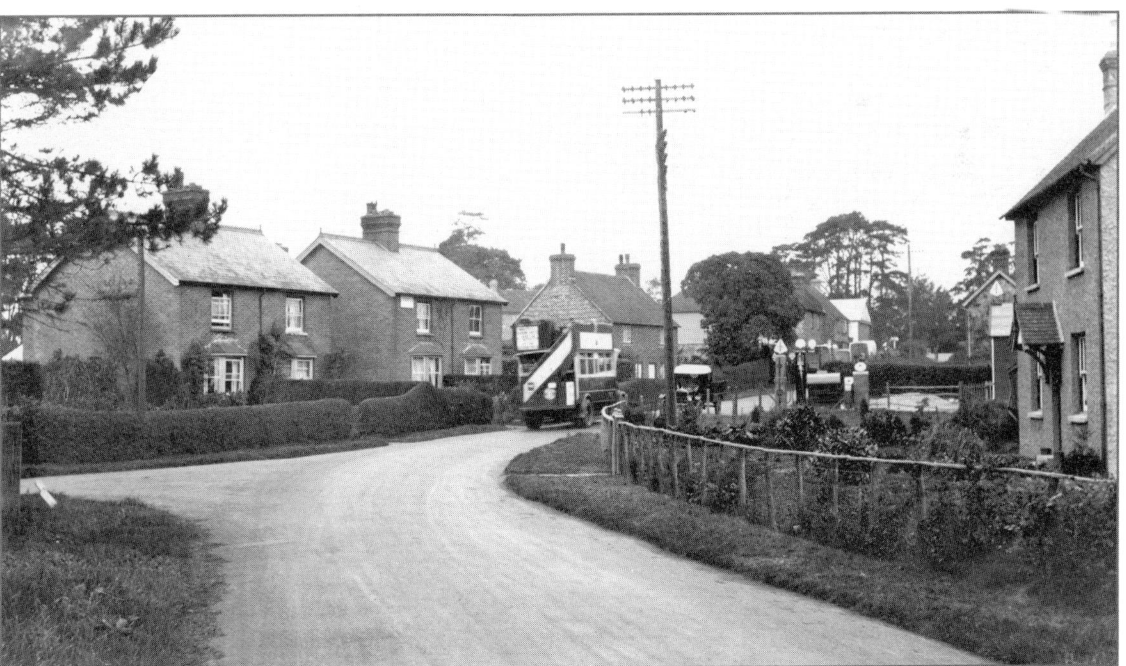

Chelwood Gate, The Village c1930 C76501
Waiting at the bus stop is a nearly new open-top Leyland double-decker bus with an outside staircase. It is on
route 92, Eastbourne to East Grinstead. A small lorry waits outside the Ashdown Garage.

▼ West Hoathly, The Village c1950 W64009

This area was connected with the Sussex iron industry in the 17th century. The forests had deposits of iron ore, and supplies of wood fuel to smelt it; the iron-making families brought much wealth to the parish. Gravetye was built in 1598: it was the home of the ironmaster Roger Infield, who specialised in making cast iron graveslabs and forged nails. The house is now the Gravetye Manor Hotel. Great House, later called Manor House, was built by the Infield family in 1627. The church of St Margaret, with a shingled broach spire, stands above the houses. The neat topiary hedge-work seen on the left is in the garden of the 15th-century Priest's House, which is open to visitors. It is still nicely kept.

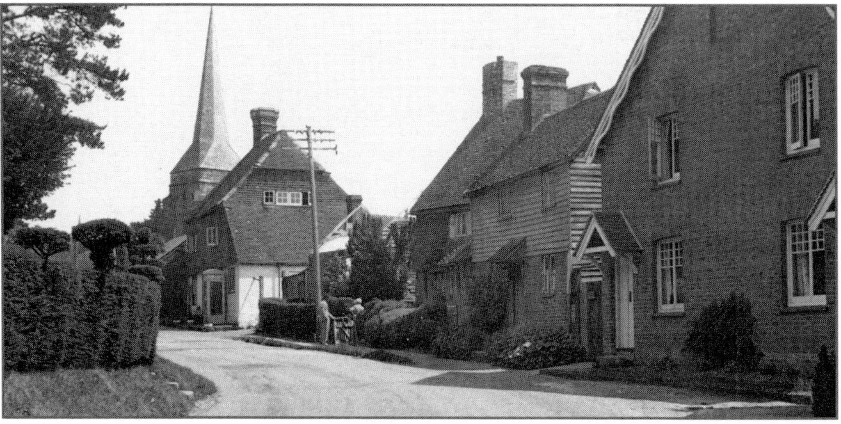

▼ West Hoathly, The Store c1960 W64065

This picture is of the same road as photograph W64009, but dates from ten years later and is taken from the other direction. The telephone kiosk is of a more modern type, and the shop front has been developed and a post box placed outside. A tall chimney on an outbuilding, leans considerably; this has now been rebuilt. The scene is similar today but there are more trees. The shop has closed and the telephone kiosk moved a short distance. Stone quarrying is a local industry and fossils have been found.

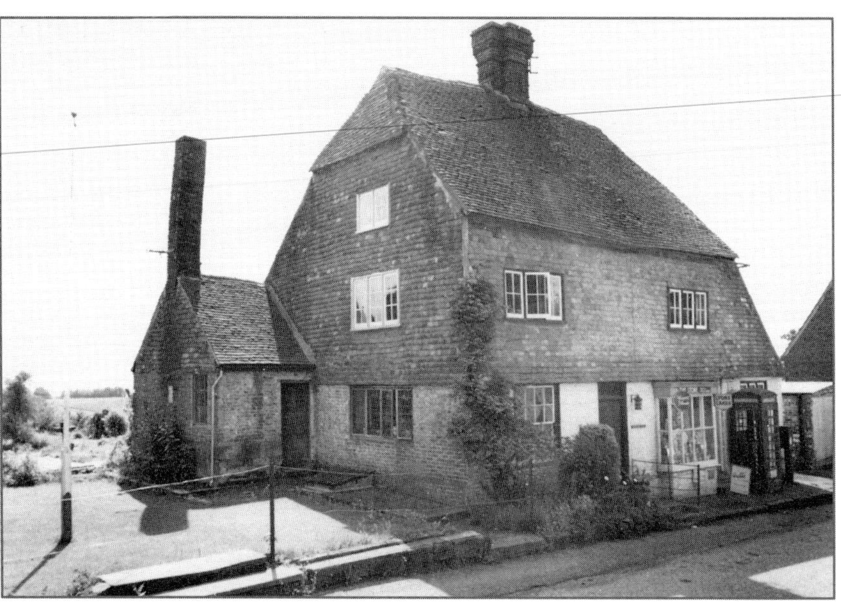

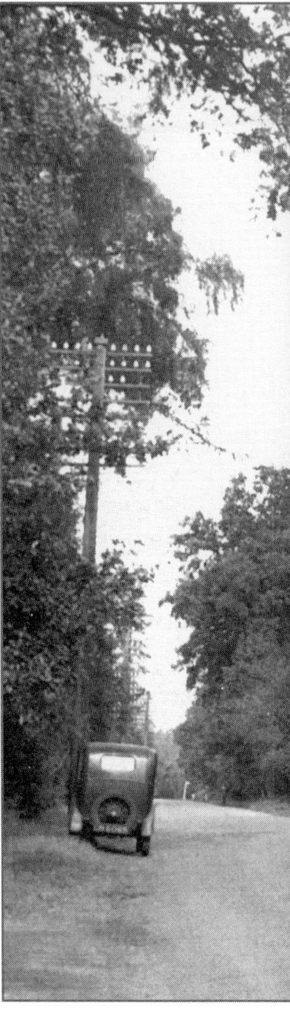

▲ Crawley Down The Village c1950

C529001

This is a small village beside an old Roman route through the Worth Forest. The Church of All Saints was built in 1843. In our photograph, the village stores and post office were sheltered from the roadway behind trimmed hedges. The old Post Office is now a house and the front gardens have been lost owing to the widening of the very busy road.

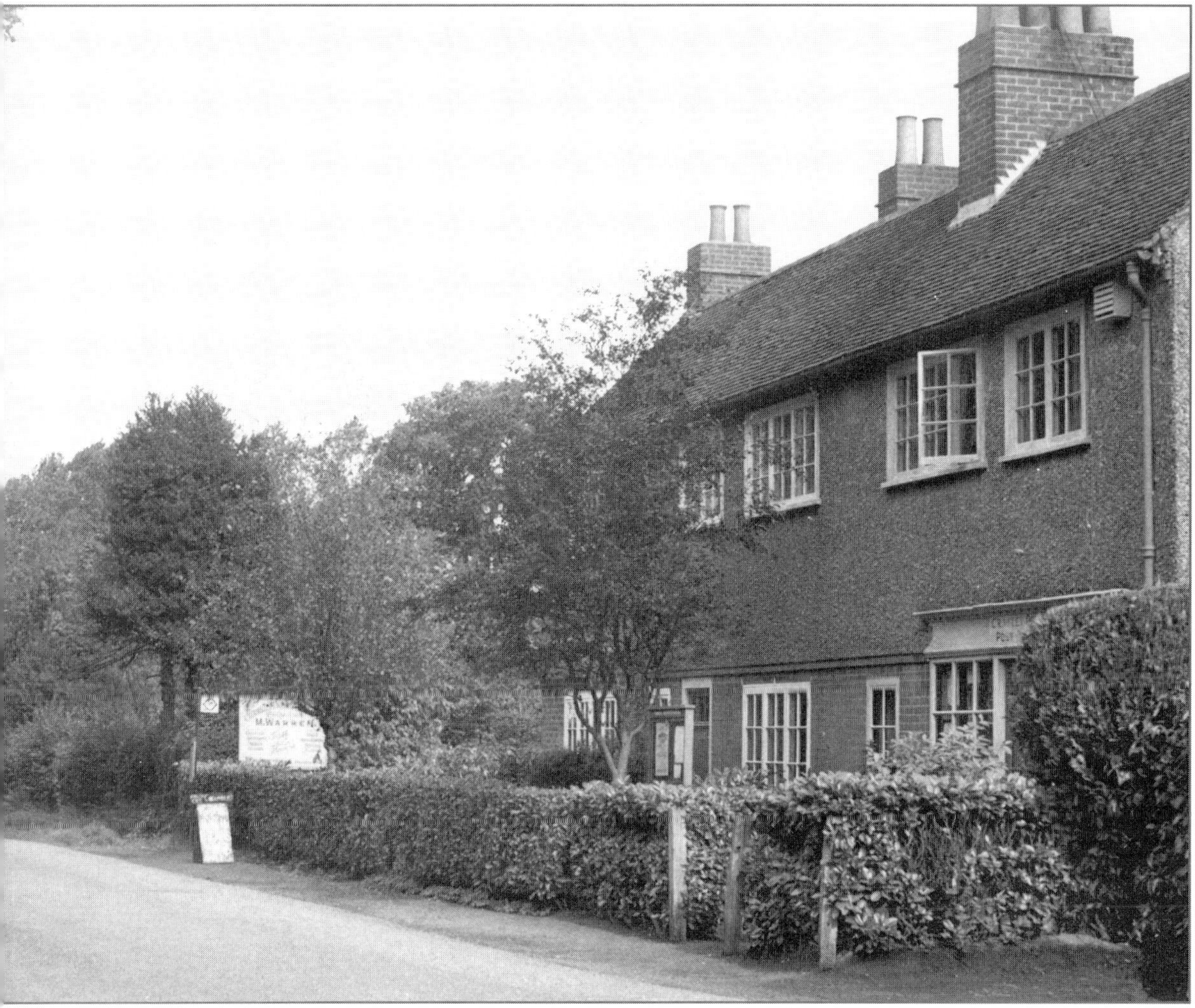

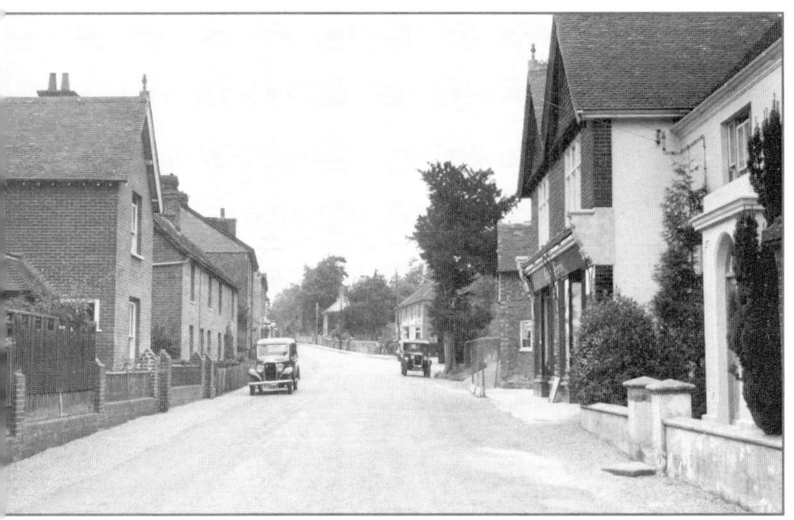

◄ **Ardingly, The Village c1950**
A207017
Ardingly is a village overlooking the Ouse valley, north of Haywards Heath. The 14th-century church of St Peter has an impressive tower. Ardingly College, situated nearby, is a notable Public School. Wakehurst Place, built in 1590, is a country estate with large ornamental gardens and tree collections. Now in the care of the National Trust and run by the Royal Botanical Gardens, Kew, it is open to visitors. The South of England agricultural showground is in the locality. Ardingly reservoir caters for the expanding needs of public water supply in the area, and has facilities for watersports.

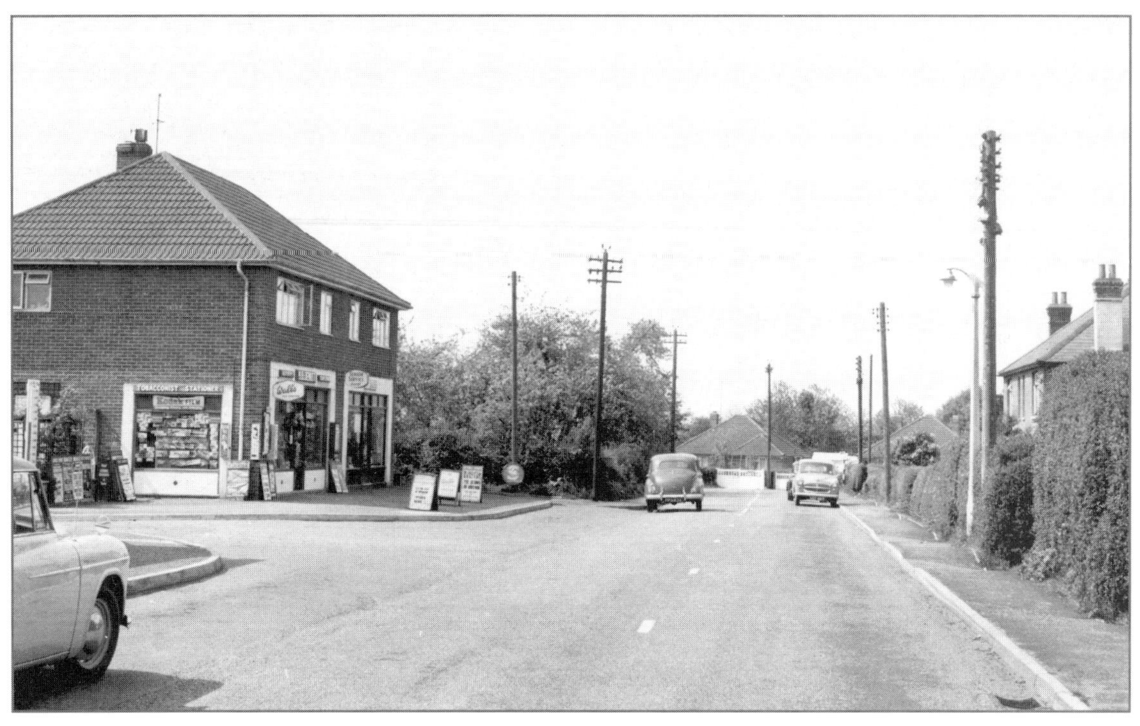

Copthorne
The Village c1955 C422038

Copthorne was a new parish, formed in 1881 out of Worth and Crawley Down. The church of St John Evangelist was built in 1877 and is just in Sussex. The picture shows local shops with a proliferation of signs of all types outside; vending machines are attached to the shopfront. An obtrusive clutter of tall poles lines the road, and a modern concrete street lamp does little to enhance the scene. The roadside has been cleared up considerably in recent years. The Prince Albert public house is at the end of the road, hidden by trees.

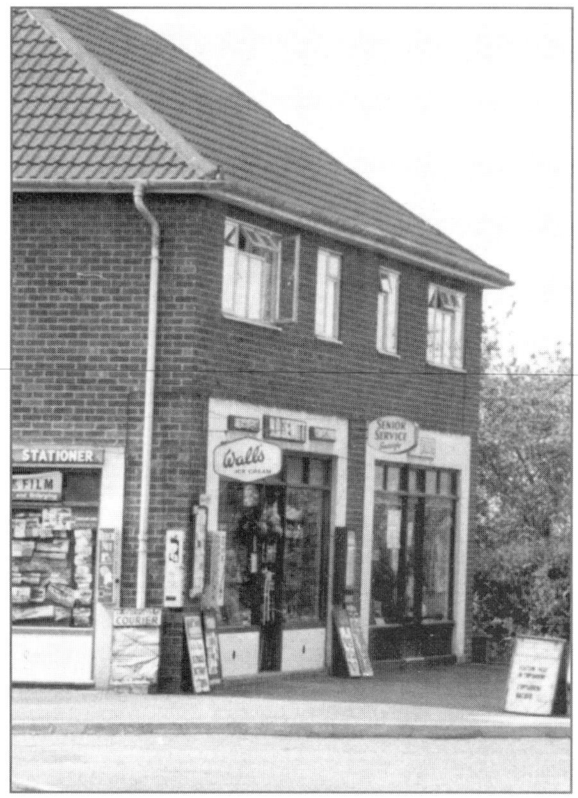

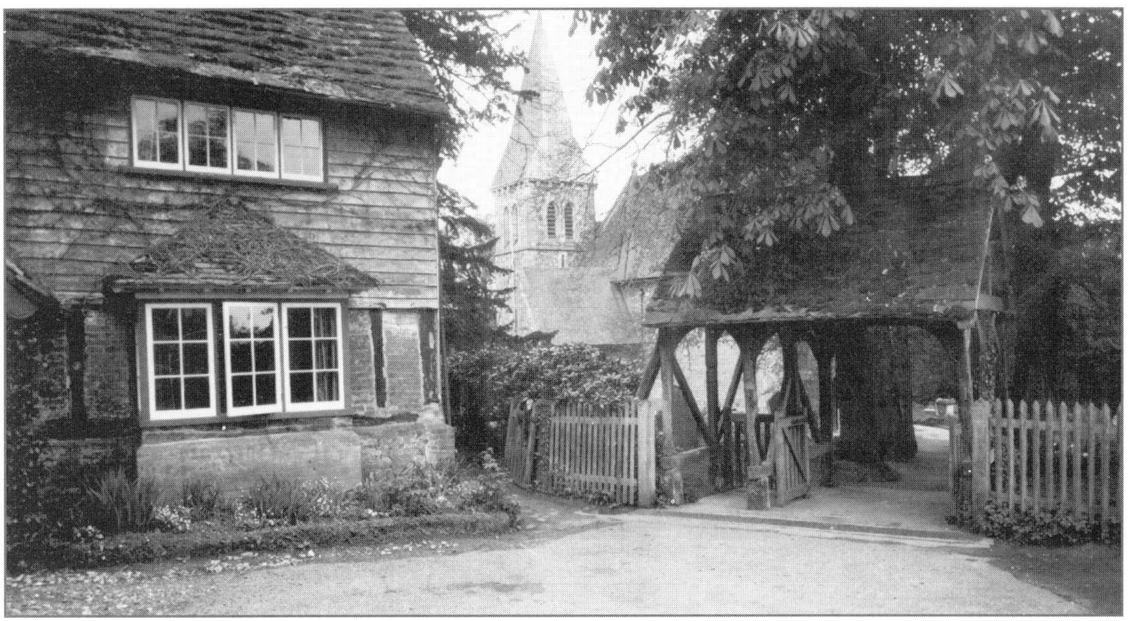

Worth, The Lychgate and the Church c1960 W146003
Worth village stands in the Forest of Worth, east of Crawley, and was a place of pilgrimage. The fine Anglo-Saxon church of St Nicholas was a principal church in pre-Conquest times. The 18th-century Worth Abbey is on the site of a town house called Paddockhurst. It is now run by the Benedictine Order as a monastery and public school. In the picture we see the Priest's House and the lychgate; both have Horsham stone roofing.

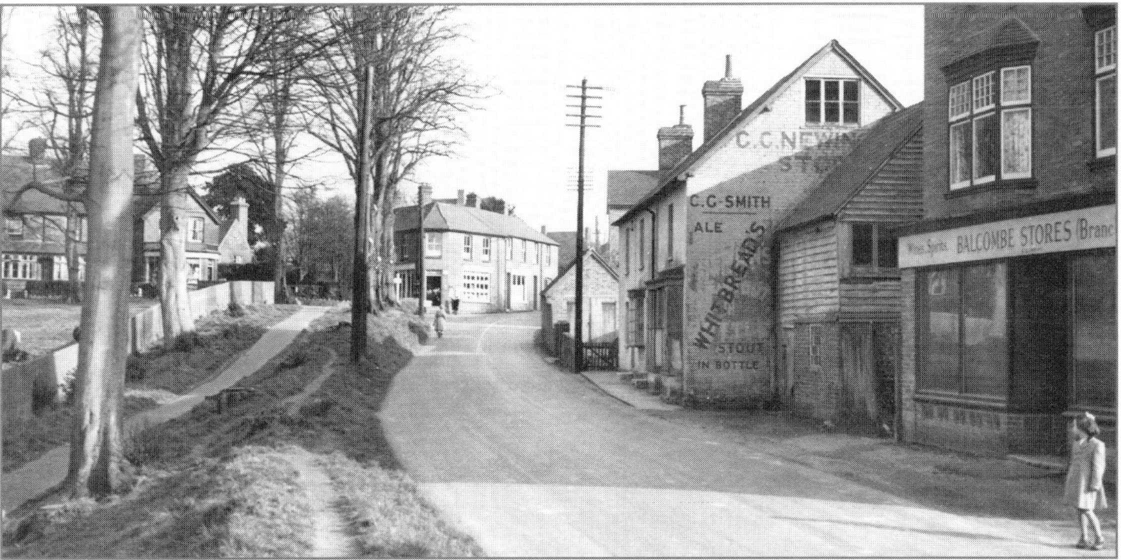

Balcombe, The Village c1955 B503006
This village is noted for its beautiful woods, a railway tunnel under the Balcombe Forest and a brick viaduct over the Ouse valley. The church of St Mary was built in 1847. Balcombe House, once called Parsonage House, is a large Tudor-style house of 1856. The 13th-century White House was run by the White Friars as a hostelry for Canterbury pilgrims. A metal pot holding 12 gold and 242 silver coins was discovered in the village in 1897. In the picture are three shops, including G G Newing Stores, later C G Smith, and Balcombe Stores, the grocer. The young girl pedestrian has little traffic to fear.

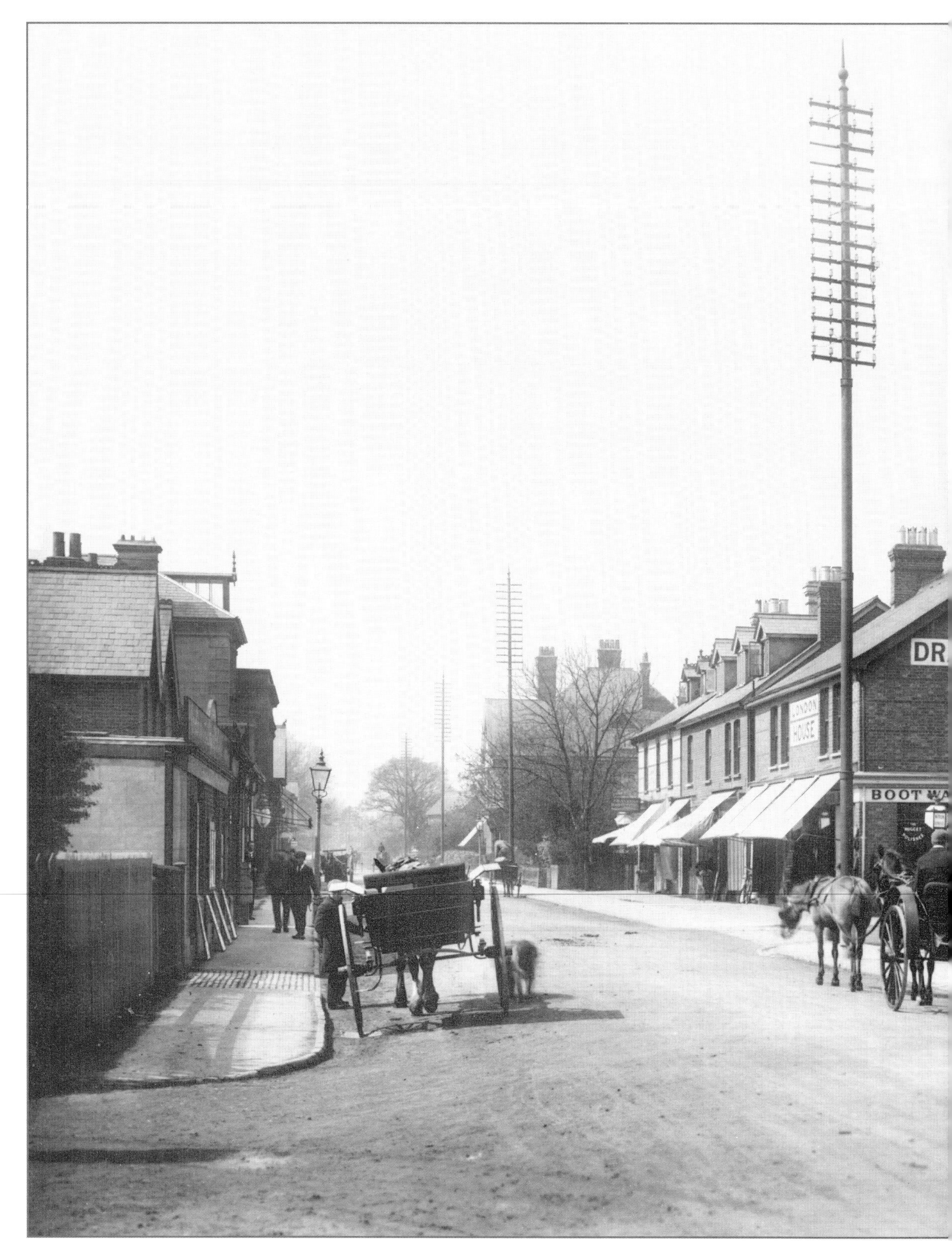

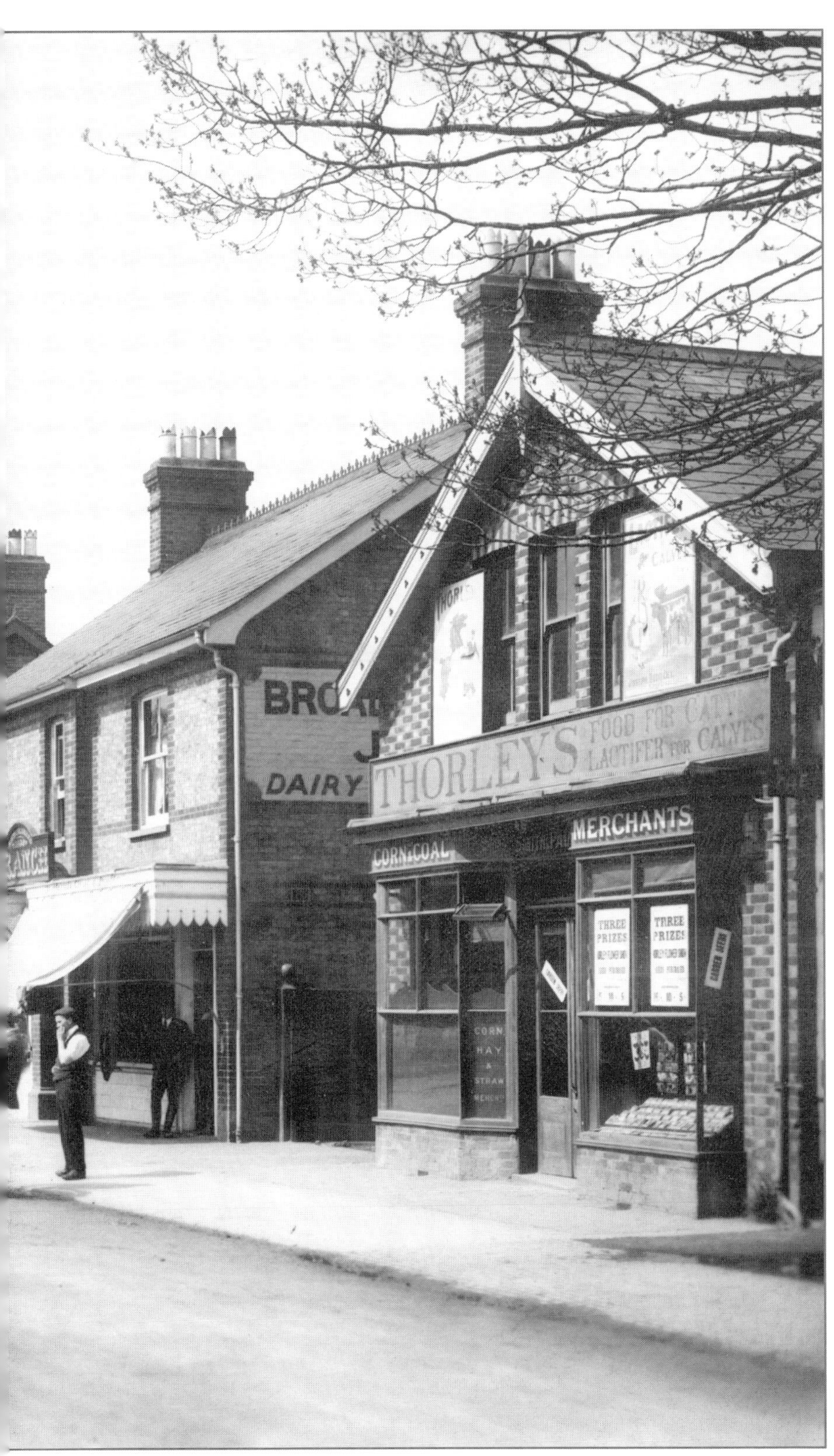

Horley, Station Road 1905 53298

Horley is on the old main London to Brighton road before it was diverted around the area of new Gatwick airport. Single and two-horse traps wait by the roadside. Corn and coal merchants sell proprietary animal feeds. We can also see London House, a draper's, Branch's shop, a dairy and a game and poultry shop. A line of very tall telegraph poles are topped with pointed finials. A gas street lamp is at the kerbside outside a shop with advertising boards on the pavement. Sunblinds are extended on the side of the street facing the sunlight.

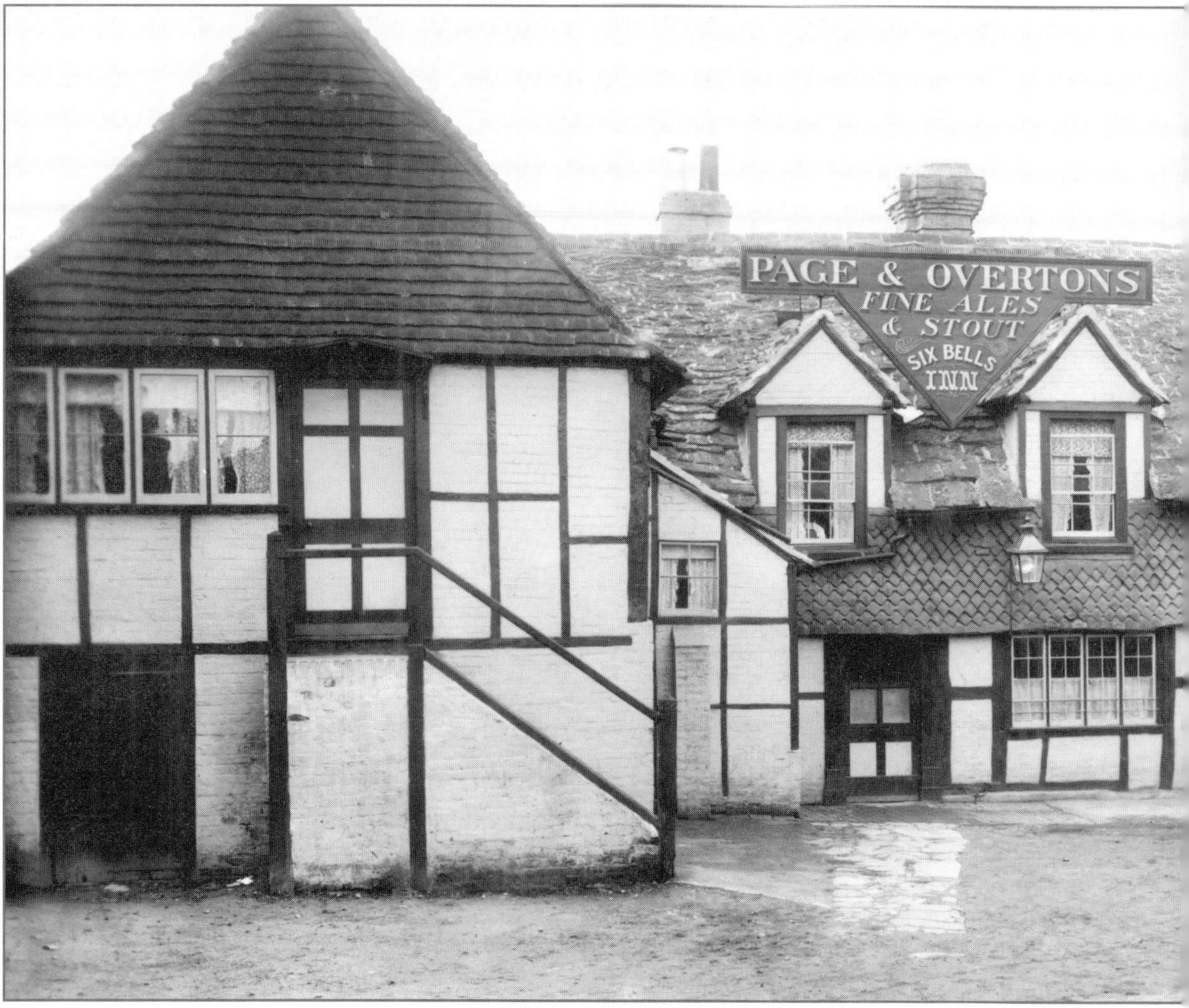

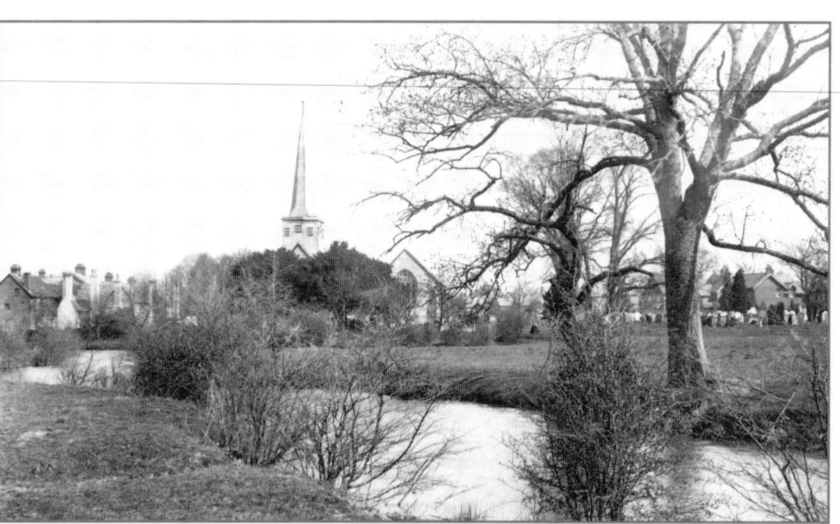

◀ **Horley, The view from the River 1906** 55373
It is wintertime with bare trees and lots of water in the River Mole. The church has a modernised tower and a shingled broach spire.

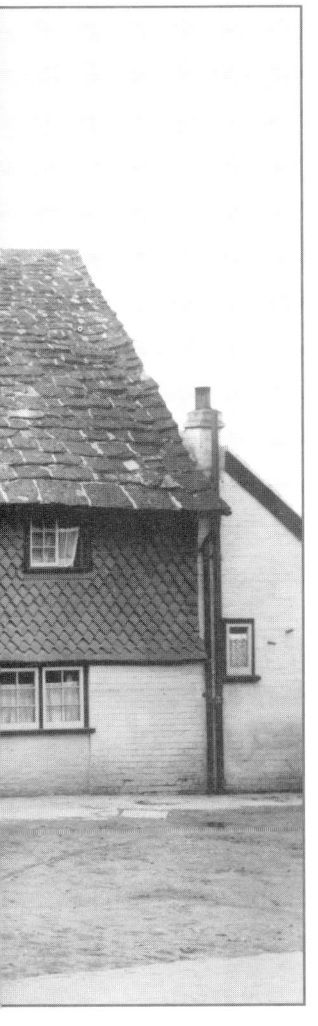

Horley, The Six Bells Inn 1905 53303

An old coaching inn on the main road. The upper storey is hung with ornate tiles, and the building has a Horsham stone roof. Horses pulling stagecoaches needed to be changed every ten miles or so. This provided business for plenty of inns with stables, which were spaced along trunk roads.

Three Bridges, Hazelwick Mill 1906 55387

The village flourmill was powered by two overshot waterwheels. The mill is pictured when it was still in working order. The overhanging lucam was used to hoist sacks of grain from a cart directly up into the bin floor. A brick arch to the right of the picture carries the London to Brighton main line railway. The mill site is now lost to Crawley New Town development.

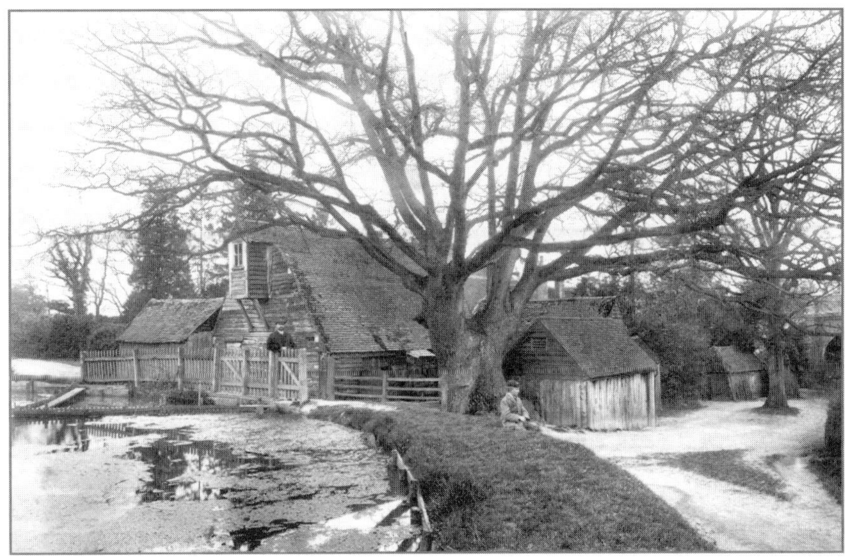

Three Bridges, The Post Office 1906 55383

The village was named after the bridges crossing the River Mole. The picture shows a well-stocked corner shop dealing in general and fancy drapery, and acting also as a Postal Telegraph office. Window displays include net curtaining, boots and shoes and hats. The shopfront and street corner have gas lamps, and the small front gardens have wood fencing. A boy waits near the shop doorway for the photographer.

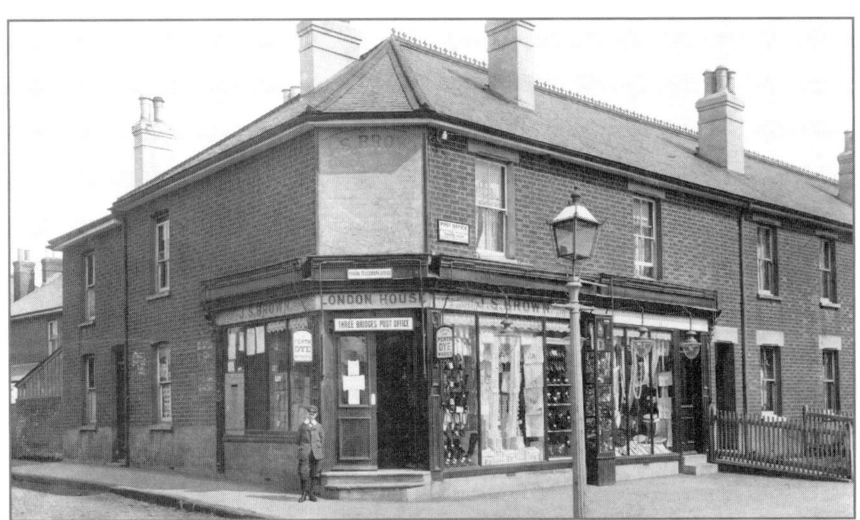

▼ Lowfield Heath, The Church and the Village 1905 53328

Lowfield Heath is near the old London to Brighton main road. The White Lion Inn, left, also serves teas. The Stores, run by J F Mitchell, has the front door open awaiting customers. In the background is St Michael's church. Built in1867, it has a square tower and a pyramidal spire. The whole area is now very close to the greatly expanded and very busy Gatwick Airport, which was built in the 1960s partly on the site of the old Gatwick racecourse.

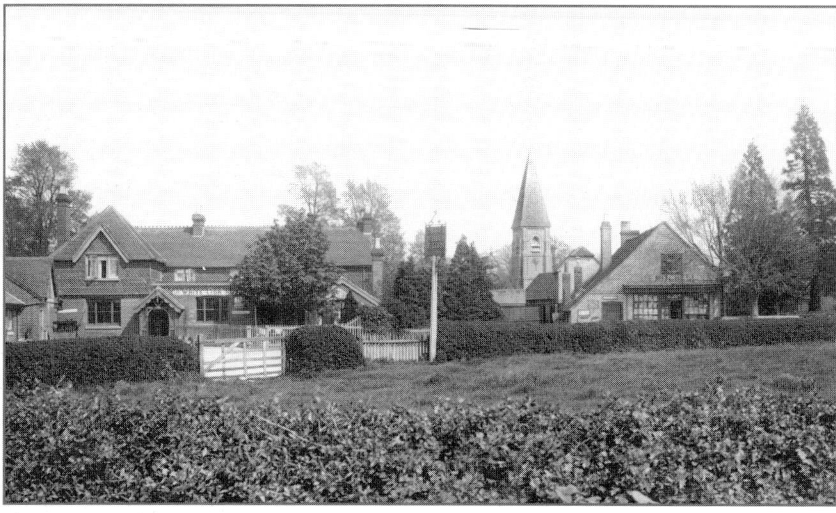

▼ Handcross, High Street c1950 H311003

A village on the eastern edge of the St Leonards Forest at a high point on the London to Brighton trunk road. The Red Lion, c1550, is an old coaching inn. Nymans Gardens has an ornate dovecote and is in the care of the National Trust and open to visitors. Handcross Park house is now a school. The buildings in the photograph are little changed today. The village was by-passed in 1959.

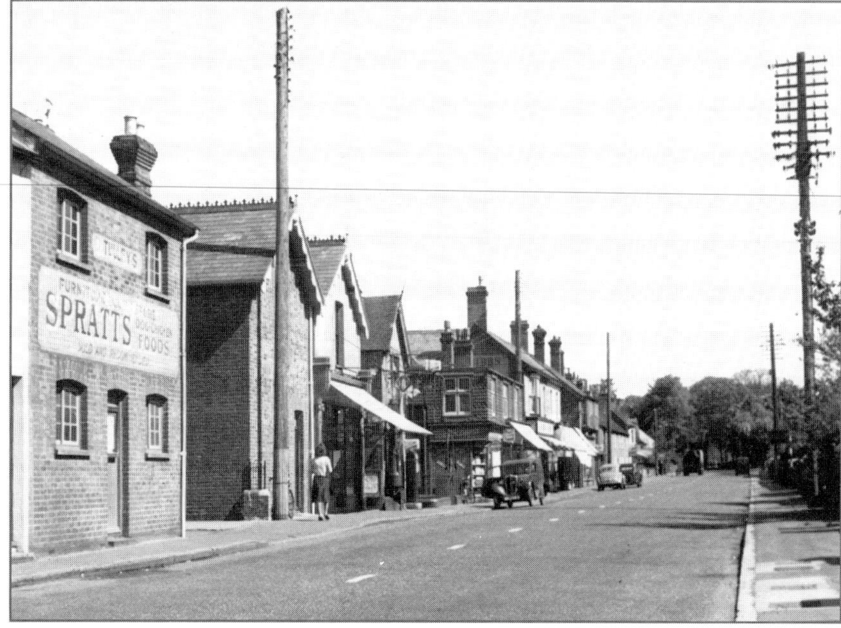

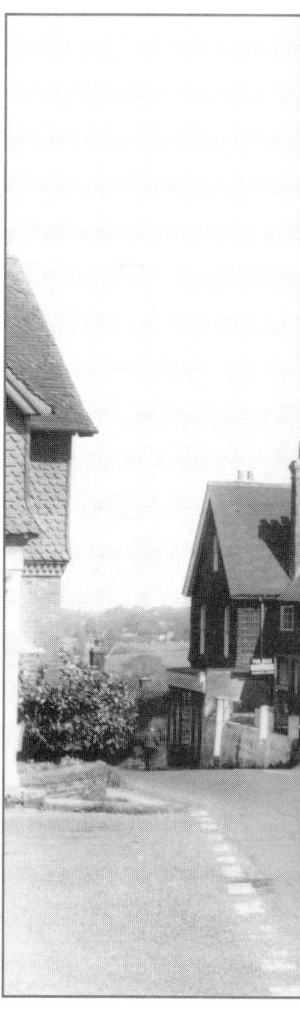

▲ Turners Hill, The Corner Shop and the Chapel c1960 T248044

A hilltop village on the southern edge of the Worth Forest with distant views of both the North and South Downs. St Leonard's church was built in 1895. The Crown is a 16th-century coaching inn and has a turnspit and crane in a fireplace. The corner shop is located on a crossroads at the highest point in the village. A large chapel is nearby. The scene today is very similar.

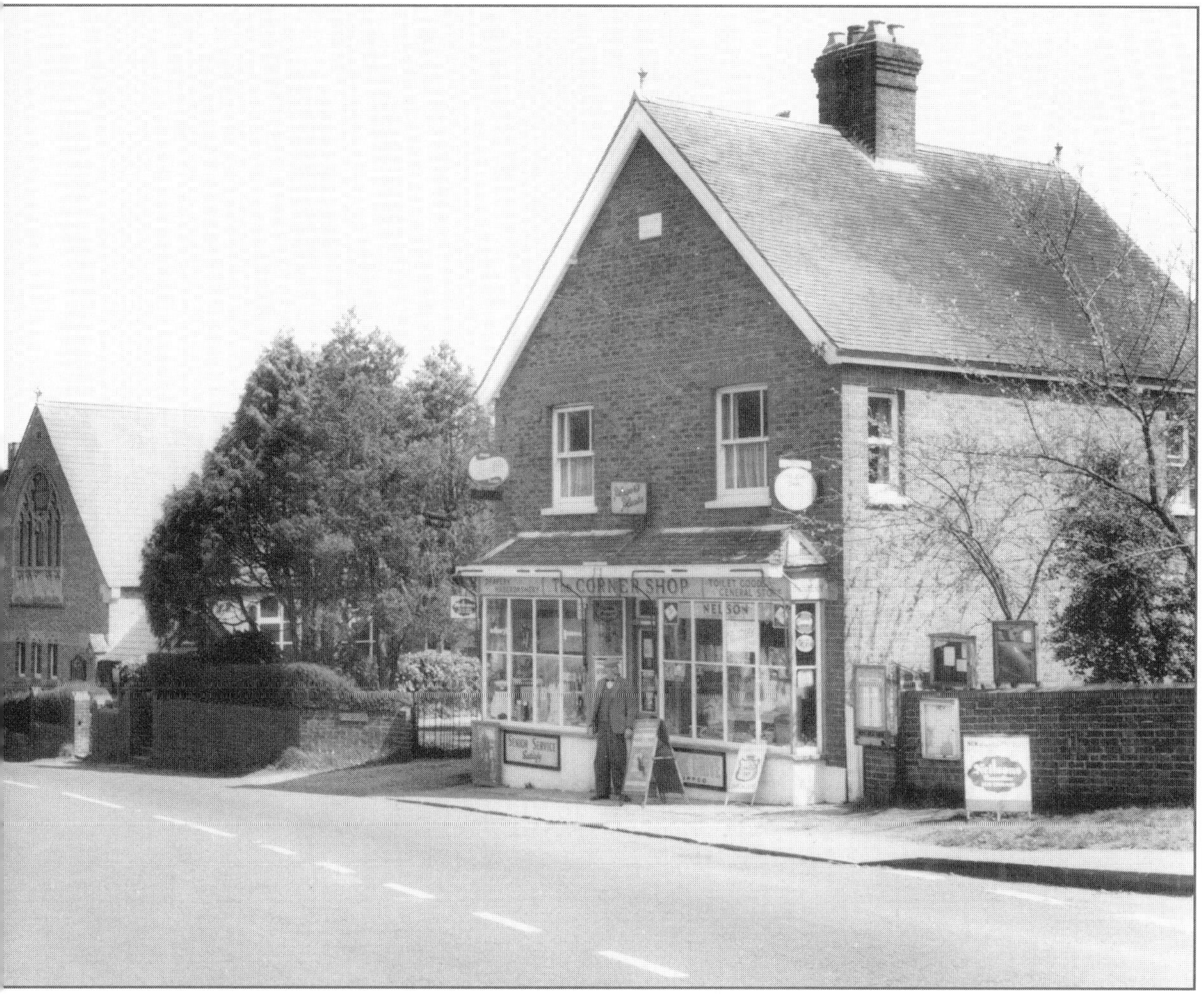

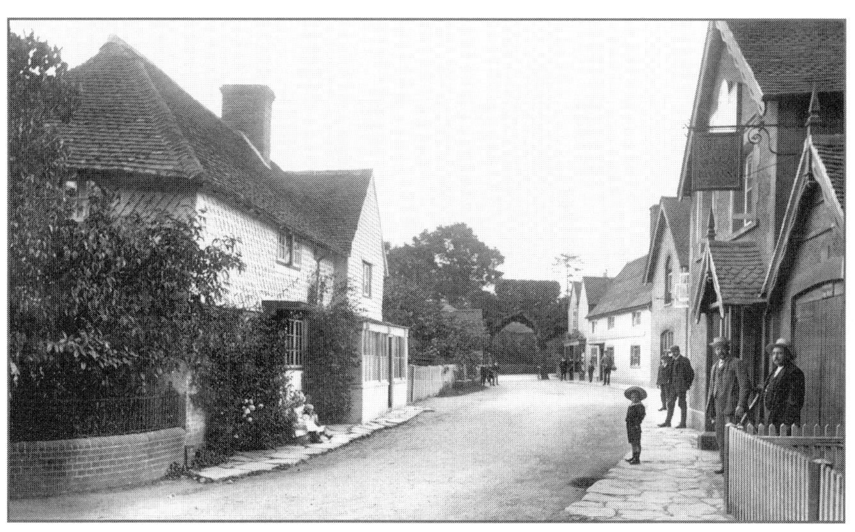

◄ Charlwood, The Street 1904 52386
Charlwood was in Surrey until the 1970s administrative boundary changes. A feature of the scene is the limestone paving flags that neatly line The Street, and the trimmed trees forming an arch across the roadway. The Half Moon Inn (landlord W Teasdale), awaits customers. A few villagers stand still for the photographer, while children sit in the dust of the pavement.

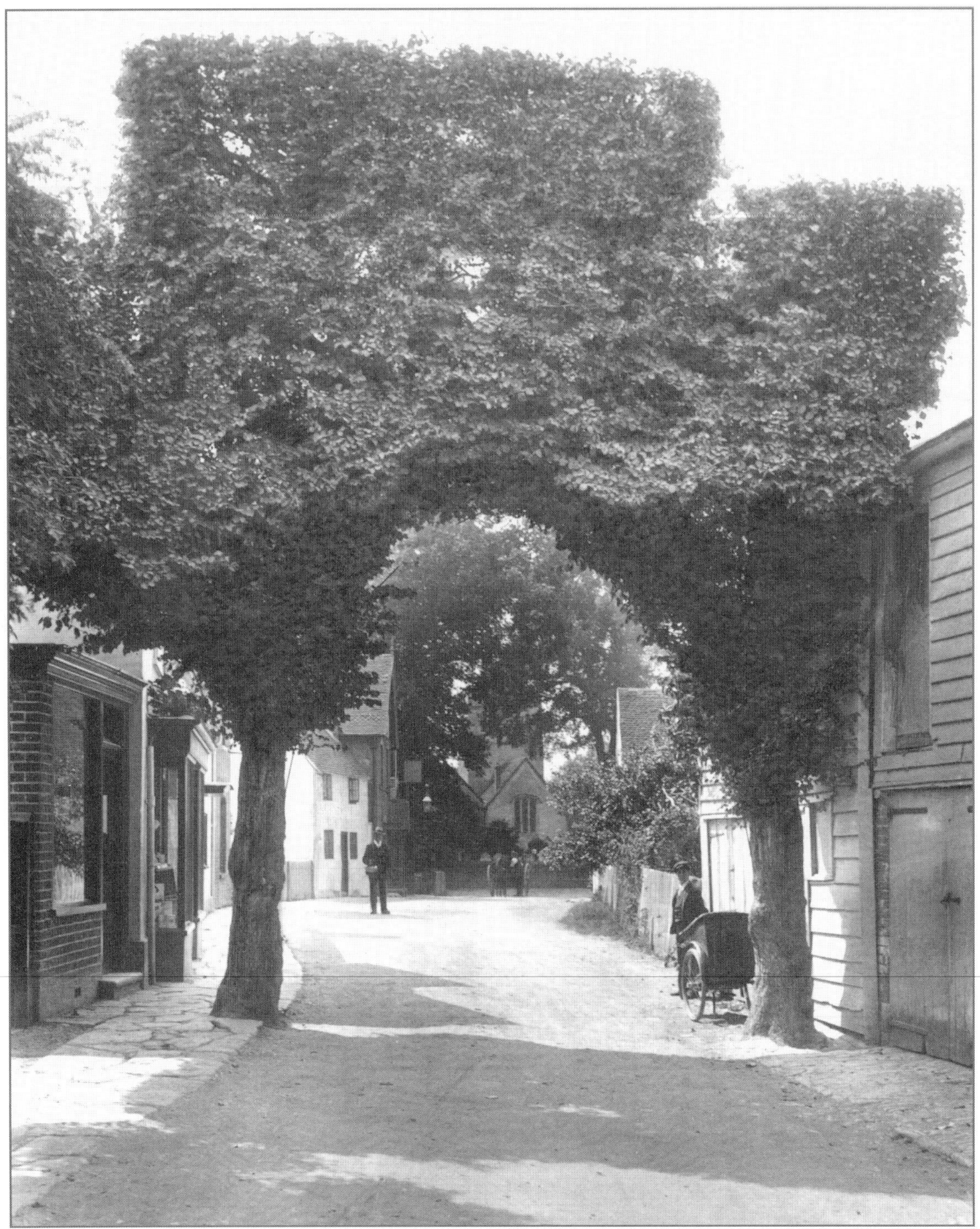

Charlwood, The Archway 1906 54173
A close-up view of the roadside trees forming an arch. The Norman church is just visible through the trees, beyond a horse and cart. Charlwood House was the home of Nicholas Sander, a scholar and talker, who was a Roman Catholic conspirator against Queen Elizabeth I. After the Queen's accession he became a fugitive.

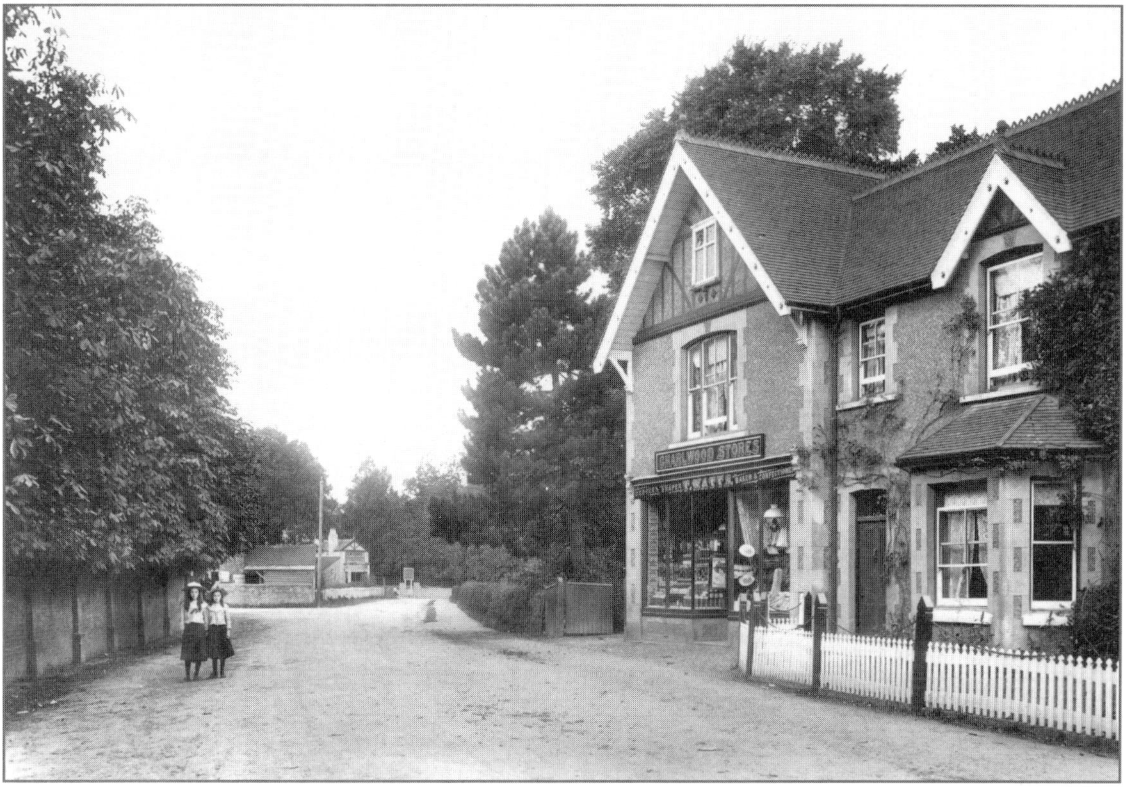

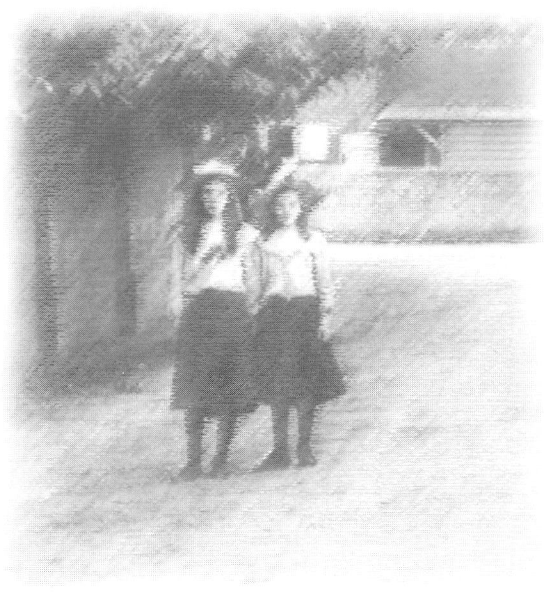

Charlwood
High Road 1904 52387
The photograph shows Charlwood Stores,
whose sign reads 'T Watts, Grocer, Draper,
Baker and Confectioner'. A post-type windmill
has been moved from Lowfield Heath and
reconstructed in full working order, and is
open to visitors. The village is now very close
to the ever-expanding Gatwick Airport.

▼ Faygate, The Village 1929 82454
A small village at the western edge of St Leonards Forest, on the main road and railway line between Horsham and Crawley. Local legends say that dragons and serpents inhabited the forest. Charcoal-making was a forest industry until the 1960s, and was carried out on sites within the forest. There were two brick works in the village. A road of brick cottages is seen next to the Wesleyan church. The scene has now altered: the left-hand side of the road has been developed with houses and bungalows, and the church is now converted to a house.

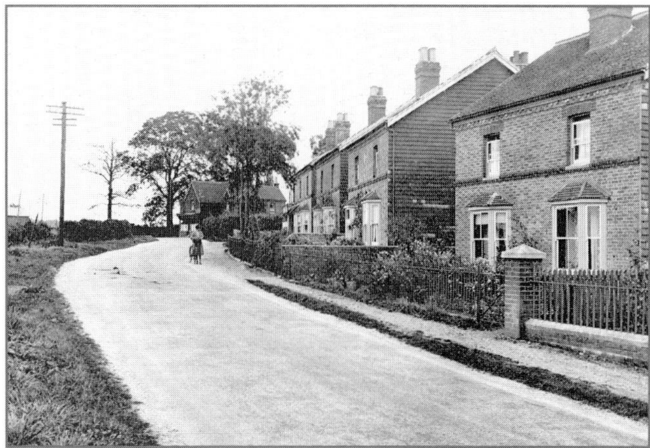

▼ Rusper, The Village 1909 61383
A small village on minor roads near to the Surrey border. The church of St Mary Magdalene has two historic 14th-century brasses. In the 12th century, a small Benedictine convent known as Rusper Priory was founded by a small number of nuns. The last remnants of the convent were demolished in 1781, and a house called 'The Nunnery' was built on the site. Avery's is a c1550 half-timbered house. Ghyl Manor, a 17th-century house, is now an hotel. The picture shows Friday Street, with the historic Plough Inn on the left, obscured from view by a large tree. The village store is on the right halfway down the road. The scene is similar today.

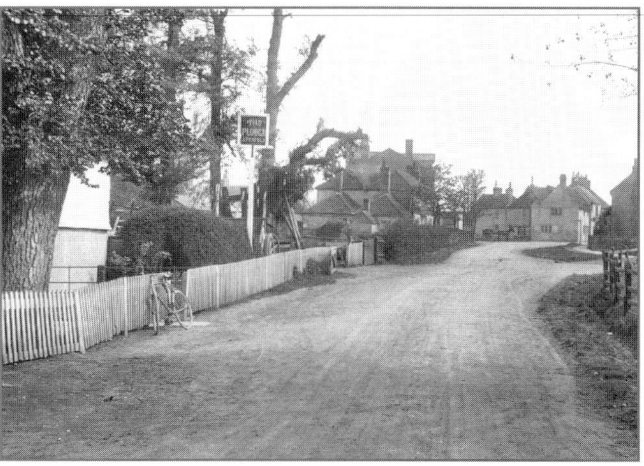

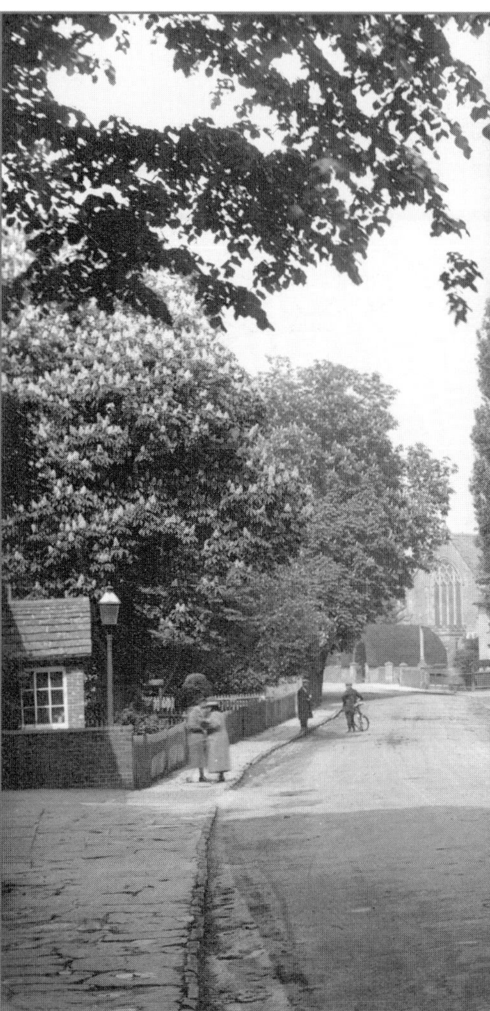

▲ Warnham, Topiary Work 1928 80850
We are just north-west of Horsham. The church of St Margaret's has a neatly clipped yew tunnel at the churchyard entrance. Inside is an elaborate monument to the memory of John Caryll, an ironmaster. Warnham watermill is on the site of an iron furnace; it has been nicely restored to workable order. Warnham Mill Pond is a beautiful iron industry water source with a large earth dam behind the mill. The picture shows a neatly sculptured hedge forming decorative peacocks. Stone flag pavements line the road. Brickmaking is an important local industry: a hundred million bricks were made a year in the 1970s. The topiary yew hedge is now grown out; otherwise the scene is still similar.

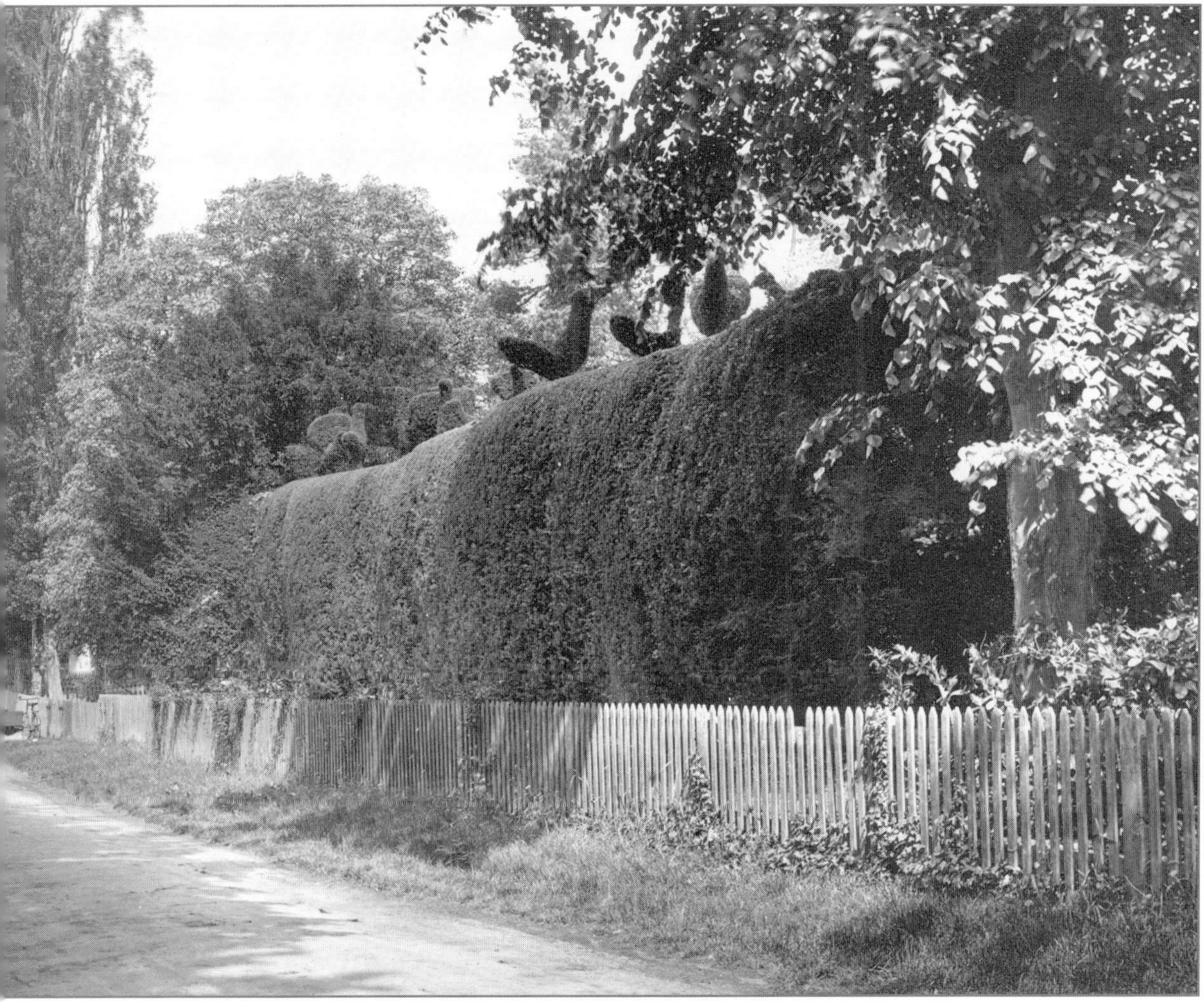

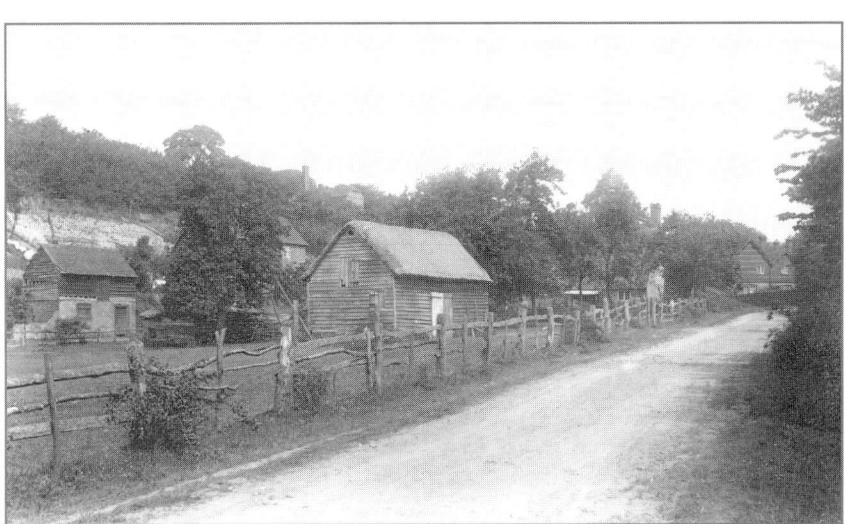

◄ Rake, The Village 1901
46605

A small village with a common on the Portsmouth to Guildford main road near the Hampshire border. There is chalk quarrying being carried out on the hillside on the left. Vernacular fencing surrounds the paddock of the smallholding, which has a small weather-boarded barn with a thatched roof. There are more houses among the trees on the hillside.

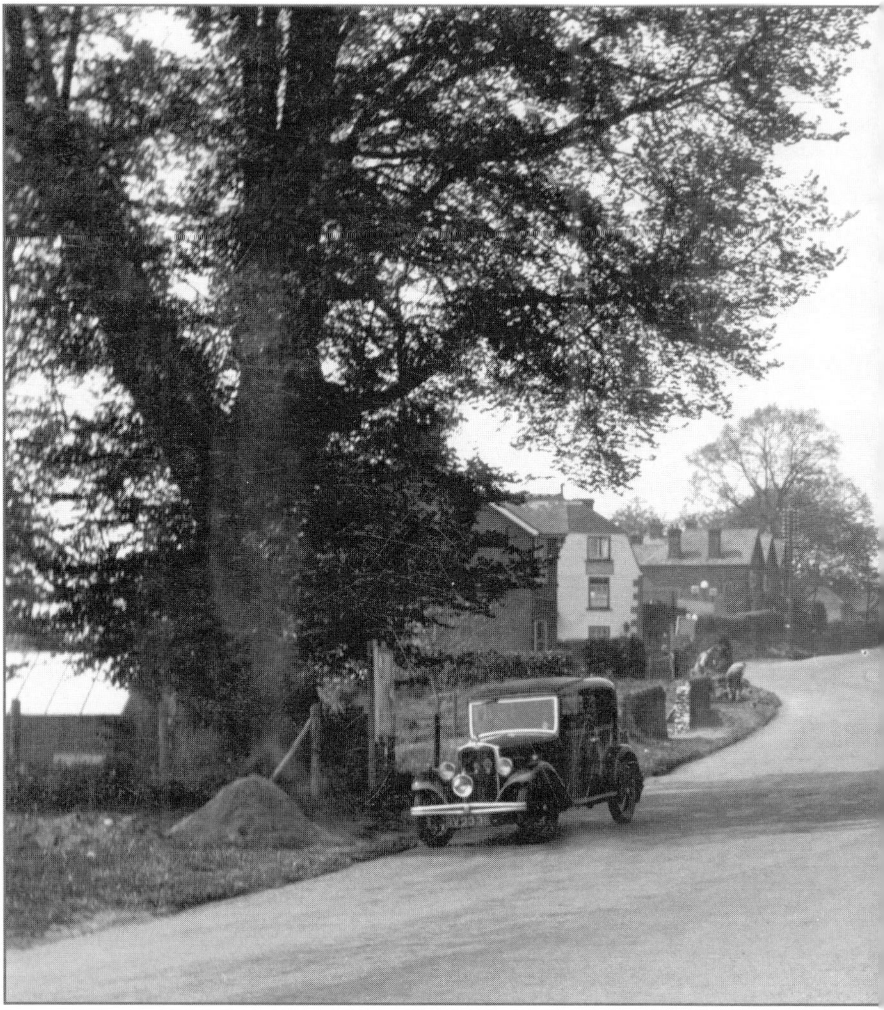

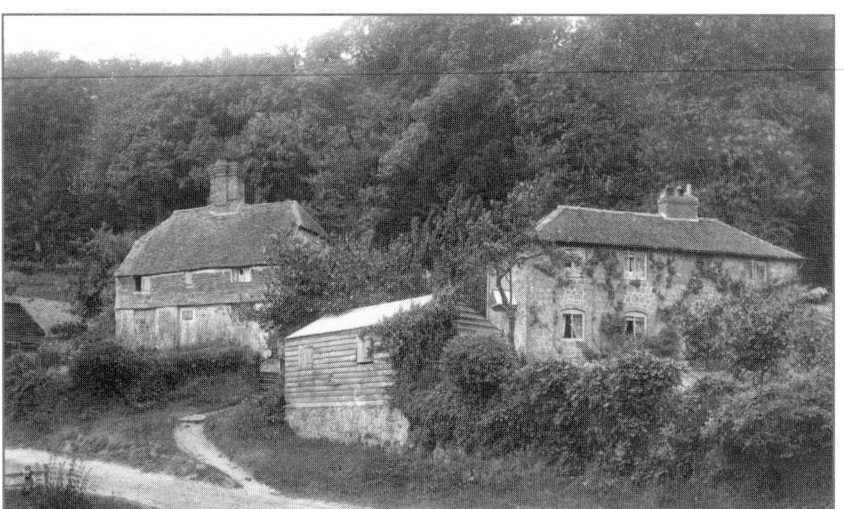

▶ **Rake**
The Flying Bull 1934
86051
We are now right on the border - part of the inn is in Hampshire. The name of the inn comes from two stagecoaches, 'The Fly' and 'The Bull', which plied the road. Cars of the early motor age travel along the road, or wait at the side. Large telegraph poles line the road.

◀ **Milland**
Cottages 1901 46598
An estate village of Hollycombe, a Tudor-style house of c1900. Chapel Common has a quaint 16th-century chapel in a wood, with a new church of St Luke built nearby in 1878. In the picture an old farmhouse stands next to farm buildings; the two semi-detached stone cottages alongside probably housed farm workers.

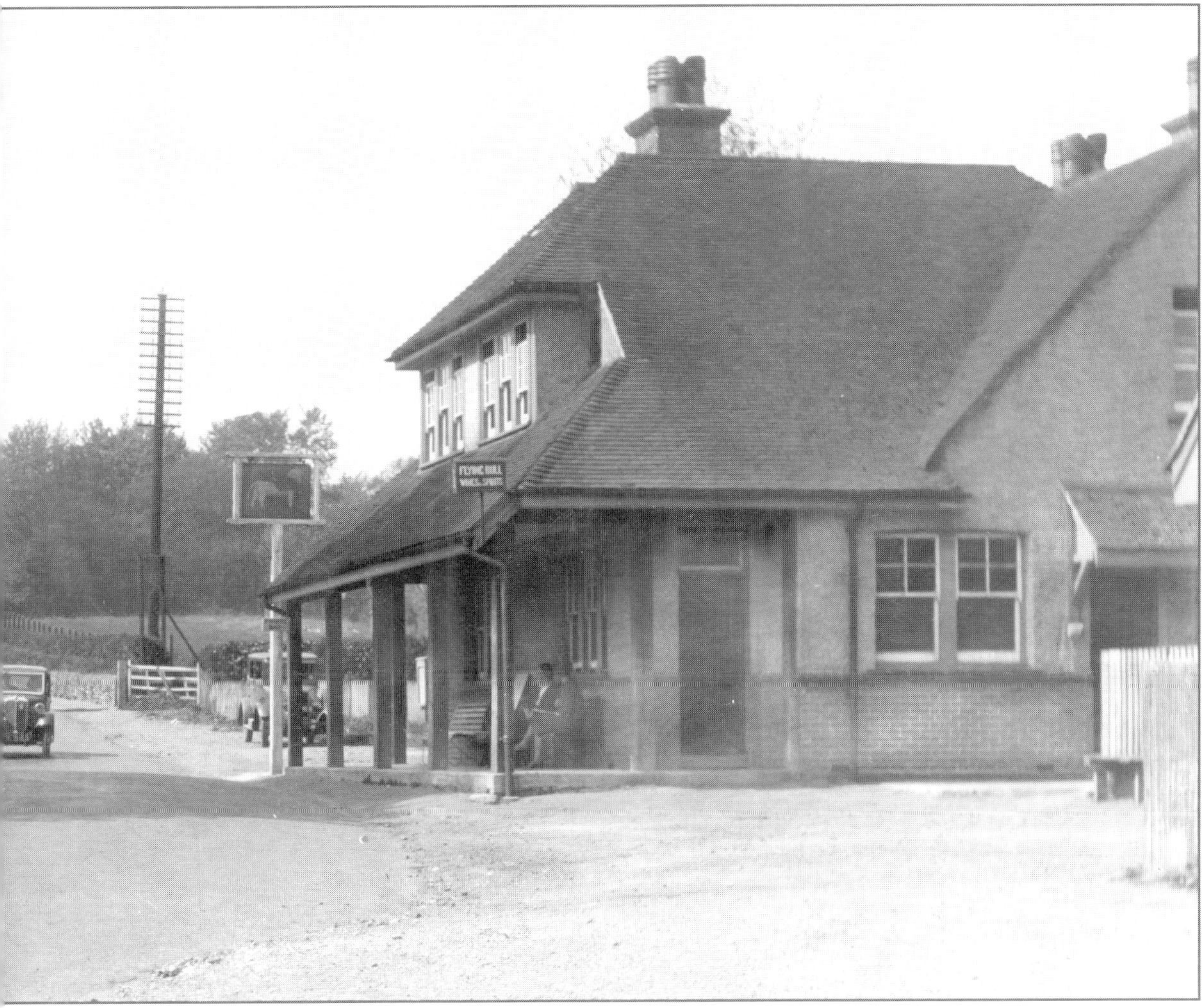

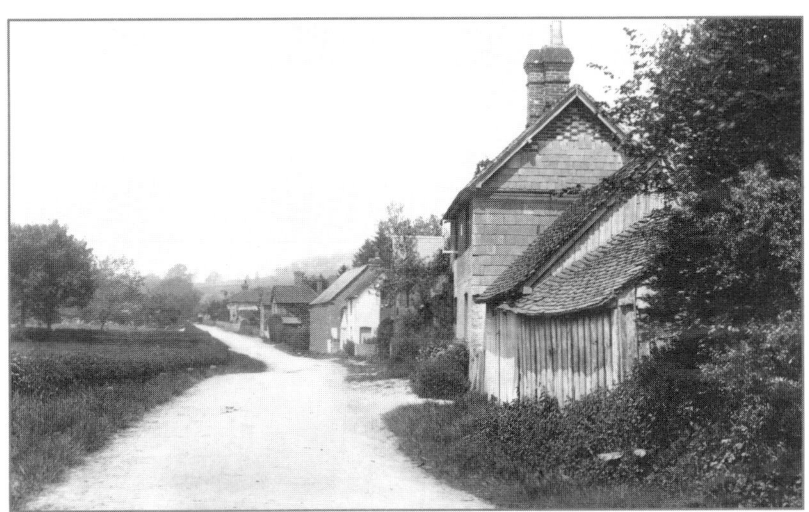

Fernhurst, Vann Road 1908

59675

The village was a Roman settlement with a tile works. It later became a centre for the iron industry with a furnace, a forge and a cannon foundry. The church of St Margaret has Norman walling and windows. Hawksfold was the home of Anthony Salvin, an eminent architect. The Verdley Place Estate of 1870 is now occupied by an agricultural chemical manufacturer. Blackdown is a great sandstone hill 918 feet high, and Blackdown House is a Tudor-style manor house of 1640.

▶ **Kingsley Green Hindhead from the Toll House 1910** 63047
The Sussex Turnpike Trust was set up in 1749 to maintain the road from Hindhead Heath to Chichester with a tollgate at Kingsley Marsh (now Green). Regular users of the roads became skilled at dodging toll collection points. The picture could easily be mistaken for a more modern scene. There is nothing visible that gives clues to the real date.

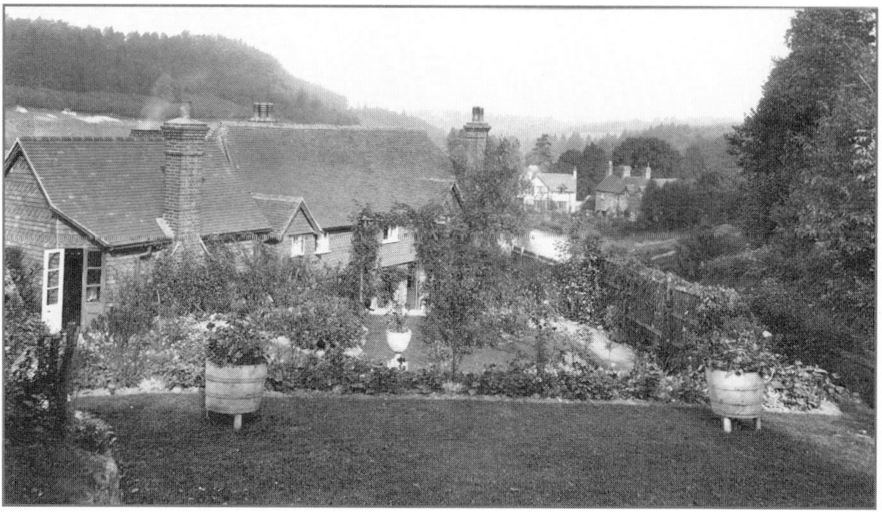

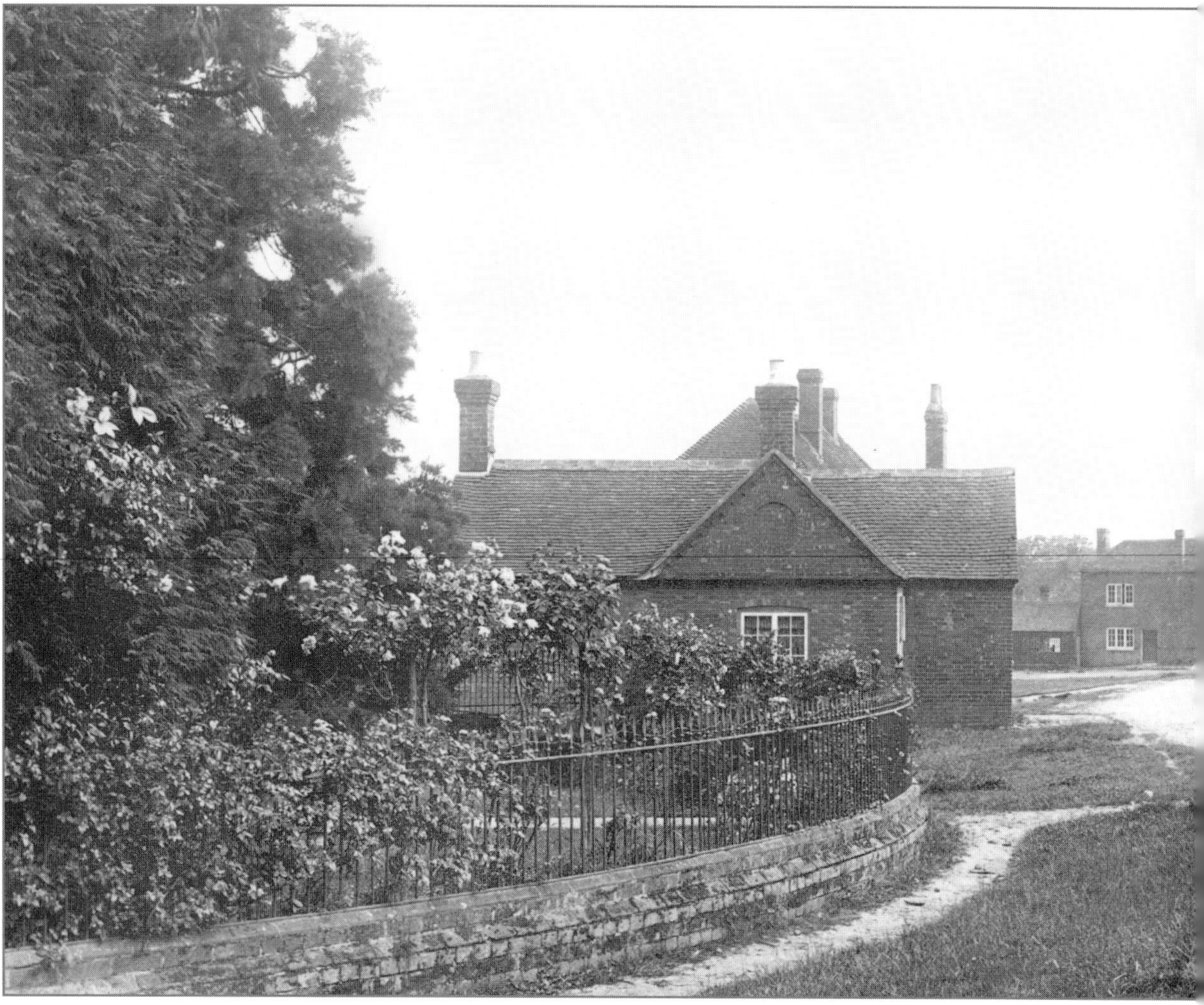

▶ **Kingsley Green Hindhead from the Toll House 1910** 63047

► **Northchapel, The Village 1902** 48370
This is taken further down the same road as 48369. The Swan Inn advertises 'Good Accommodation for Cyclists', and another sign offers 'Horse and Trap or Wagonette for Hire'. Cycling would have been hard going on the rough roads. Horse chestnut trees stand at the side of the road. In front of the inn is a triangular area of little-worn roadway. The scene is similar today, but the Swan is now called the Deepwell Inn.

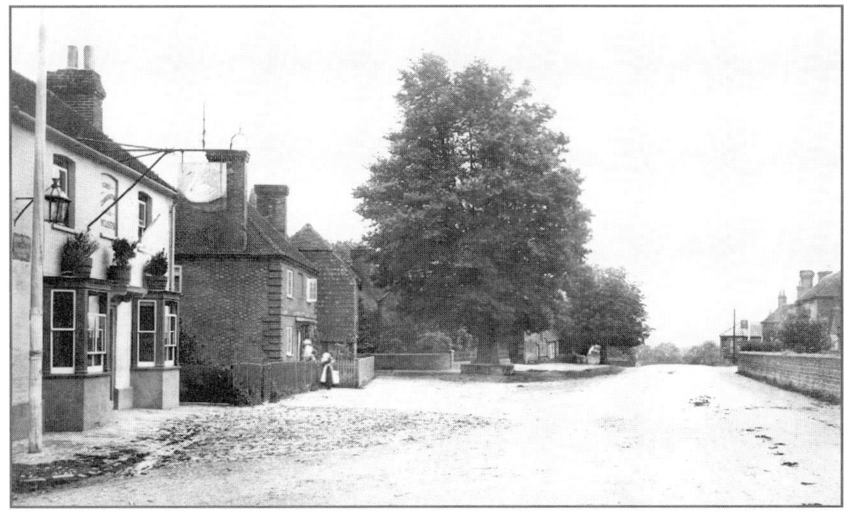

◄ **Northchapel
The Village 1902**
48369
We are on the Petworth to Guildford main road. The church of St John Baptist was rebuilt in 1877; it has a strange-looking font dated 1662. Goff's Farm is a good example of a 17th-century Wealden farmhouse. The Half Moon is a 16th-century inn. The Swan Inn can be seen down the road beyond the horse-drawn vehicles that are waiting for the photographer.

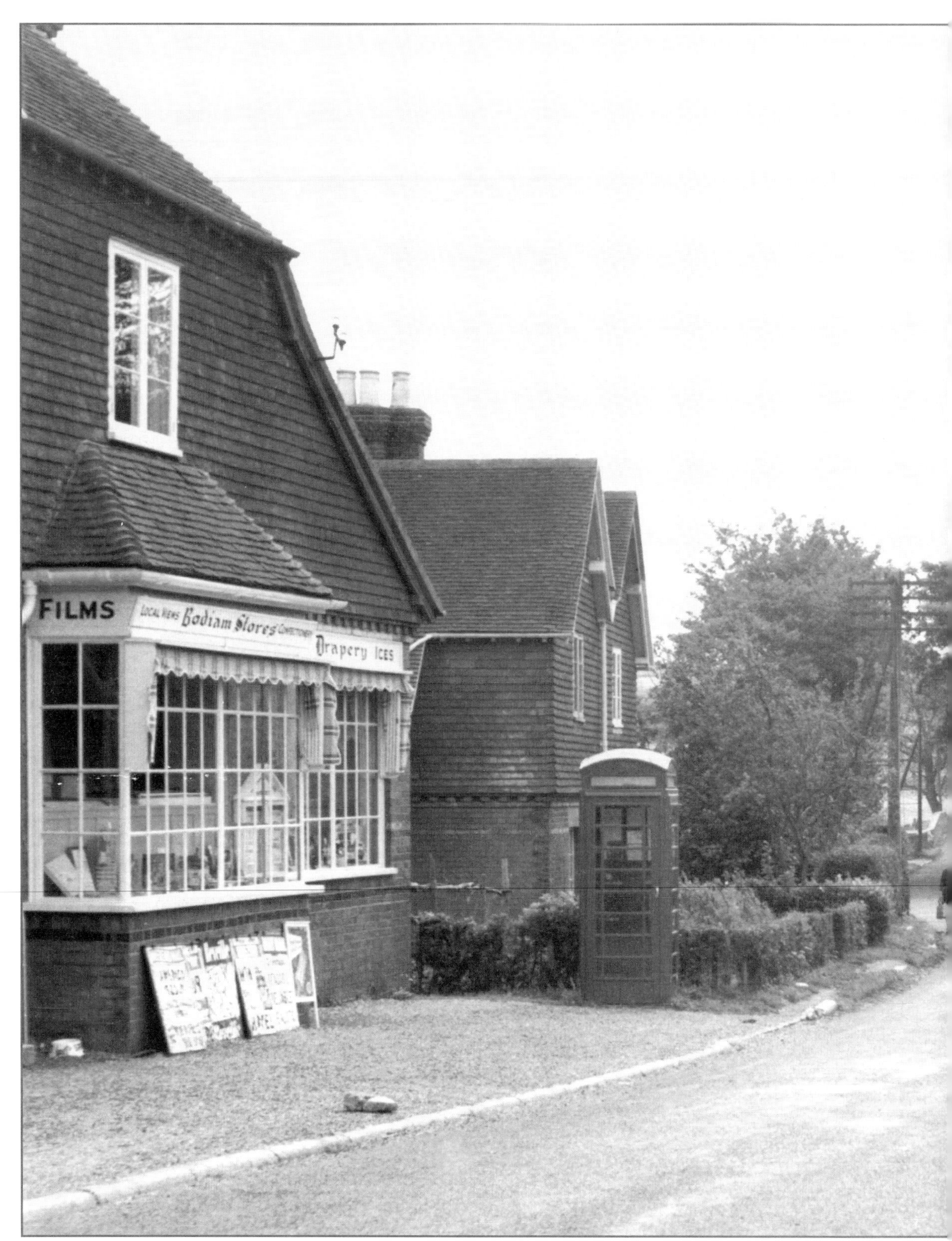
FILMS
LOCAL NEWS
Bodiam Stores
Drapery ICES

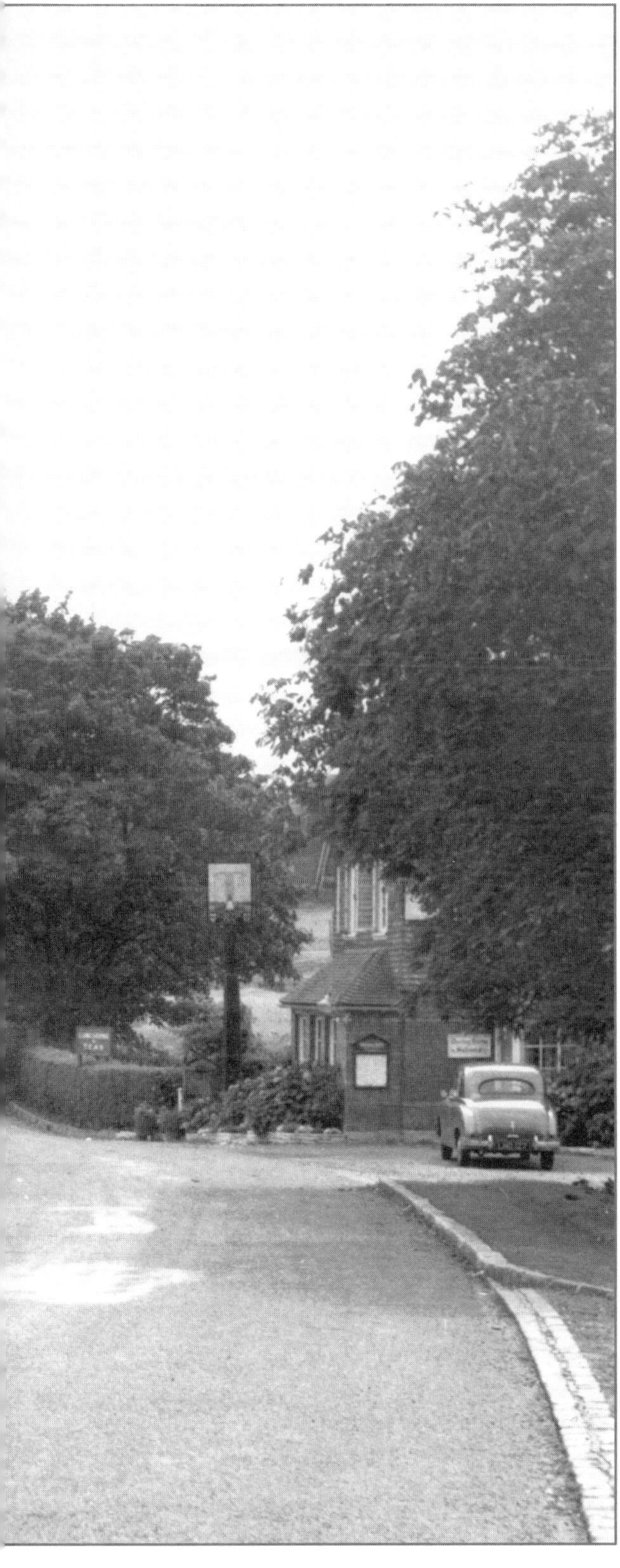

The Weald

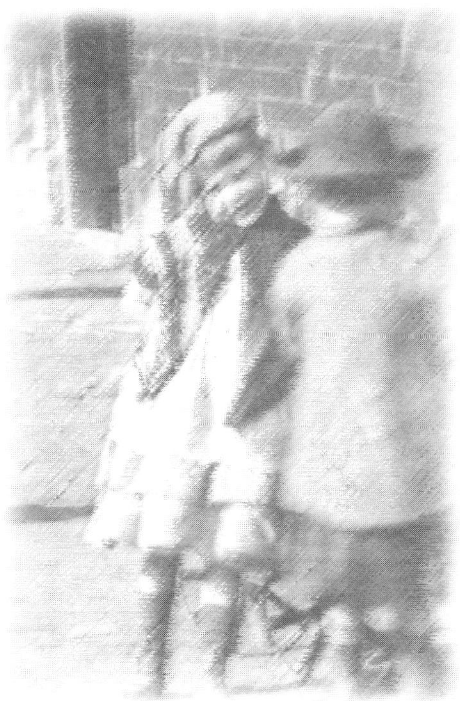

Bodiam, The Village c1955 B128015
Bodiam is located on the River Rother and was once
a port that shipped iron ingots and cannon, which
were made in the area. Bodiam Castle was
constructed in 1388, the last castle to be built in
England for coastal defence. It is well conserved
and set within a moat, and is in the care of the
National Trust and open to visitors. In the picture we
can see the 14th-century Castle Inn on the right
and Bodiam Stores on the left. The scene is similar
today, but the shop is now a tearoom.

Robertsbridge
High Street c1955 R332034

Robertsbridge is a medieval village near the Kent border. There is no church in the village, the nearest being at Salehurst. An iron-smelting furnace, controlled by the Churchill family, made cannon in 1754. The Seven Stars Inn, a picturesque 15th-century timber-framed building, is seen on the right, with a temporary sign. At Abbey Farm the remains of a Cistercian abbey are now part of a house and farmyard. The area is noted for making high quality cricket bats from locally-grown willow trees.

Flimwell
The Village 1903 49363

Flimwell is centred on a crossroads near the Kent border. Its church, St Augustine's, was built in 1873. Seacox is a French chateau-style house built in 1871 for the Goschen family, who were great benefactors of the village; they built many cottages for estate staff. Sir Edward Goschen was British Ambassador in Berlin in 1914 when the war began. Seacox Park has a magnificent collection of trees and shrubs.

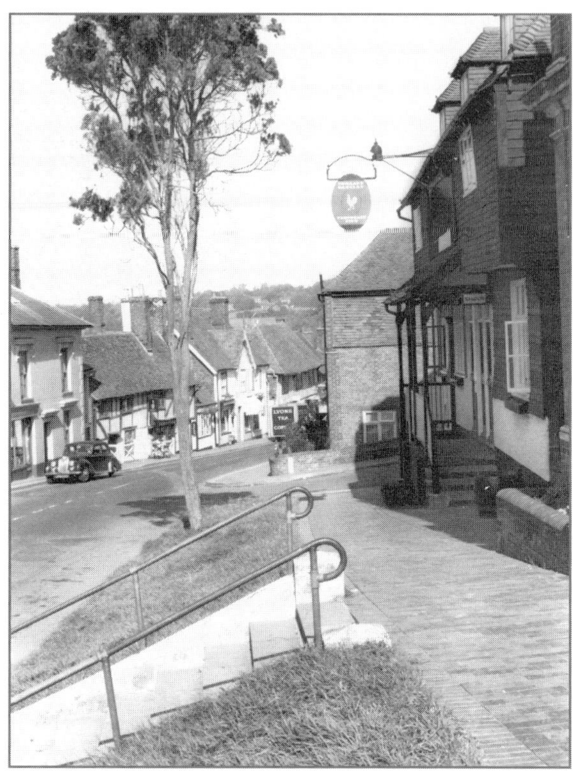

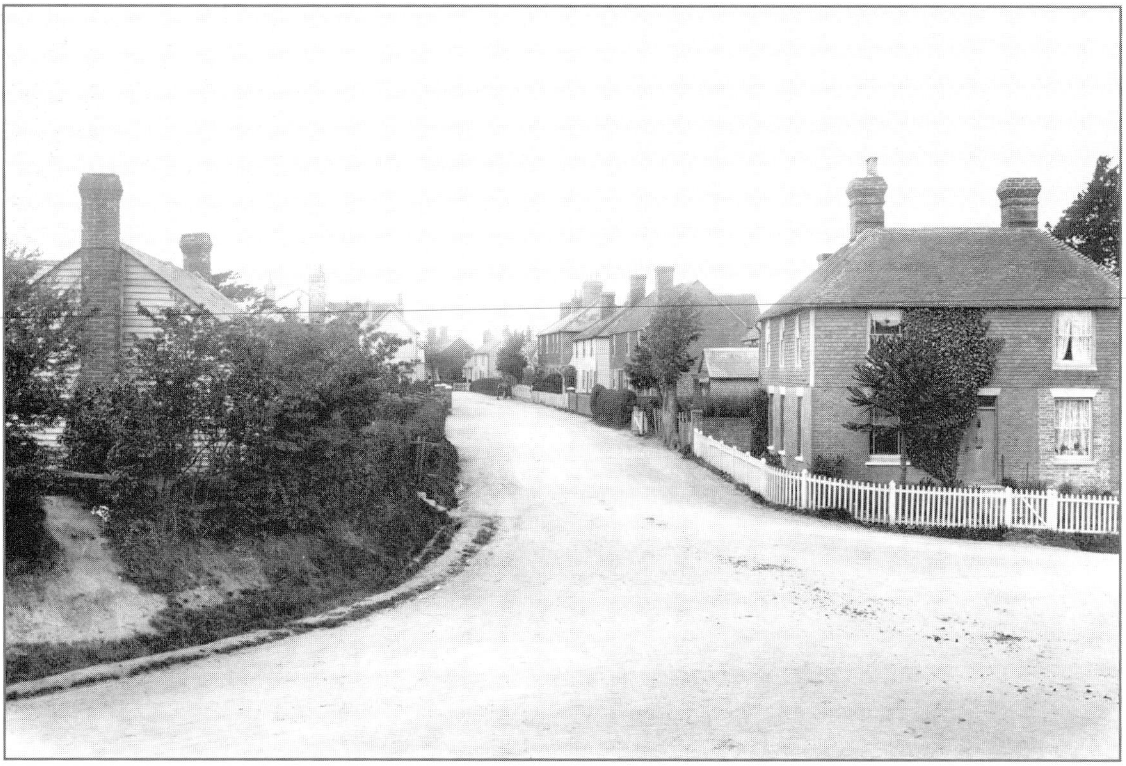

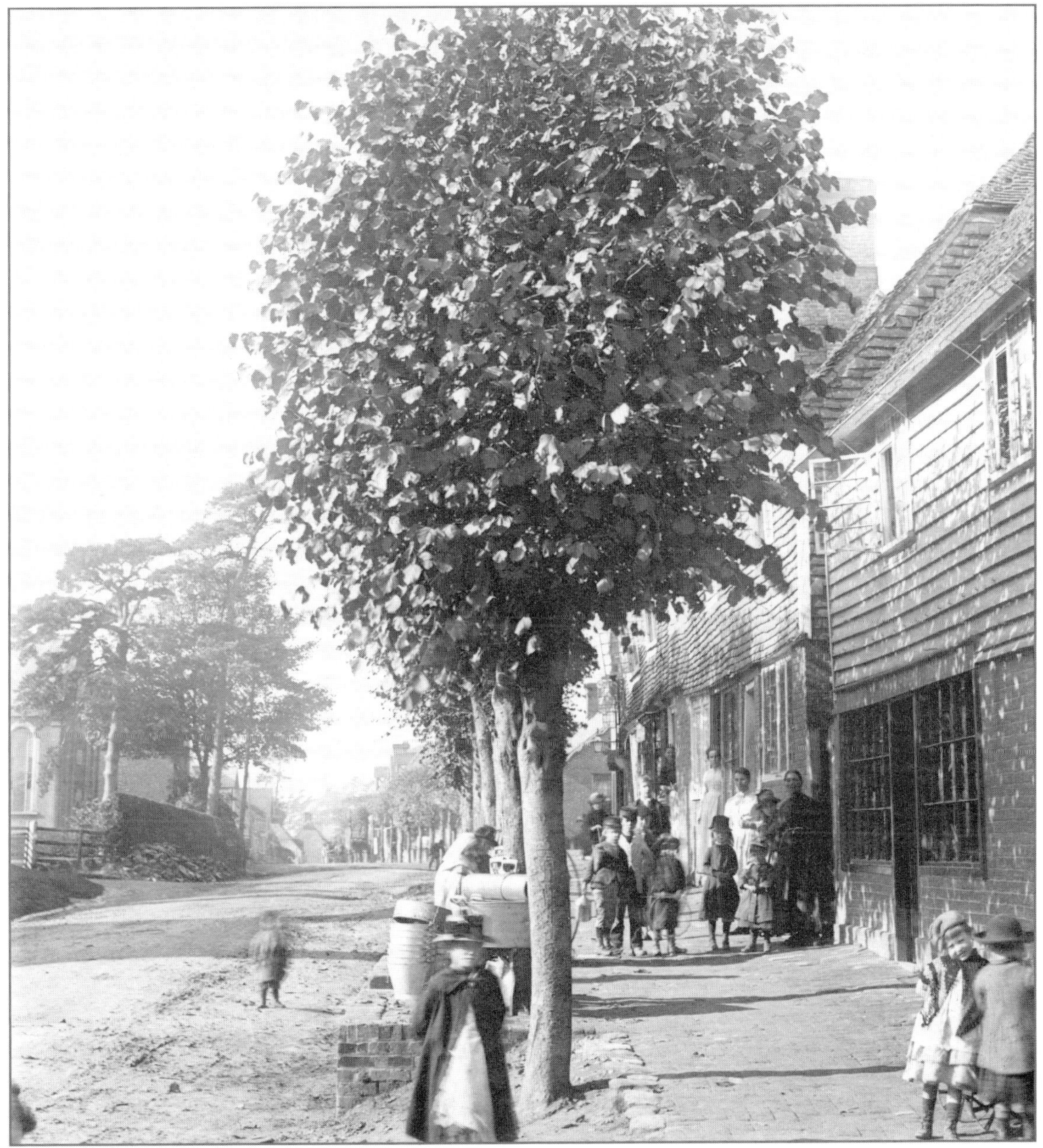

Burwash, The Village 1889 B291501

Burwash was a centre for Sussex iron making. After the iron industry ceased production, the locality was less prosperous; the common became notorious for 18th-century lawlessness. Batemans was built in 1634 for an ironmaster; later it was the home of Rudyard Kipling (1902-1936). It is a beautiful Jacobean house, now in the care of the National Trust and open to visitors. Kipling's literary work 'Puck of Pook's Hill' (1906) is set in the area. Park Mill, a watermill built in 1795, became part of Batemans and is restored to working order. Burghurst manor house is opposite the church. Rampydene is a fine brick house built in 1699. The church of St Bartholomew is on the left of the picture, partly hidden by Scots Pine trees.

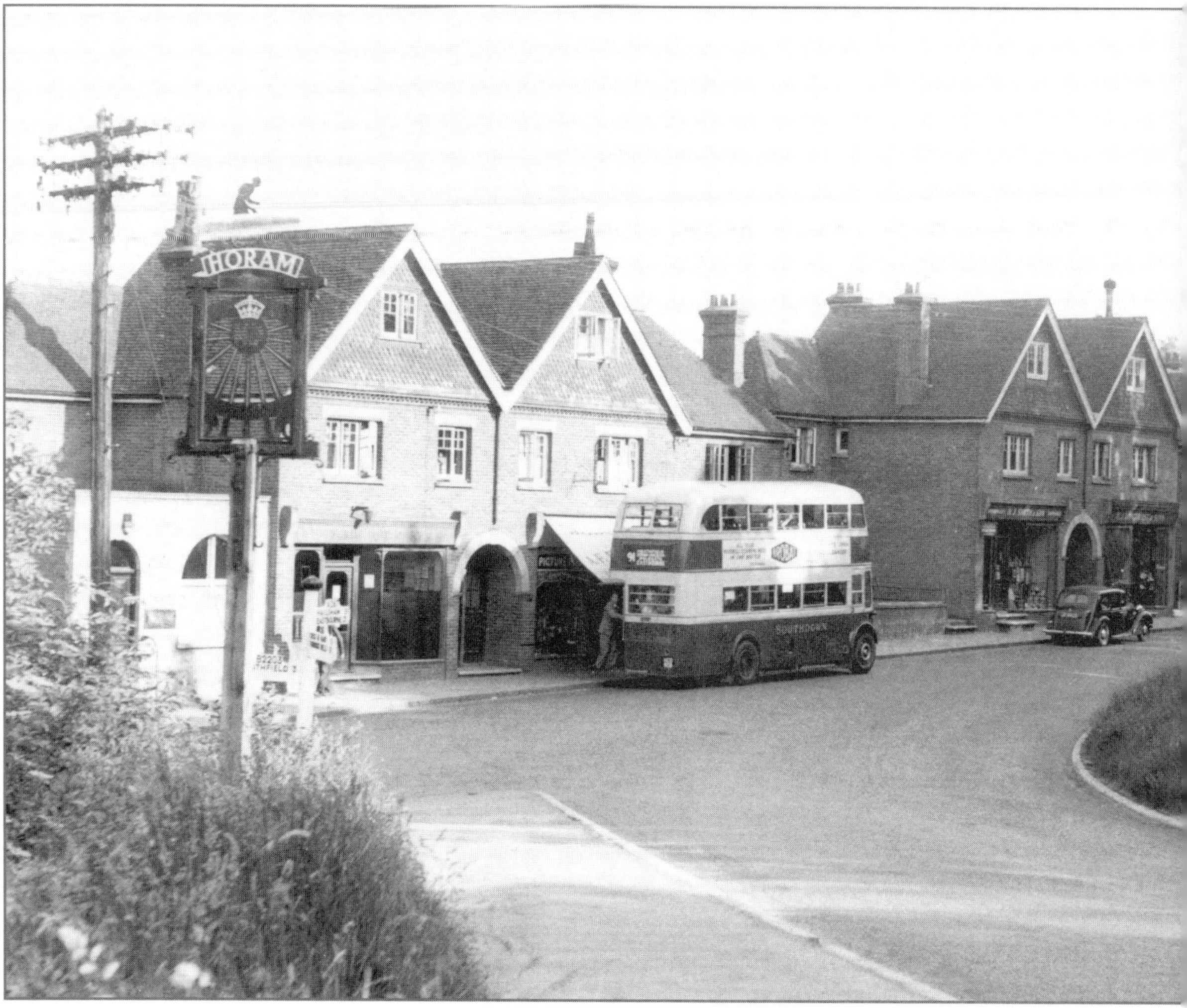

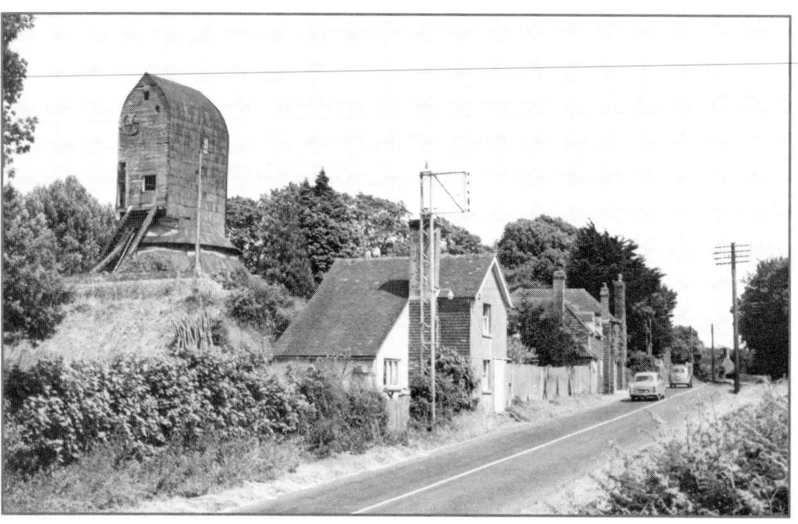

◄ Windmill Hill
c1965 W448005
Windmill Hill is near Herstmonceux. It is a post-type windmill where the body is turned to the wind by means of a long tailpole. The front and sides of the mill body and the roundhouse roof are clad in sheet iron. It is the tallest windmill of this type in Sussex. Built in 1814, it ceased working in 1893, when the sails were taken off. There was a bakery by the mill house. The mill is now being restored by its owner. Iron electricity poles line the road; they are of a type only seen in this part of Sussex.

◄ Horam, The Post Office c1955
H329009

The 'Cuckoo Trail' for cyclists, walkers and the disabled connects Horam to Heathfield and Polegate via the route of an old railway. Old industries in the area were iron ore mining and brickmaking, which is expected to be revived soon. Horeham Manor is noted for making Merrydown vintage cider. The village sign is in the left foreground of the picture. Passengers board the route 91 Southdown bus, en route from Uckfield to Eastbourne.

▼ Five Ashes, The Five Ashes Inn c1960 F172002

The village is named after five ash trees on the green. Twits Gill was once the home of Sir Austen Chamberlain, who was Chancellor of the Exchequer in 1903 and Foreign Secretary in the 1920s. He assembled a vast collection of rock plants from all over the world. At the time of the picture, the Five Ashes public house was offering customers ales from Tamplins, Brighton Brewery.

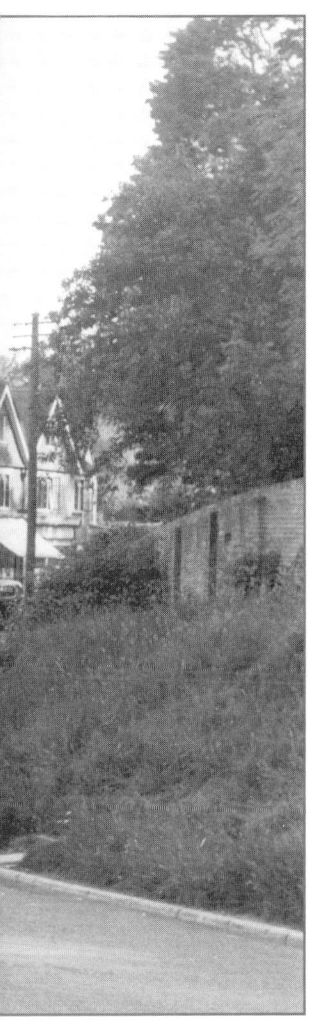

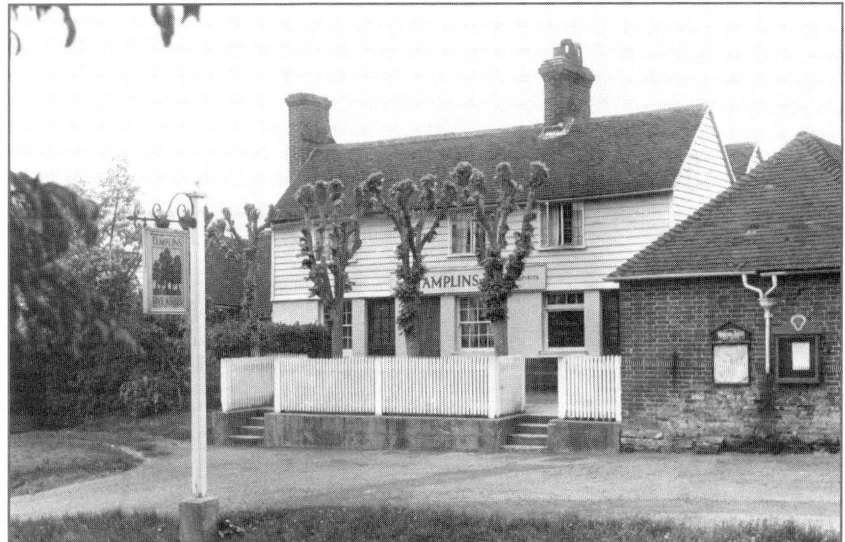

◄ Upper Dicker, The Plough Inn c1950
U50004

We are in the Cuckmere Valley, with fine views of the scarp side of the Downs. The Dicker, behind the brick wall and trees beyond the pub, is a rather odd-looking mansion, built by Horatio William Bottomley, a politician and journalist. It is now St Bede's School. Dicker Pottery made bricks, tiles and pottery. Not far away is Michelham Priory, founded in 1229 for 13 Augustinian Canons. King Edward I spent a night here on his way from Lewes to Battle. After the dissolution it became a farmhouse. Restoration of the buildings was commenced in 1927; recently it included a watermill that has been restored to working order. The inn in the photograph is offering Tamplins Brighton Ales.

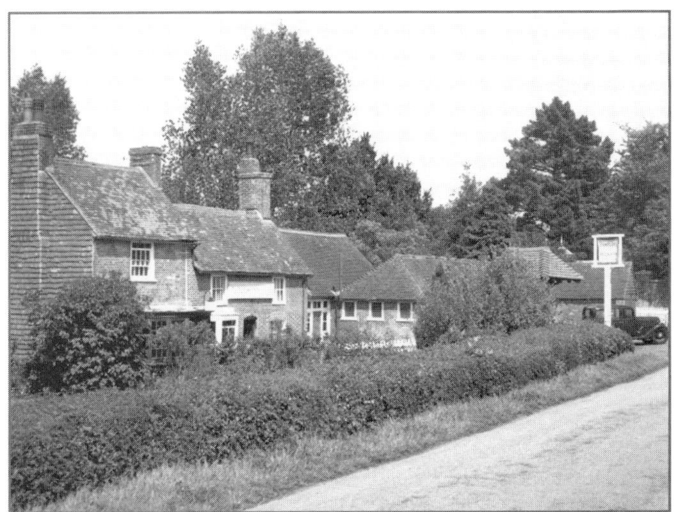

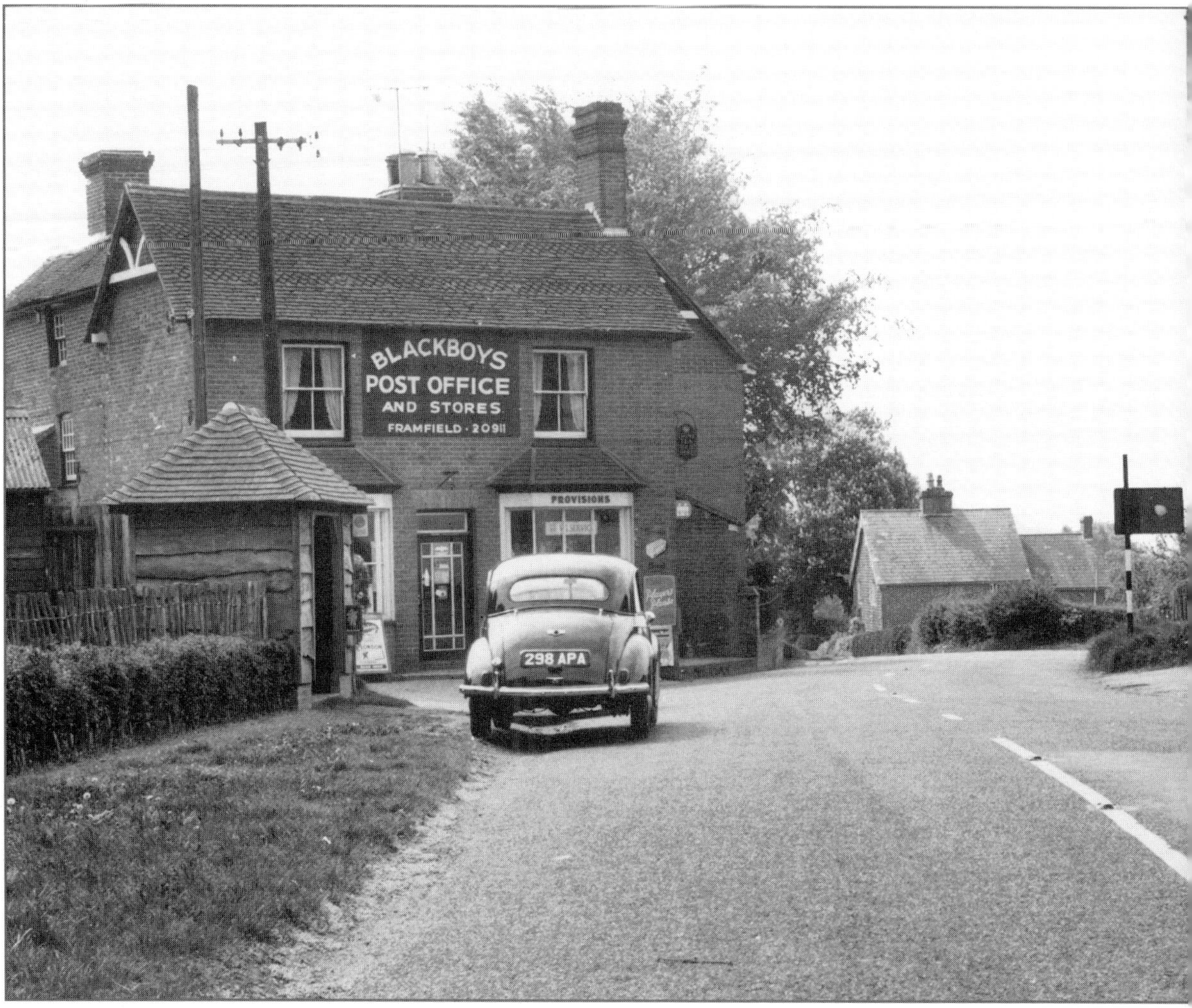

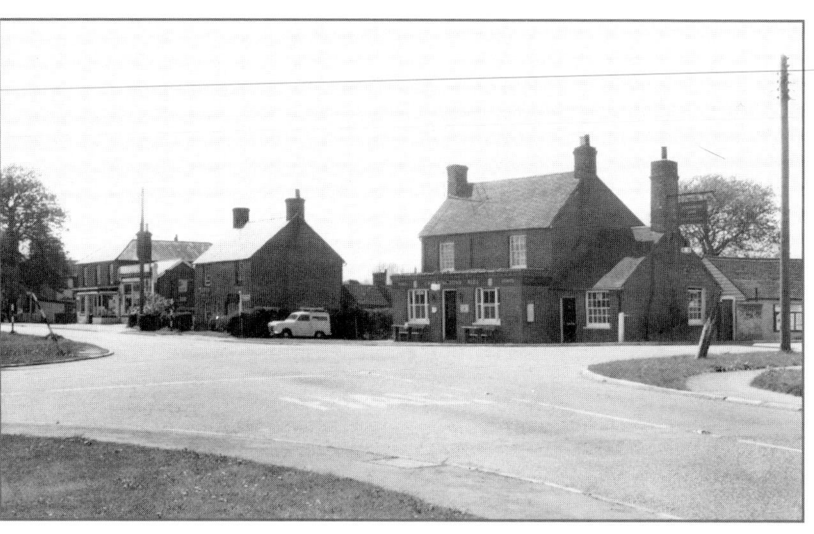

◀ **Halland, The Cross Roads c1965** H327014
We are on the Eastbourne main road, south of Uckfield. Halland Park Farm is the remains of the mansion built in 1595 to replace Laughton Place as the principal house of the Pelham family, who were earl, duke, bishop, lords, knights and baronets. The Blacksmith's Arms is made out of extended and altered buildings, with a house at the core. The village store has been added to the front and side of what was once a large house.

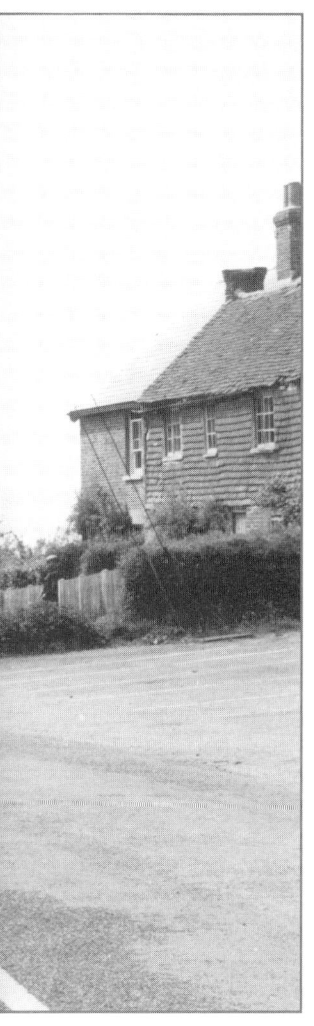

Blackboys, The Post Office
c1960 B566034

Blackboys is a small iron industry village. Its name is believed to have come from the appearance of charcoal workers as they emerged from working in the woods. Tickerage Wood was the site of a smelting furnace and forge hammer, and later a corn watermill. The village also had a well-known post-type windmill, which was sited by the main road. The 14th-century Blackboys Inn has been recently restored after fire damage.

Maresfield, The Mill Pond
1902 48216

One of many millponds used by the Sussex iron industry. The ponds stored water to drive waterwheels for powering furnace blowers, forging hammers for working wrought iron, and for driving lathes for boring cannon. Boringwheel Mill is nearby; it finished work as a corn mill site. The spire of the church of St Bartholomew is just visible on the hilltop. The Chequers is an old coaching inn built in 1734.

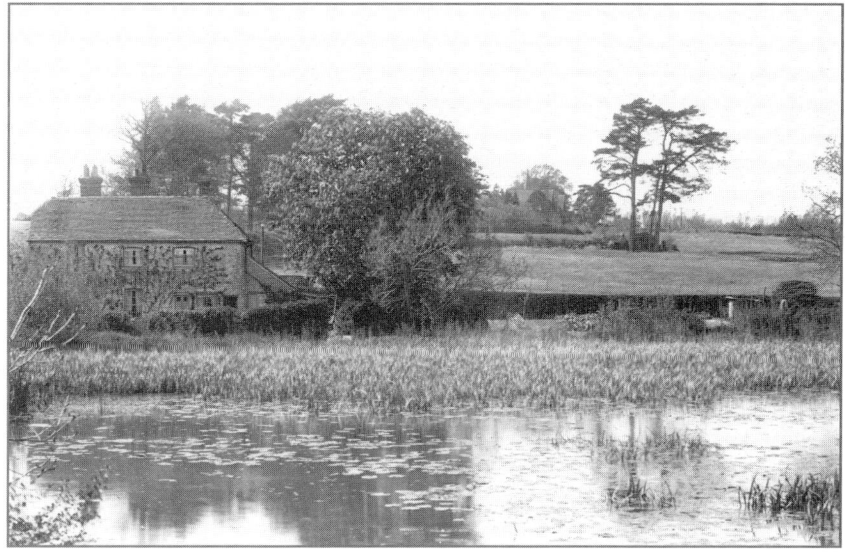

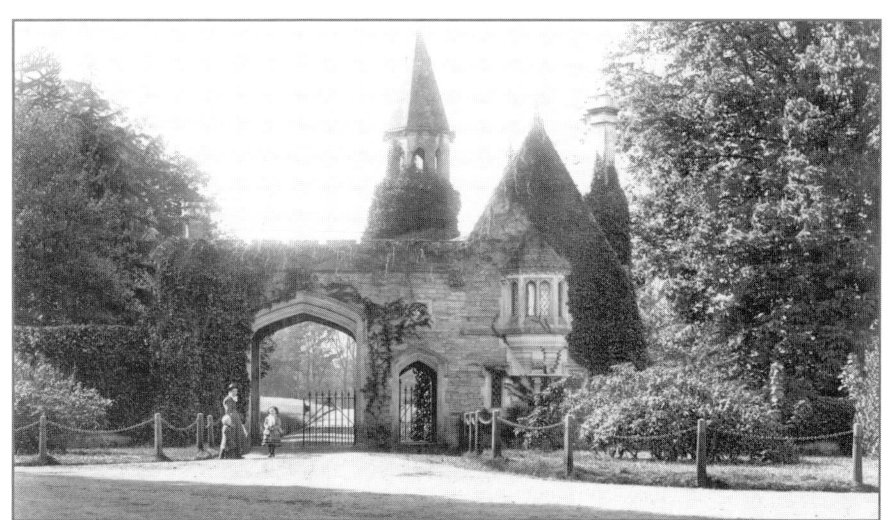

Maresfield
The Park Entrance
1902 48217

The 19th-century Gothic style gatehouse to The Park has a turret and plenty of ivy growing up the stone walls. Park House is now nearly all demolished. The woman and children are dressed up and stand still in the sunshine waiting for the photographer to complete his work.

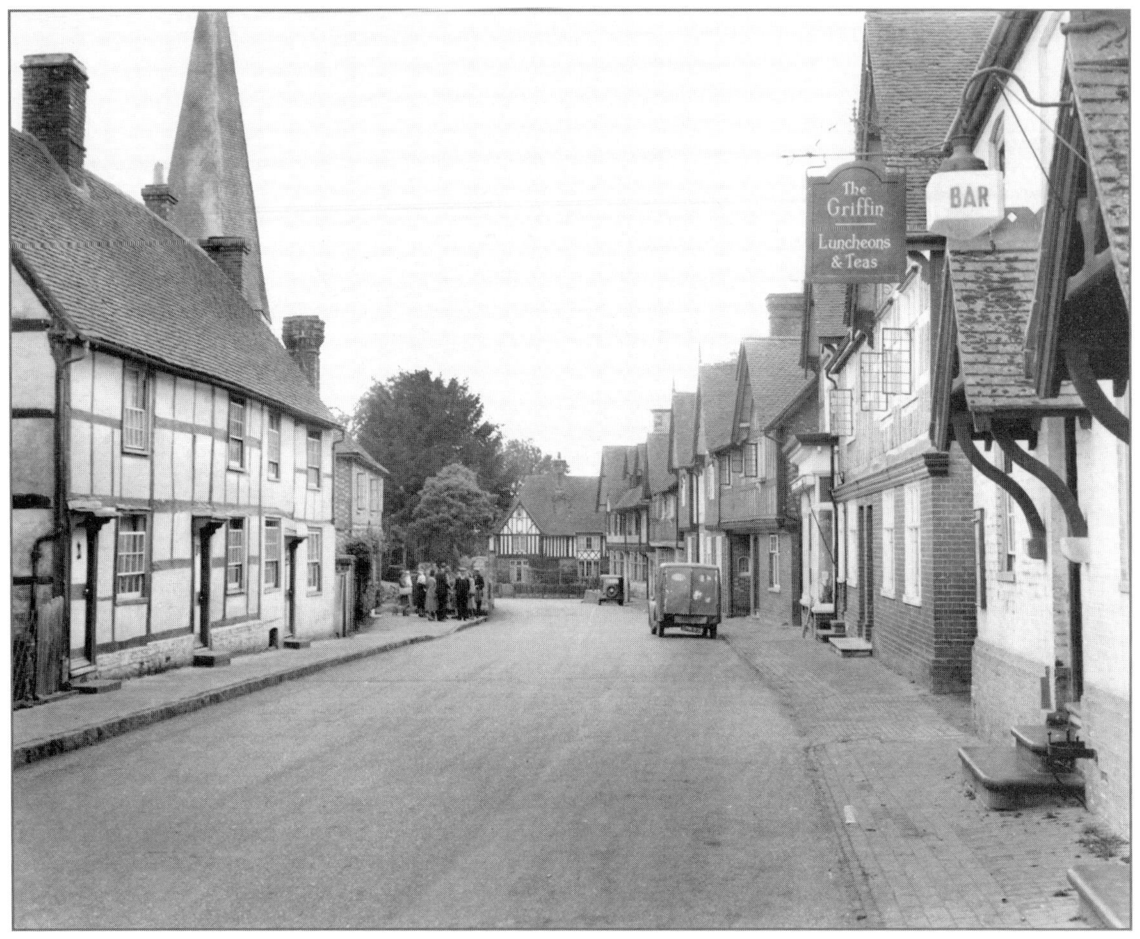

Fletching
The Street c1950 F138005
Simon de Montfort's army lay here the night before the Battle of
Lewes in 1264. The area was made notorious by the 'Piltdown
Man' fake archaeological discoveries in the 1910s. The nearby
Sheffield Park estate built the modern mock half-timbered houses
at the end of the street. Sheffield Park Gardens were magnificently
landscaped by Capability Brown and are open to visitors. The
gardens also contain the National Pinetum collection of pine trees.
The southern terminus station of the Bluebell Railway to
East Grinstead is nearby.

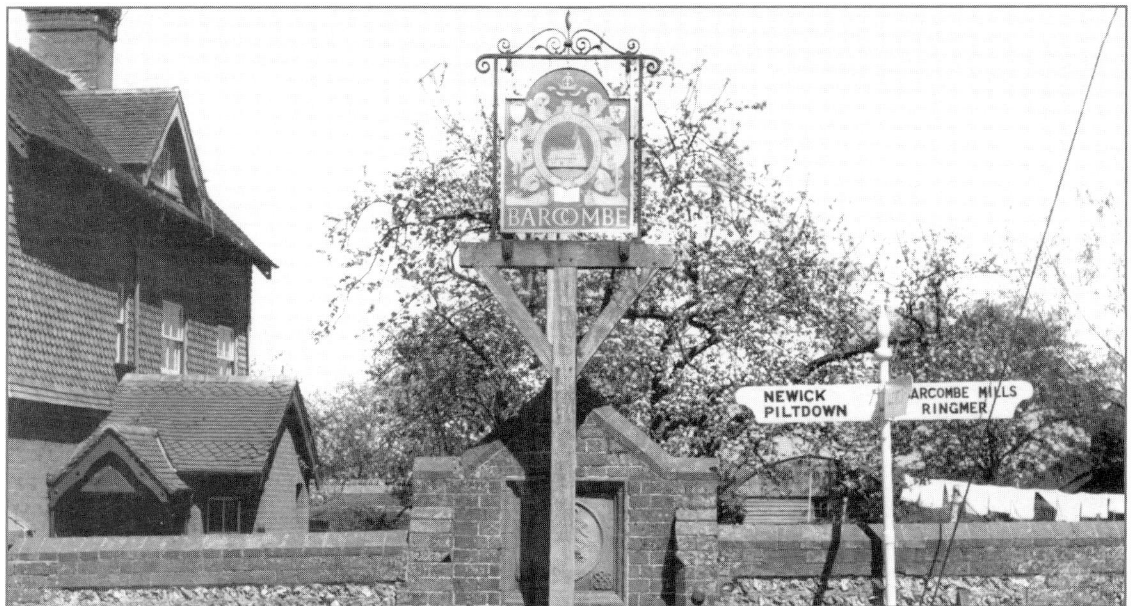

Barcombe, The Village Sign c1955 B18031

We are on the navigable River Ouse and an old Roman road. The flint-built church of St Mary is over-restored, with little of the original remaining. Court House is an altered 15th-century hall-house. The picture shows the village sign and a modern road sign. All road signs were removed during World War Two to confuse invaders. They were replaced soon after the war finished, in time for the great expansion in post-war tourism.

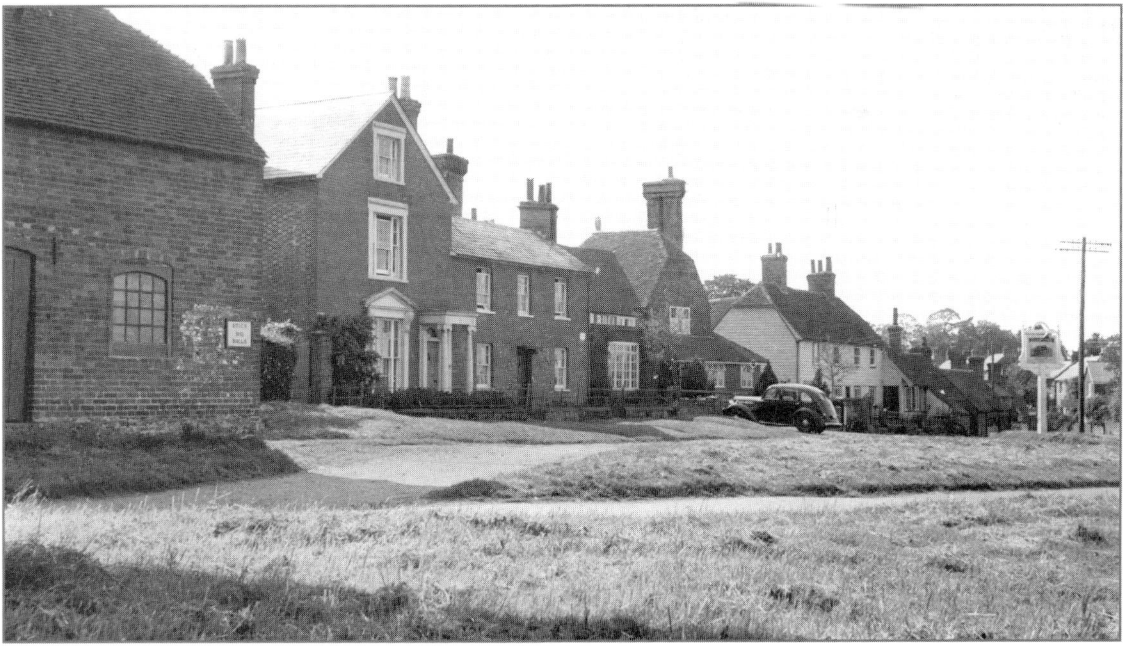

Newick, The Green c1955 N90009

Newick is situated halfway between two great Christian centres of worship - Canterbury and Winchester - so the village was used as a resting-place for pilgrims. A range of different building styles is seen in the picture, including the Bull Inn, whose sign stands on the green in front.

Chailey, The Village Green c1965 C437004
A scattered village on a hilltop in the centre of Sussex. Friendly societies began here at the Five Bells Inn in 1782. The Heritage is a specialised health care institution for disabled children with buildings in several locations around the area. High Common was famous for potteries, and bricks are still made in the area. North Common has a white smock windmill reckoned to be the exact centre of Sussex. A temporary World War Two fighter airfield was constructed at Chailey in 1943, with grass runways.

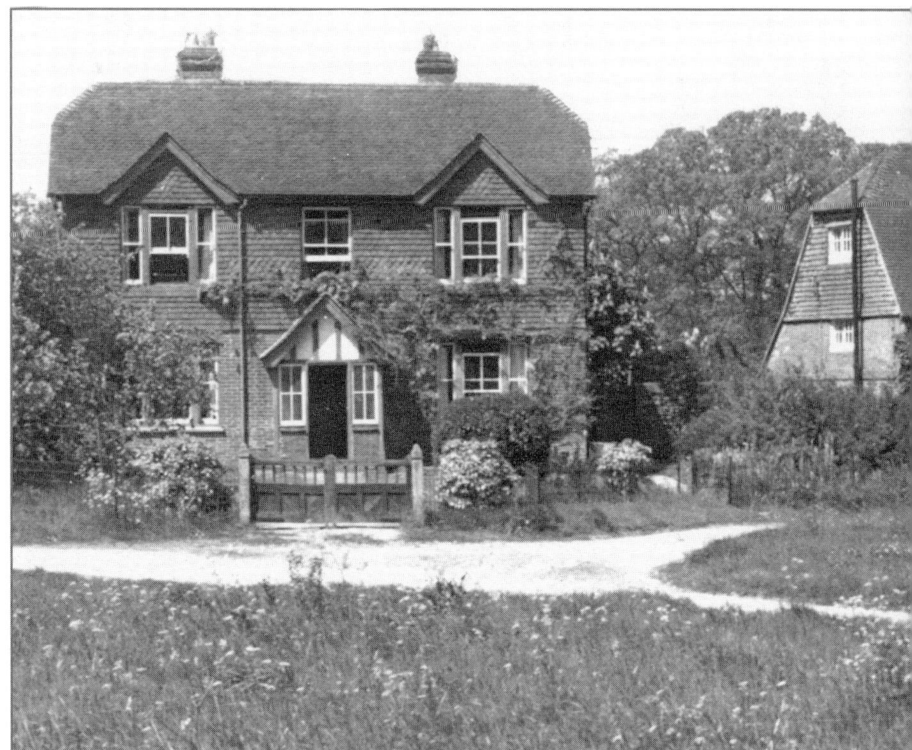

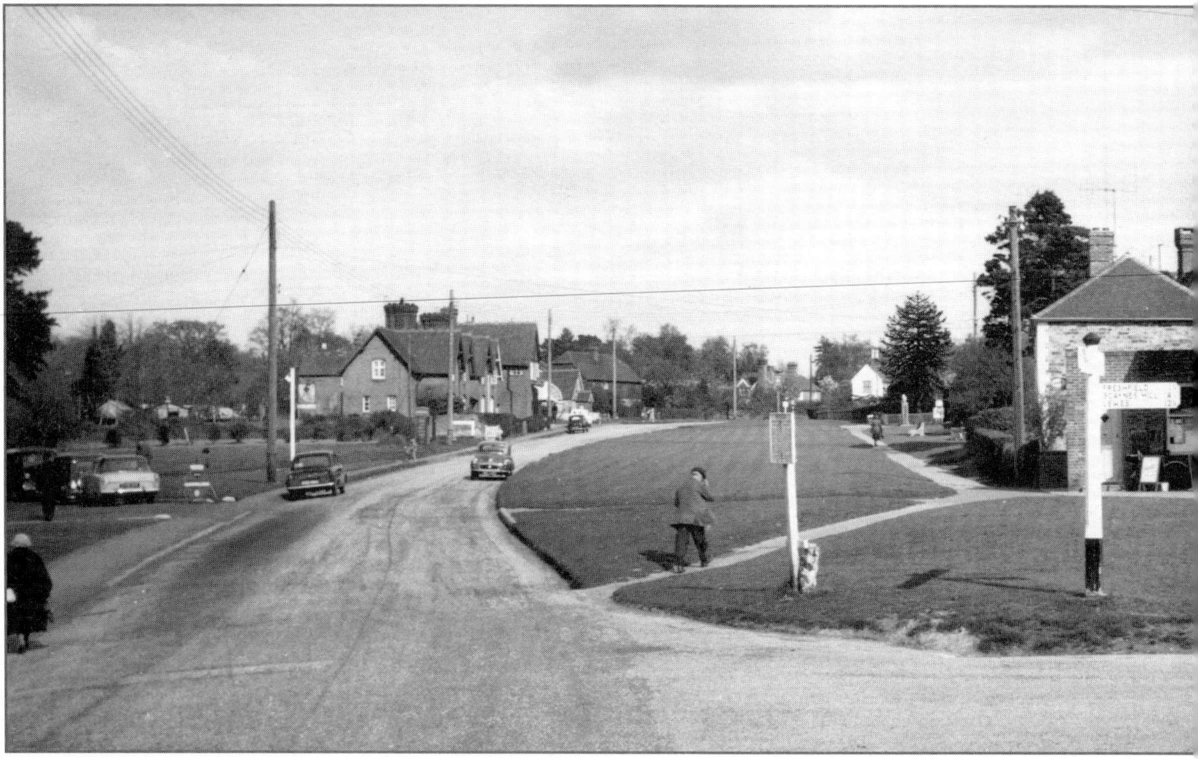

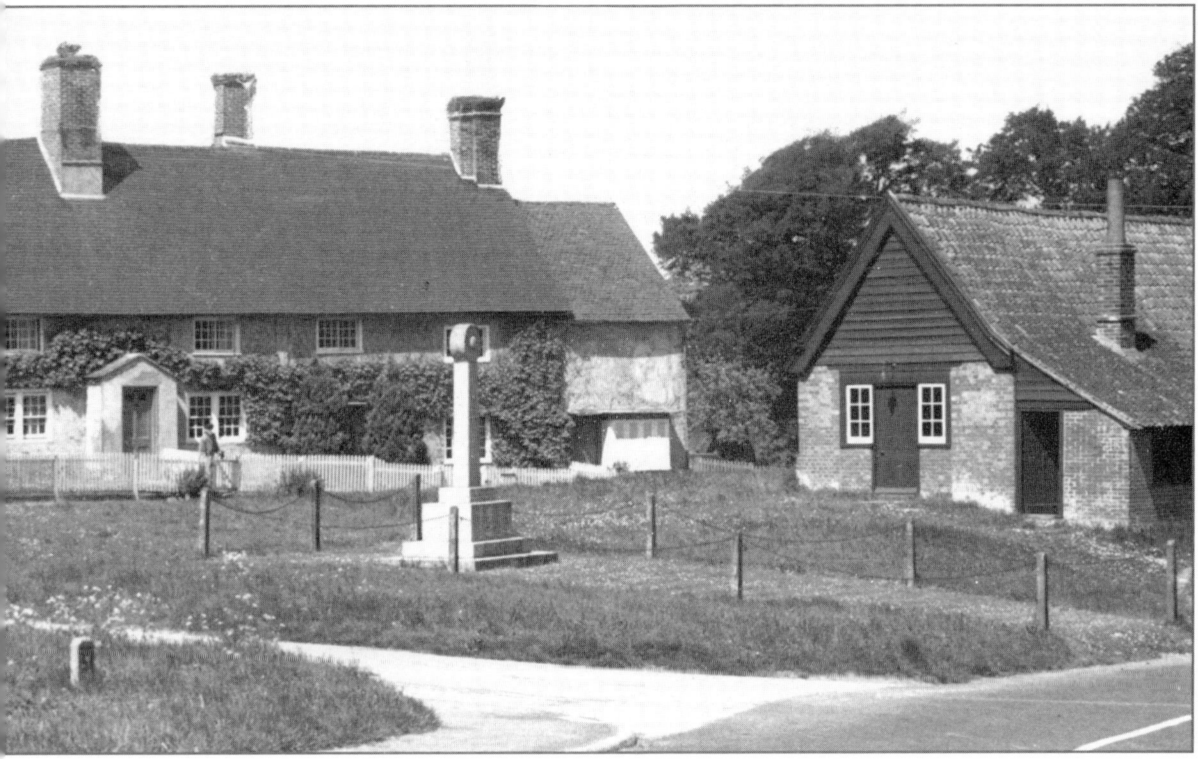

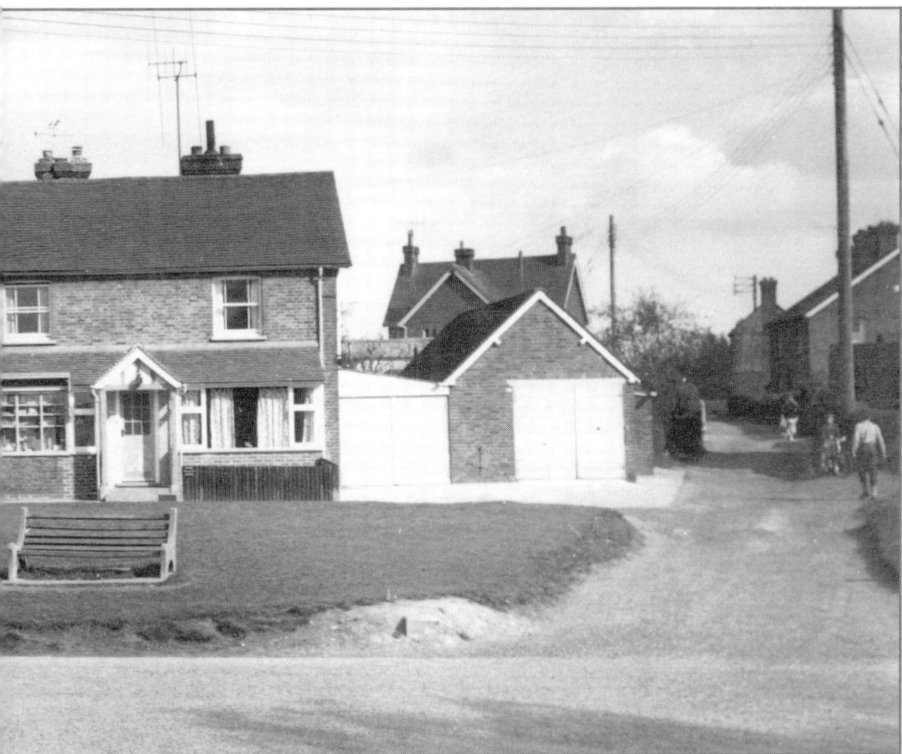

Horsted Keynes
The Green c1965
H359017

There are connections with the Sussex iron industry, for an ironmaster once lived here. The 17th-century house Birch Grove was the home of Harold Macmillan, the former Prime Minister. Ludwell Grange, built in 1540, is a fine half-timbered house. The Norman church of St Giles is at the north end of the village. Along a footpath nearby is a well-restored watermill with a wooden overshot waterwheel. The railway station is on the Bluebell Line to East Grinstead. The village stores has been made by adapting a house.

▼ **Lindfield, The Bower House and the Church c1955** L221060

The church of St John the Baptist is mainly 13th-century and has a wood-shingled broach spire. The village has many historic houses. The Bower House is a timber-framed hall house with a kingpost roof. The Tiger public house was once Church House - behind the brick façade it has a king post roof and a 15th-century hall. The half-timbered Thatched Cottage was built c1390 by the Chaloner family, who were French immigrant broadloom blanket weavers. Humphrey's Bakery, High Street, has been dated 1332.

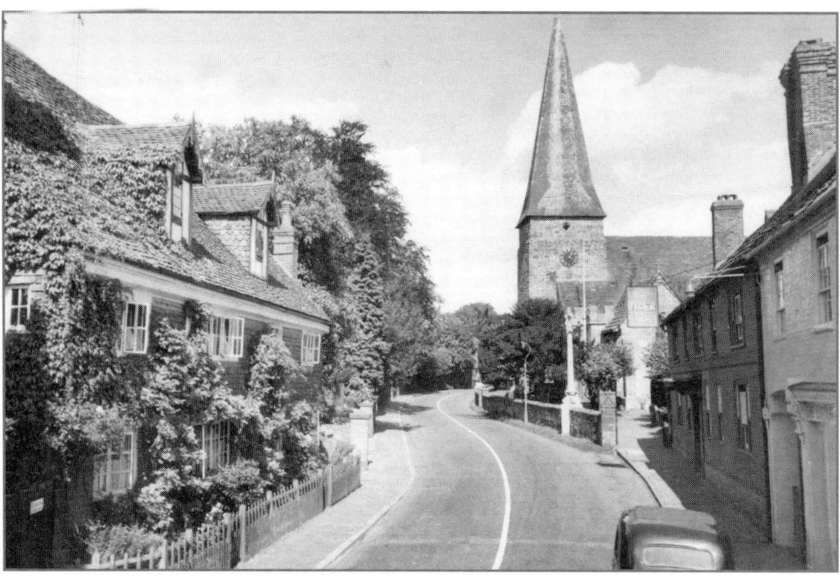

▼ **Keymer, Keymer Road c1960** K127028

Keymer is at the foot of the Downs near Hassocks. The Norman church of St Cosmos and St Damian was re-built in 1866. Ockley Manor is an 18th-century brick house, with a dovecote. Oldland post windmill is being slowly restored to a good state of repair. On the left of the picture is the signboard of the Greyhound, a Watneys house. It has a fireplace dated 1595.

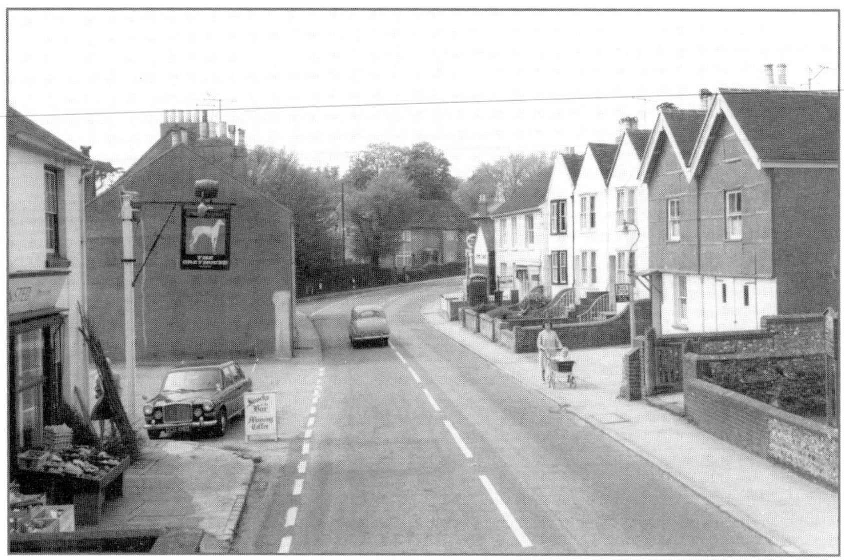

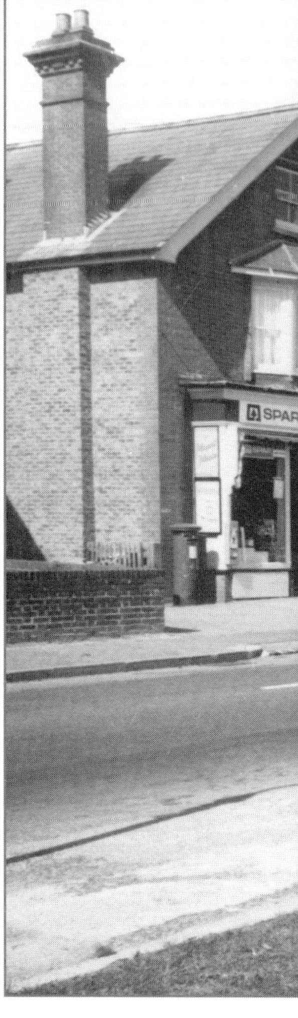

▲ **Whitemans Green The Village c1965**

W452011

A small village to the north of Cuckfield, Whiteman's Green was once on several bus routes - a single-decker bus is just visible at the bottom of the hill. A village sign is on grass verge. It is nice to see a village scene with no visible overhead wires and poles.

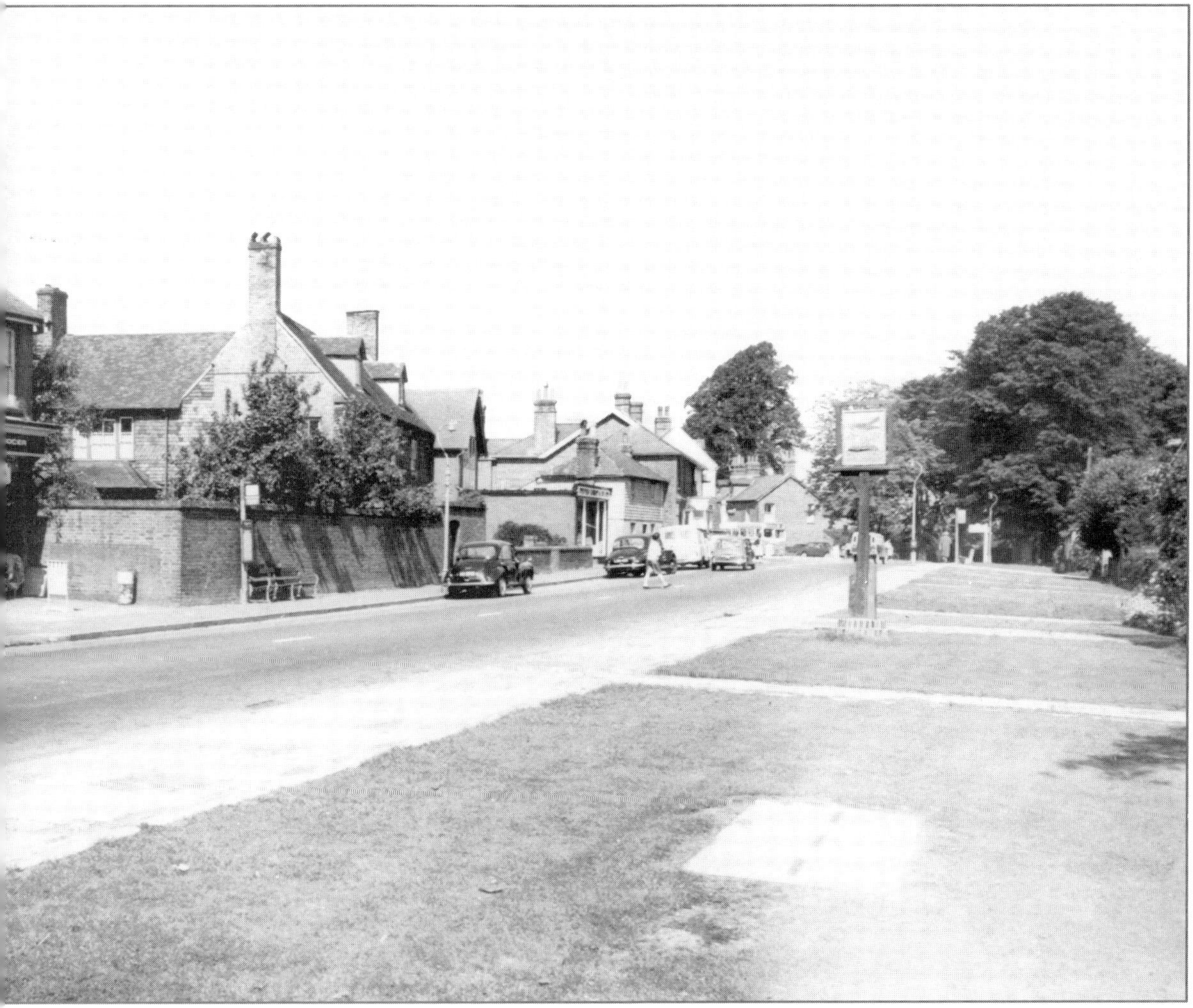

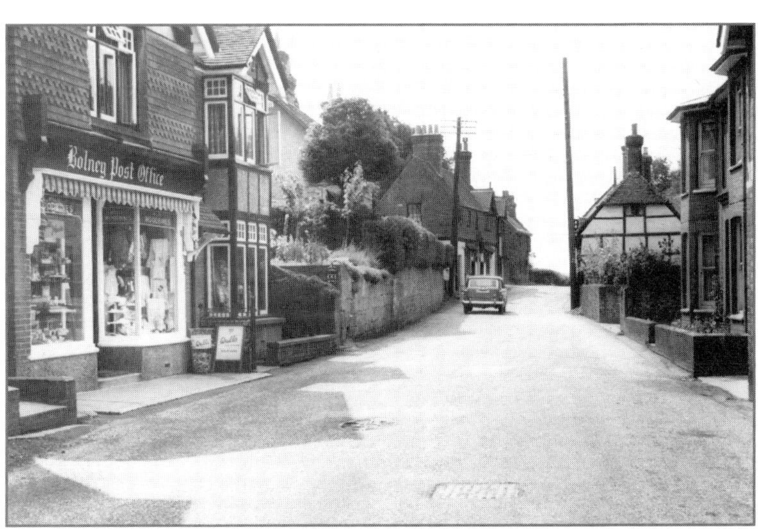

◀ **Bolney, The Post Office 1957**
B507050
Bolney is a quiet village, located just off the main London to Brighton trunk road. The 13th-century church of St Mary Magdalene has a massive 16th-century tower with rounded pinnacles, which houses a peal of eight bells. The public house is appropriately named the Eight Bells. A timber-framed Tudor Tea House is located on the main road. Wykehurst is a French-style chateau with conical turrets and elaborate ornamentation. It was built in 1872 for Henry Huth, a famous collector of rare books. A new vineyard was planted in the village in 1973.

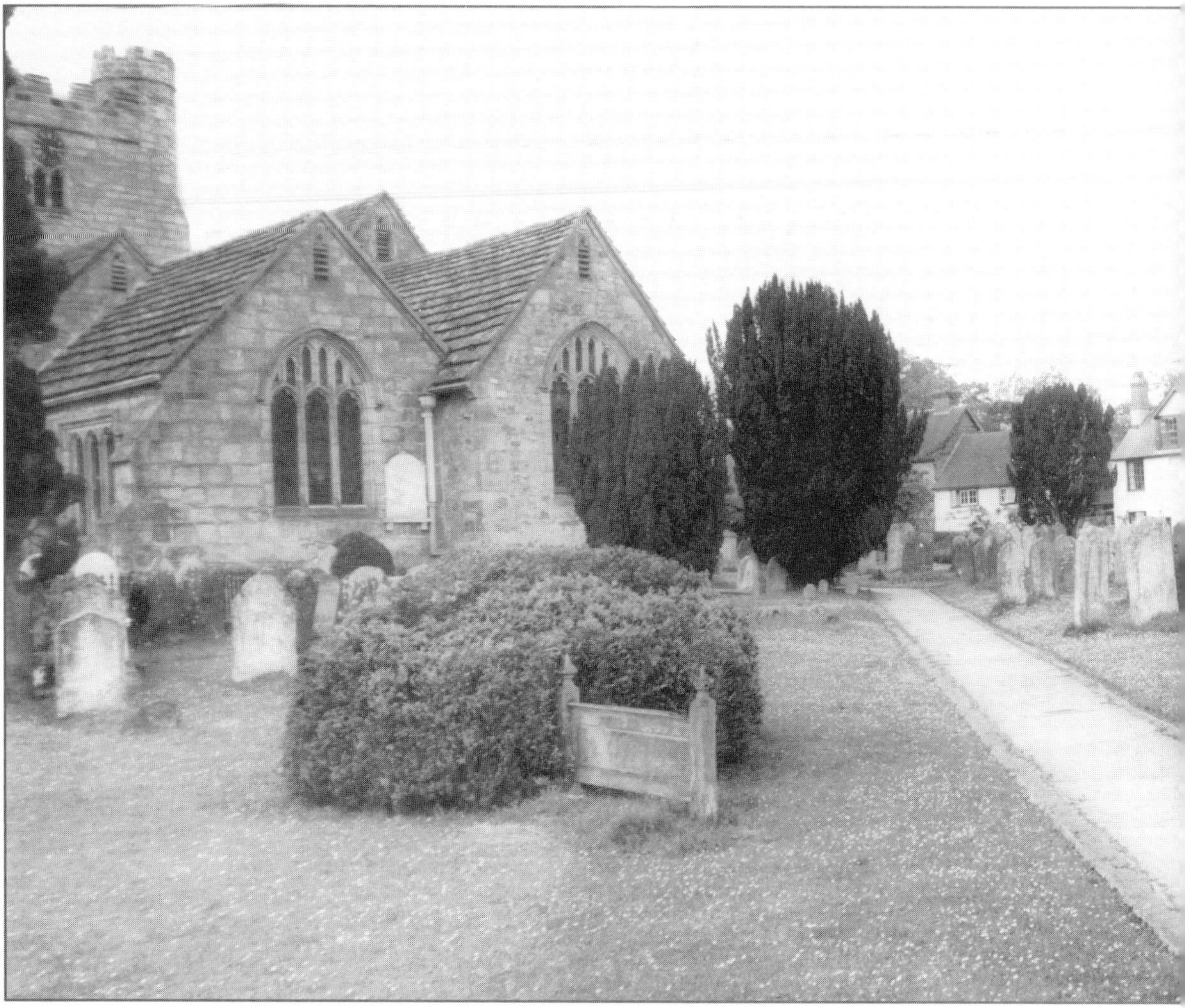

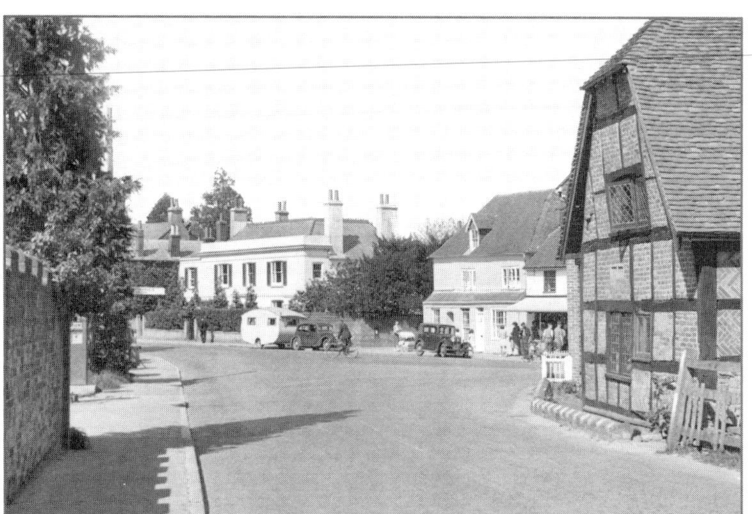

◀ **Henfield, Golden Square
c1955** H313002
Henfield is a main road village
midway between Horsham and
Brighton. St Peter's 13th-century
church was rebuilt in 1870.
Nearby is the Cat House, a
quaintly decorated half-timbered
residence. Brickmaking was quite
a large local industry. A common
on the Brighton Road has a fine
cricket pitch and reed beds.
There are two old coaching inns in
the High Street: the 14th-century
George and the White Hart. In the
picture an old-style touring
caravan hitched up to its towing
car waits at the roadside.

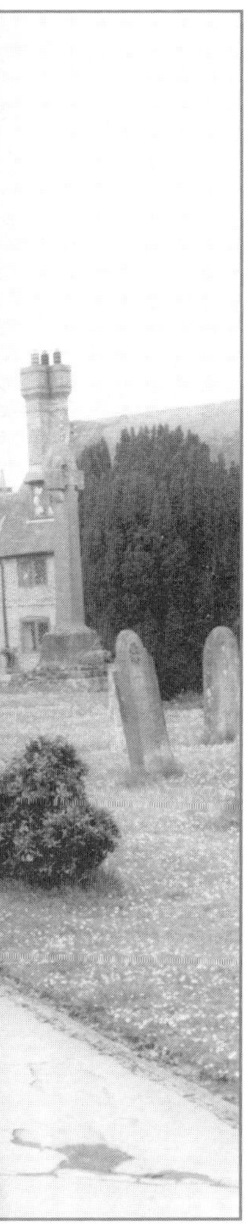

Cowfold, St Peter's Church c1960 C425022

This village has grown around a road junction on the Horsham to Brighton road. The church has a fine Horsham stone roof and a large brass on the floor of the nave to Thomas Noland, Prior of the Cluniac St Pancras at Lewes, who died in 1433. A line of large and small cottages face onto the churchyard, which has many old yew trees. St Peter's Cottage, once a priest's house and now a restaurant, has an inglenook fireplace with a cast iron Sussex fireback of 1657. To the south, St Hugh's Carthusian monastery, consecrated in 1880, has a very visible tall spire. The monastery is still in use.

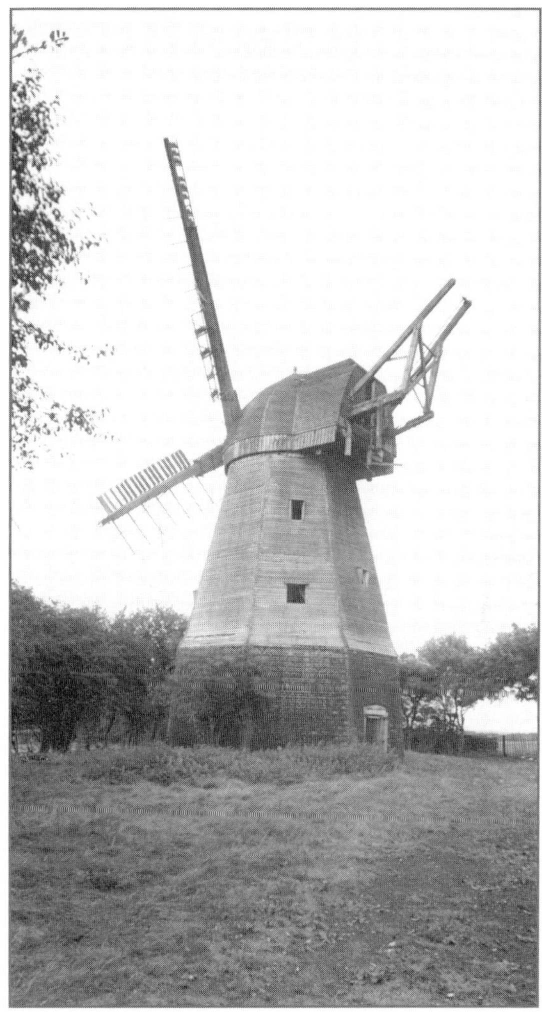

Partridge Green ▶ The Mill c1950 P603001

Jolesfield smock windmill was built in 1788 and ceased work in 1928. It was dismantled in 1959 and the parts were taken to County Oak, near Gatwick Airport, but have not been reassembled. The tarred octagonal single-storey brick base remains on site and is used as a storage building.

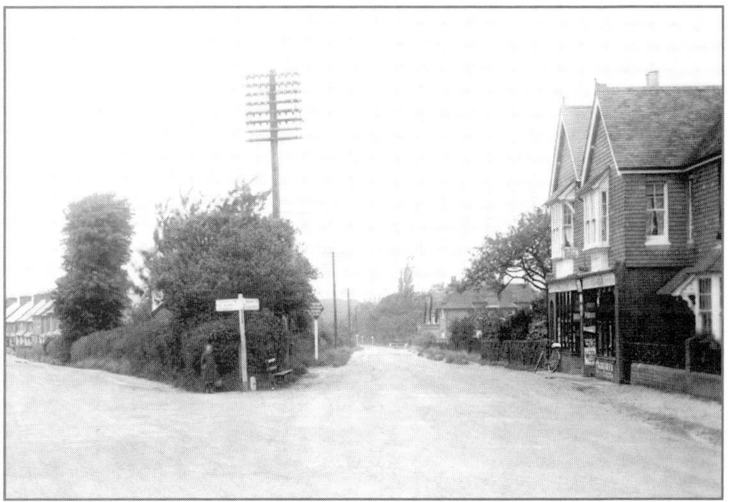

◀ Broadbridge Heath, The Portsmouth and Guildford Roads 1924 75469

The village was created at the turn of the century to house construction workers for the very large brick-built Christ's Hospital school nearby. The famous poet Shelley was born at nearby Field Place. Broadbridge Mill is an ancient mill site by the River Arun. It was a prosperous business powered by two waterwheels that drove six pairs of millstones. Horsham Baptist Church used the millpond for baptismal purposes. The village is now cut off by the new Horsham by-pass that takes most of the traffic out of the village. The scene in the picture is still recognisable. The Shelley Arms half-timbered public house is nearby.

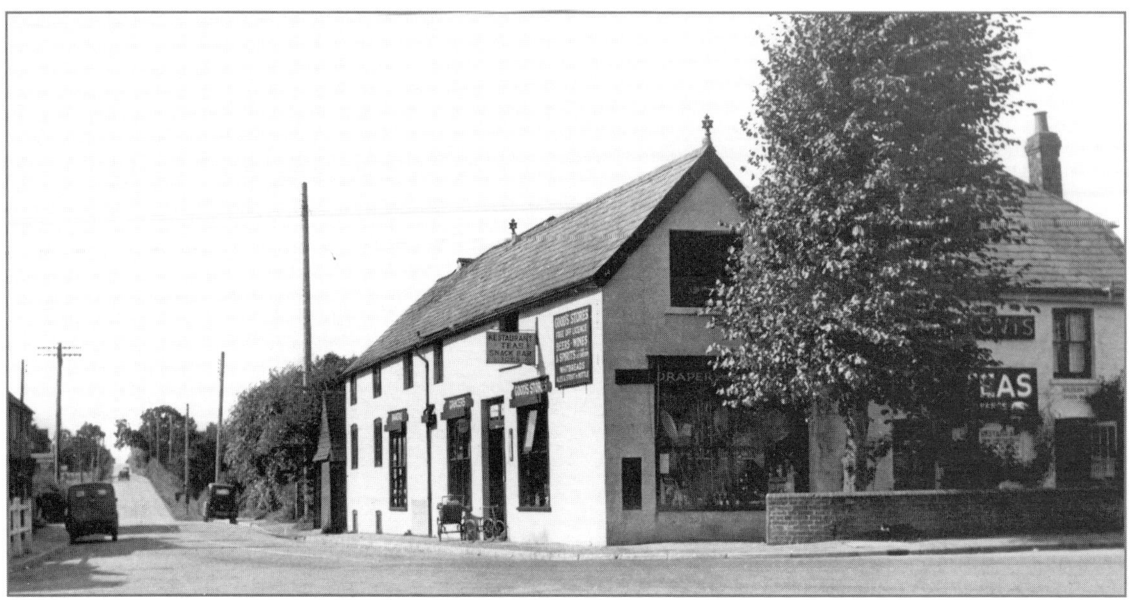

Coolham, The Post Office and Stores c1950 C424006
Good's Stores, bakery, Post Office and café was fire-damaged in the 1970s. The site has now been redeveloped for housing. The Blue Idol is a Quaker Friends Meeting House and guesthouse which was converted for William Penn in 1691. The Selsey Arms Inn is half-timbered with a more recent façade. It has a dog-wheel that once drove a meat roasting spit in an inglenook fireplace. Nearby is a memorial to a World War Two fighter airfield, which was used by the American Air Force.

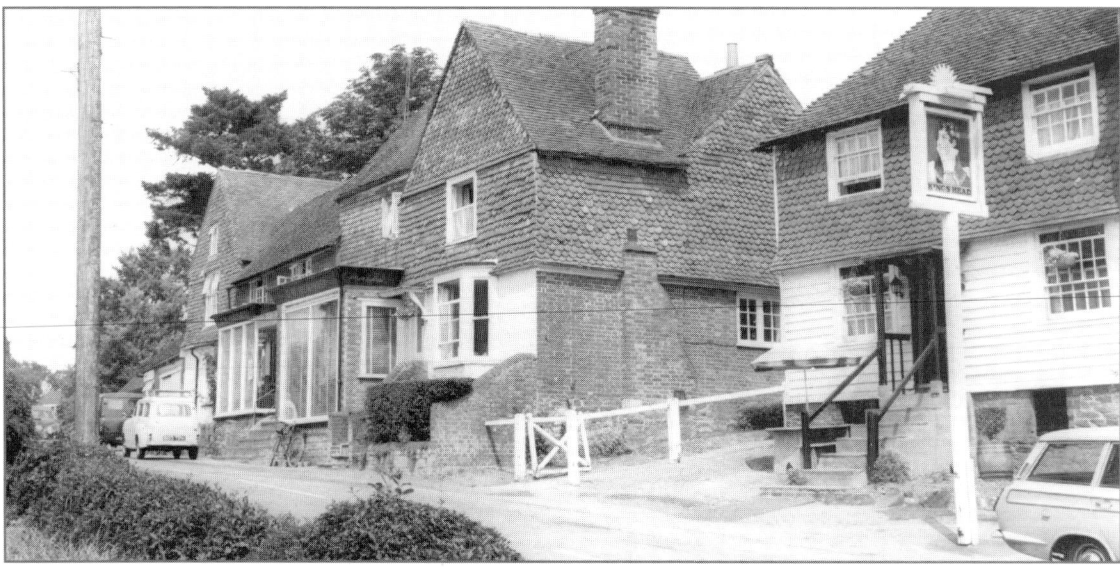

Rudgwick, The King's Head c1965 R305052
A scattered hillside village on a minor road in a wooded area near the Surrey border. At the top of the hill is the mainly 14th-century church of the Holy Trinity. The Downs Link, a long distance footpath, passes through the village on the route of the Horsham to Guildford railway line. Mushroom growing, brick making and fullers earth extraction were local industries. The King's Head was built in 1733; not originally a public house, it had a cellar to store stalls for an annual fair held nearby. The Rising Sun on top of the pub sign was a trademark of Brickwoods (Portsmouth) brewery. The scene is similar today.

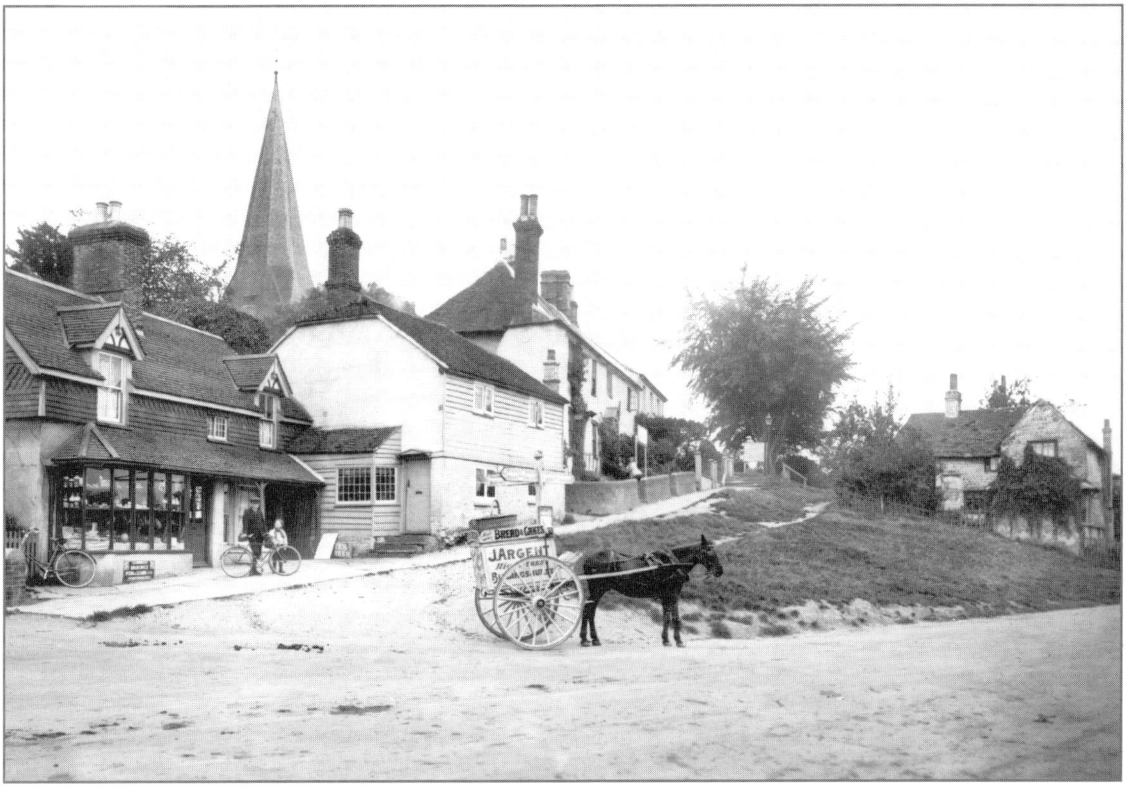

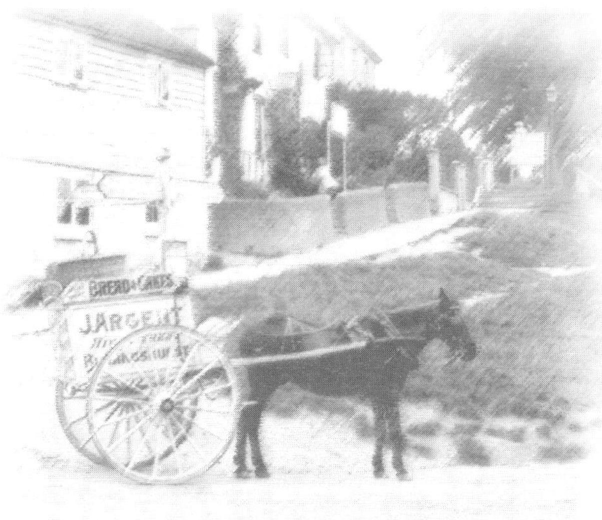

**Billingshurst
Church Causeway 1912** 64881

Billingshurst is a Roman settlement on Stane Street. St Mary's church, built on a mound with access to the churchyard via a causeway, is shown in the photograph, and has Roman bricks in the walls. The scene is similar today, but the road is metalled and very busy with motor traffic. The shop has since been converted to a private house. The main line railway station is to the south of the village centre.

▼ **Billingshurst, Ye Olde Six Bells 1923** 74918
This inn stands in the centre of the village by the side of the main
London to Worthing main road on the route of Stane Street. It is a fine
16th-century timber-framed building with a Horsham stone roof; it has
an unusual overhang along the whole length of the first floor. It is still
trading as a public house.

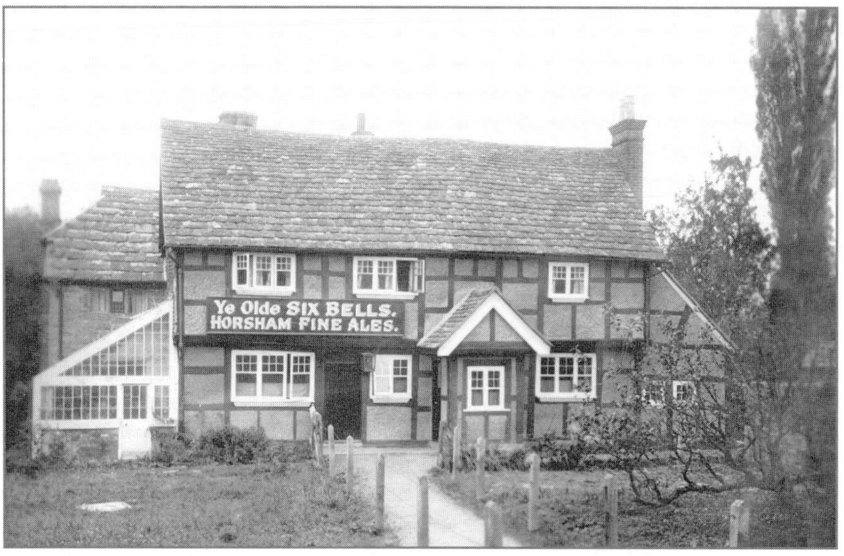

▼ **Cootham, The Village 1894** 34411
A small village, built to house Parham Estate employees, Cootham is situated
near to the foot of the downs. Nearby Parham Park has a fine Elizabethan
mansion that is open to visitors during the summer months. The picture
shows the common with the village in the background. The young girls are
dressed up and stand still for the photographer.

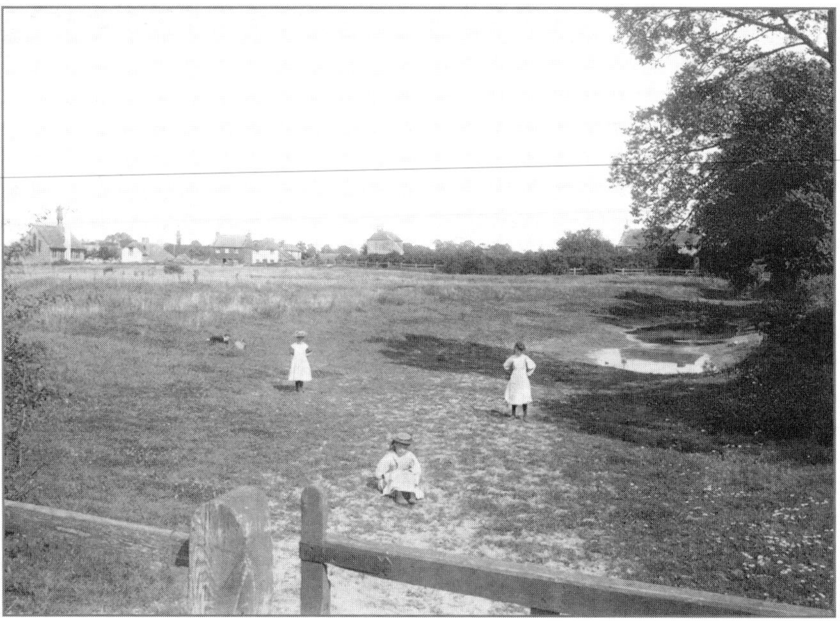

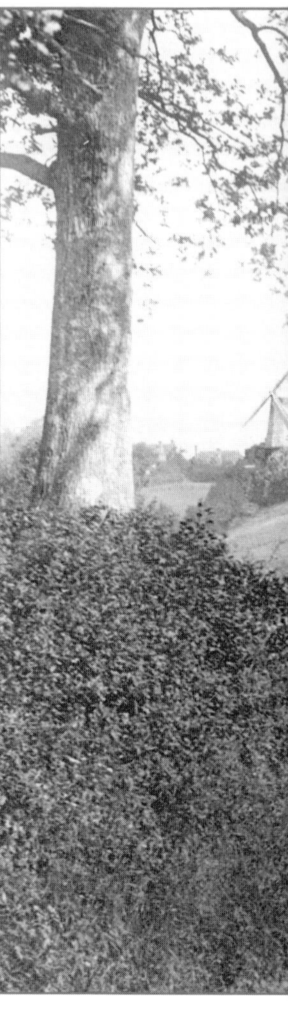

▲ **Wisborough Green
The Church and the
Village 1896** 38179
This is a fine view of a
pastoral hillside. The church
of St Peter ad Vincula has a
shingled broach spire. We
can see a fine smock
windmill in full working
order in the left distance. It
was built about 1820,
ceased work 1910, and was
demolished in 1915. The
two-storey sandstone base
is now part of a house.
Archaeologists have found
remains of 13th-century
glass-making furnaces in the
village. French immigrants
worked the glass.

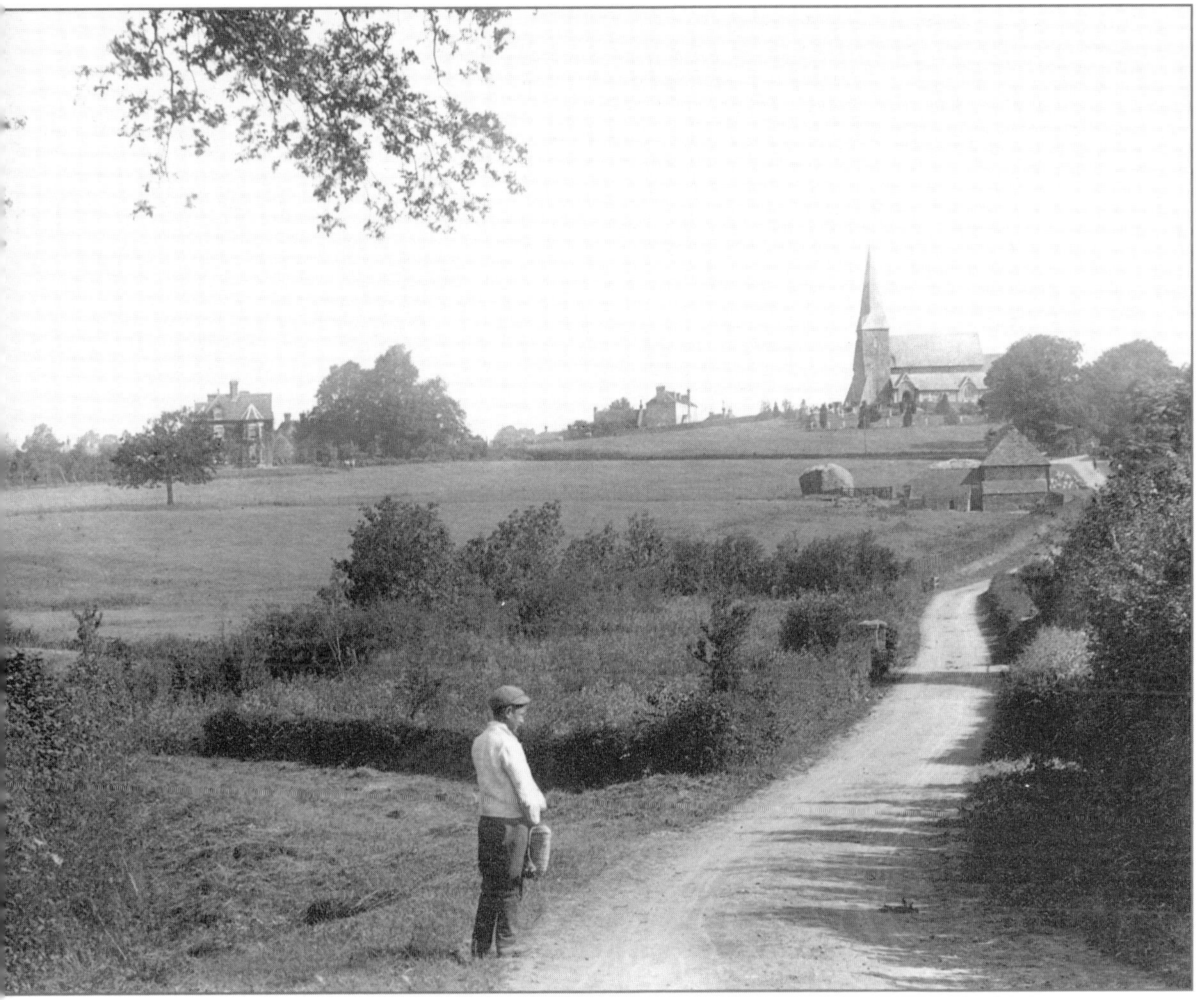

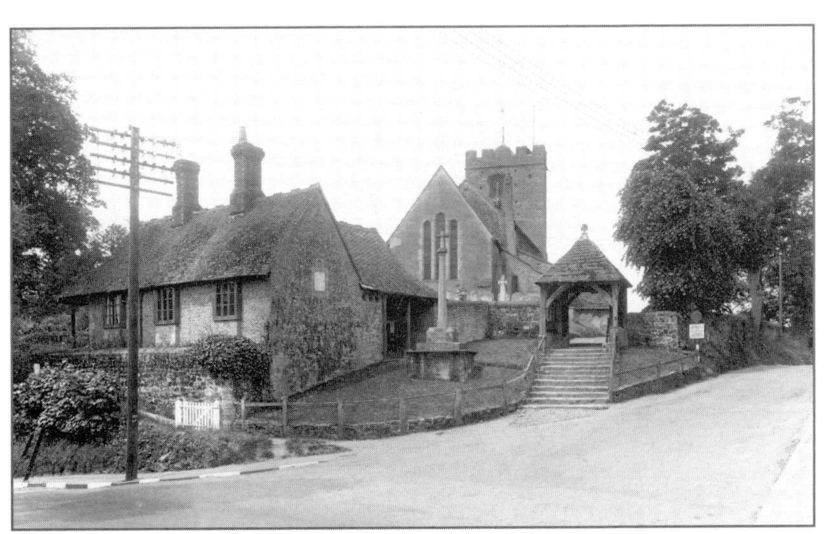

Pulborough, St Mary's Church 1939 88914
A Roman settlement on Stane Street and the navigable River Arun. The village encompasses riverside and hillside, and has a main line railway station. The 15th-century church is on the hillside. Old Place is a 15th-century manor house that was the home of the Apsley family. New Place is a stone farmhouse by the railway. The photograph shows the view from the side of Stane Street, which is now very busy. The scene now is little changed, although the almshouses have been converted into one house.

▼ **Loxwood, The Stores c1955** L304001

Loxwood is on the route of the partly-restored Wey and Arun canal near the Surrey border - 'London's lost route to the sea'. The church of St John the Baptist was built in 1898. The Onslow Arms is adjacent to the canal. The Sir Roger Tichbourne is a 16th-century inn that is now very popular with anglers. Brewhurst Mill is a complete and conserved corn watermill. The shop on the left has old enamelled metal cigarette advertising signs fixed to the wall. There is a larger shop across road. A woman waits patiently against the fence by the pond; she has just come from the swimming pool area.

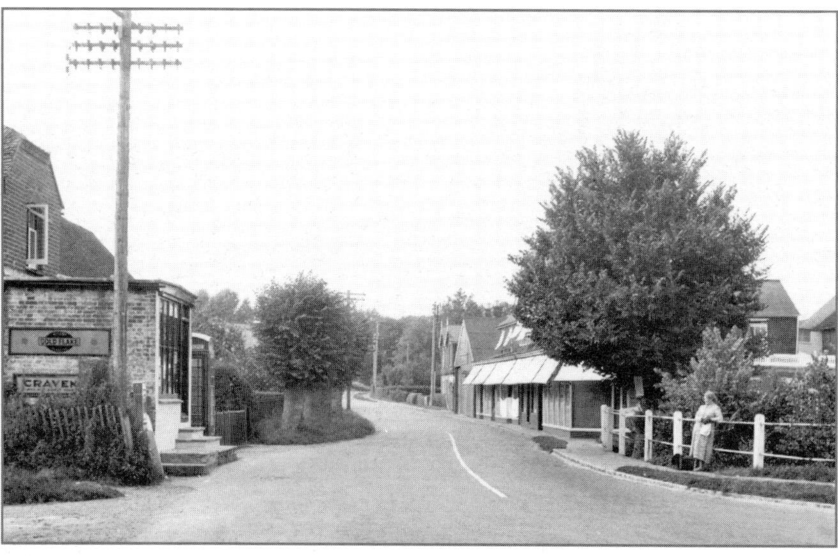

▼ **Loxwood, The Swimming Pool c1955** L304017

The swimming area is fenced off from the rest of the pond, which is situated beside the shops. The changing tents provide limited facilities for bathers. Geese watch the action from a safe distance.

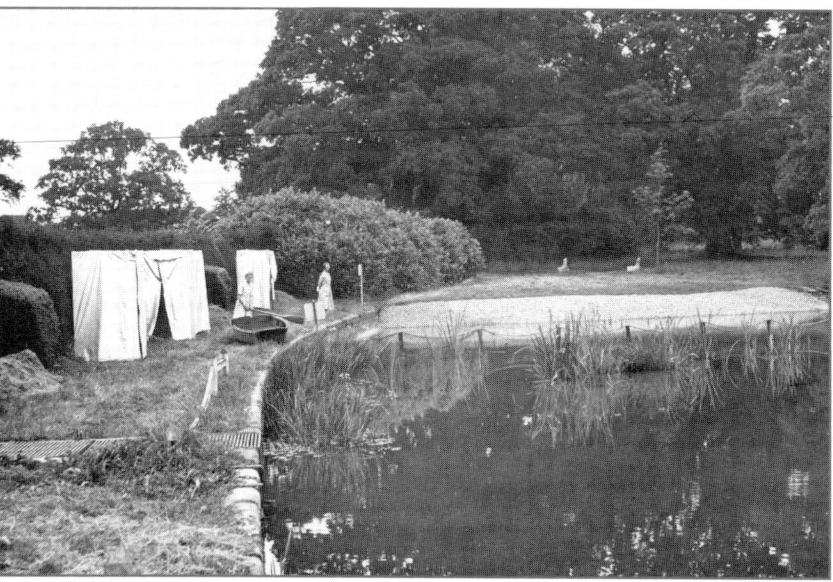

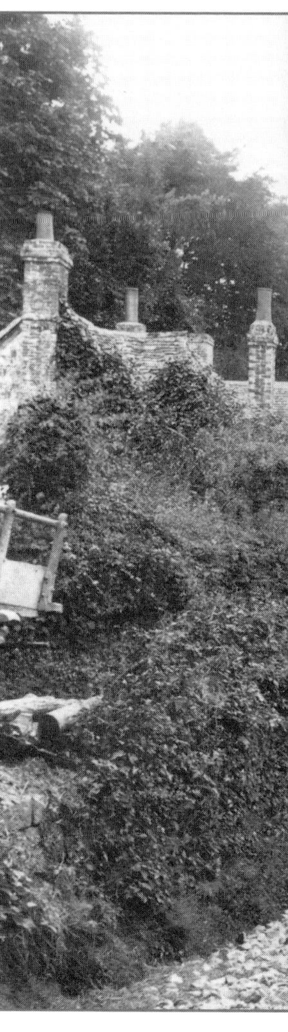

▲ **Fittleworth
The Village 1908** 60183
The local people call this 'Hallelujah Corner' because it is a sharp bend on a narrow and busy main road, near the church of St Mary. The house on the right of the picture has a chimneystack that is heavily overgrown by creeper: see the next picture - 70080.

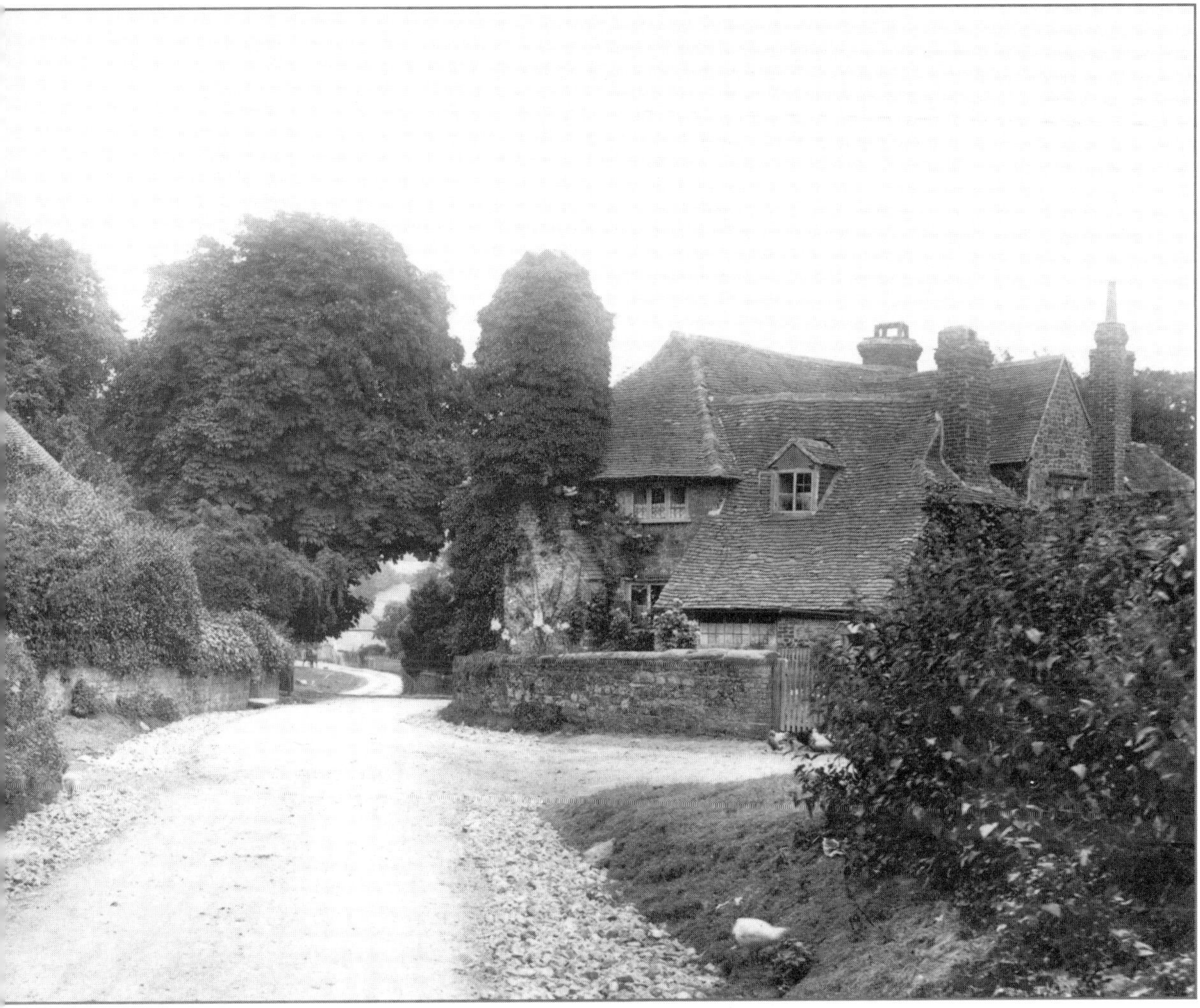

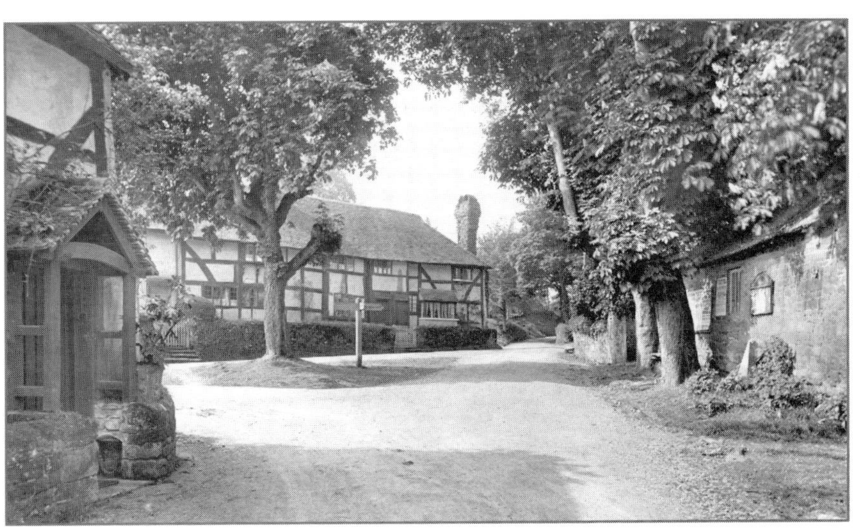

◀ **Fittleworth**
The Village 1921 70080
We are in the same position
as in 60183, but looking in
the reverse direction
thirteen years later. The
creeper on the
chimneystack has been well
trimmed, and so have the
horse chestnut trees -
although the old chimney
still shows signs of damage
caused by the creeper. A
boot scraper is visible in the
porch-way. There is an array
of noticeboards on the wall
opposite.

▼ Fittleworth, The Village c1955 F29006

Fittleworth is a picturesque village of fine old houses, commons and fir woods. On the left of the picture is the Swan, a 14th-century coaching inn with a sign spanning the main road. Nearby is a fine stone bridge over the River Rother and a picturesque house (a converted watermill) on an island in the river. The Grange is a fine house of c1700. Sir Edward Elgar, the composer, lived at Brinwell's Cottage in 1917. Coates is a crenellated Gothic-style house built c1810; during World War Two it was occupied by explosives enthusiast Colonel Stewart Blacker, who converted the cellars to develop an anti-tank weapon. The scene is still recognisable. The village stores, Harding Brothers, is now a house.

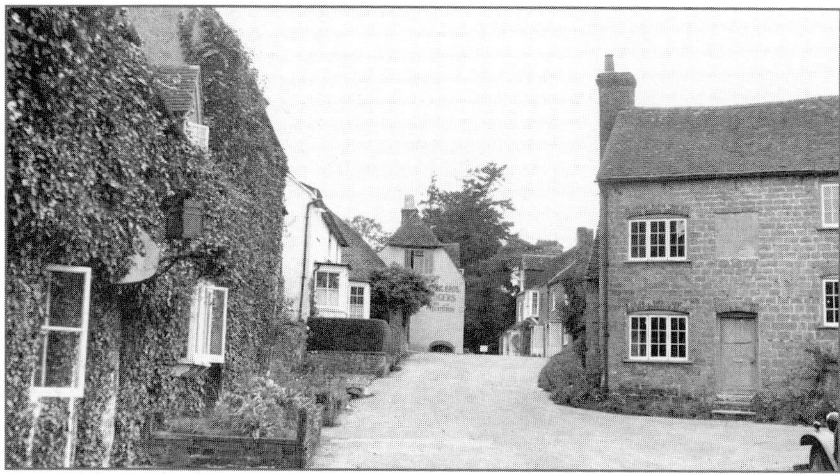

▼ Plaistow, The Village c1955 P301012

Located in a remote region north of Petworth, the village was originally formed in a clearing in the woods. The local wealden clay district is remarkable for large oak trees. In the iron industry era there were smelting furnaces and forges here; Sussex marble was also dug in the area. The 18th-century mansion at Shillinglee Park was burnt out in the Second World War; the shell is conserved. Life on the estate was documented by past residents, Lady Catherine and Lady Maria Turnour. Holy Trinity church is pictured, with turret, clock and spire and a Horsham stone roof. Outside the village store an enamelled metal sign advertises Bluebell Metal Polish. The Sun Inn is on the right behind bushes. The scene is now little changed, although the shop has gone.

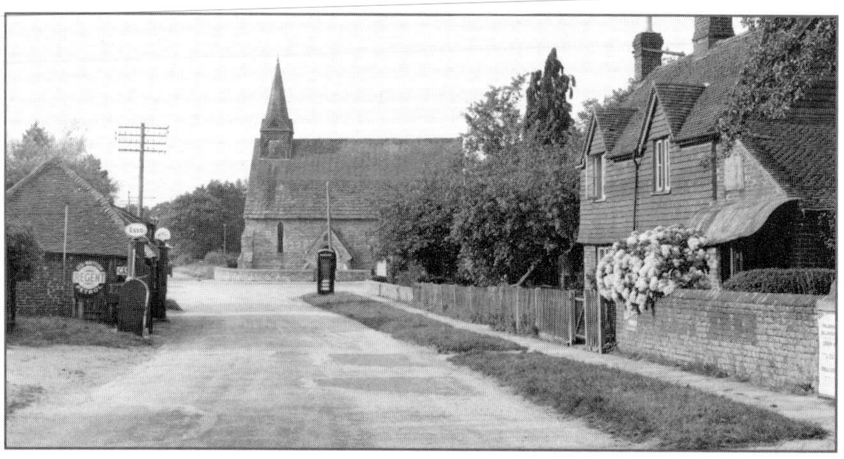

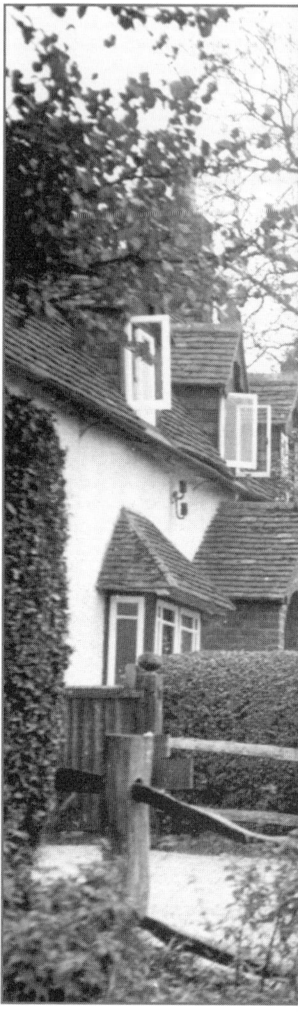

▲ Graffham
The Village c1955

G195013

Graffham is a wooded hillside village under the Downs. Pescod's Stores has a Hovis sign on a painted wall.

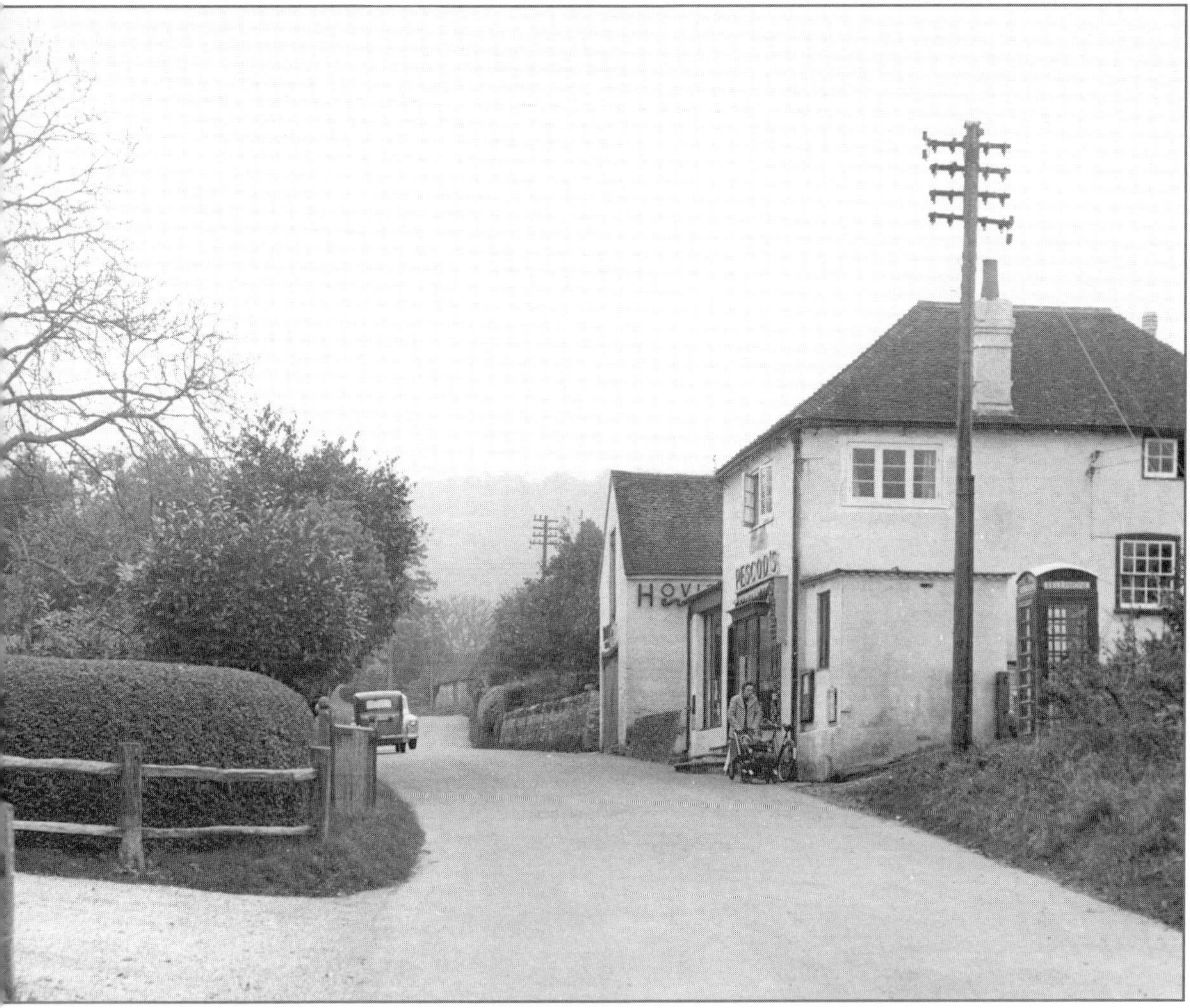

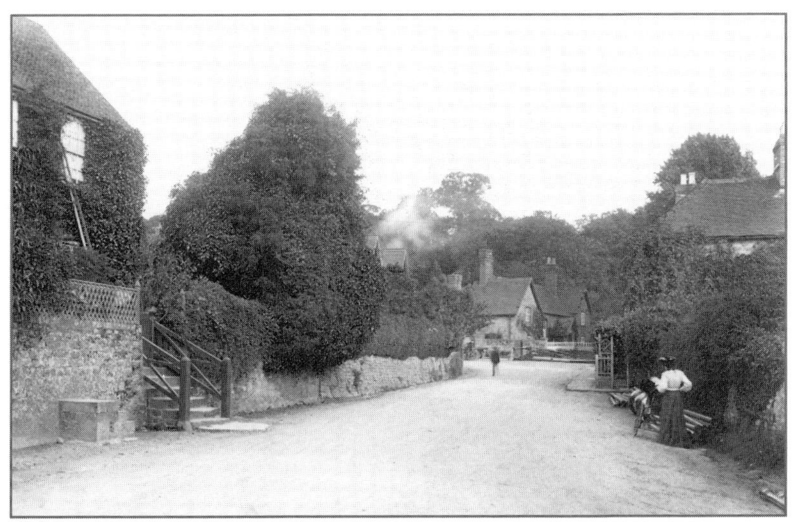

◄ Easebourne, The Village 1906
54380
This village near Midhurst was built
mainly to house employees of the
Cowdray Estate, famed for the
landscaped park and polo playing.
St Mary's church stands near the
park gate and contains the tomb of
the first Lord Montague, who
entertained Queen Elizabeth I at
Cowdray House. The conserved
ruins of the house, a Tudor
mansion damaged by fire in 1793,
are situated near the River Rother.
Beside the church is Easebourne
Augustinian Priory. After the
Dissolution, the buildings continued
in use as a private house.

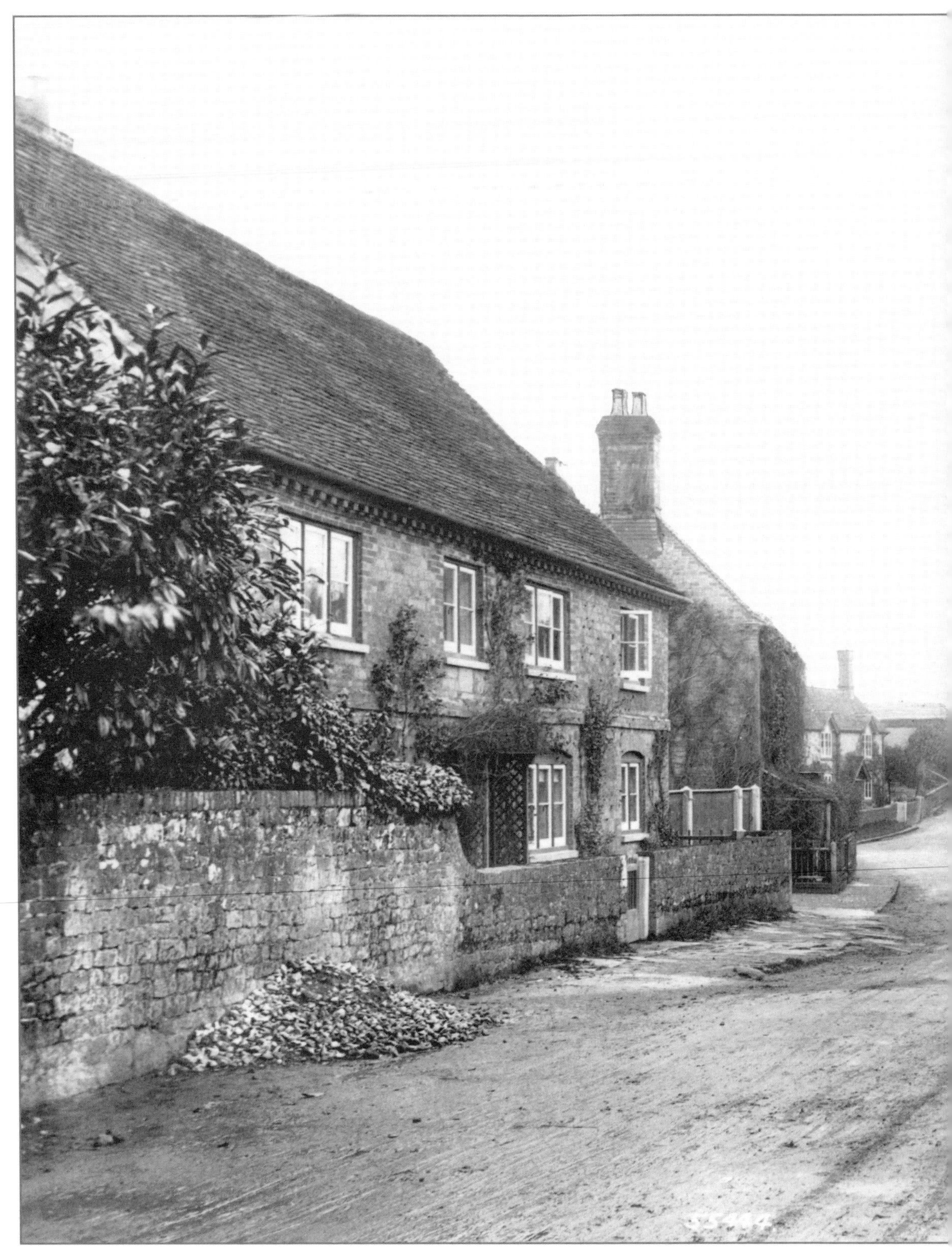

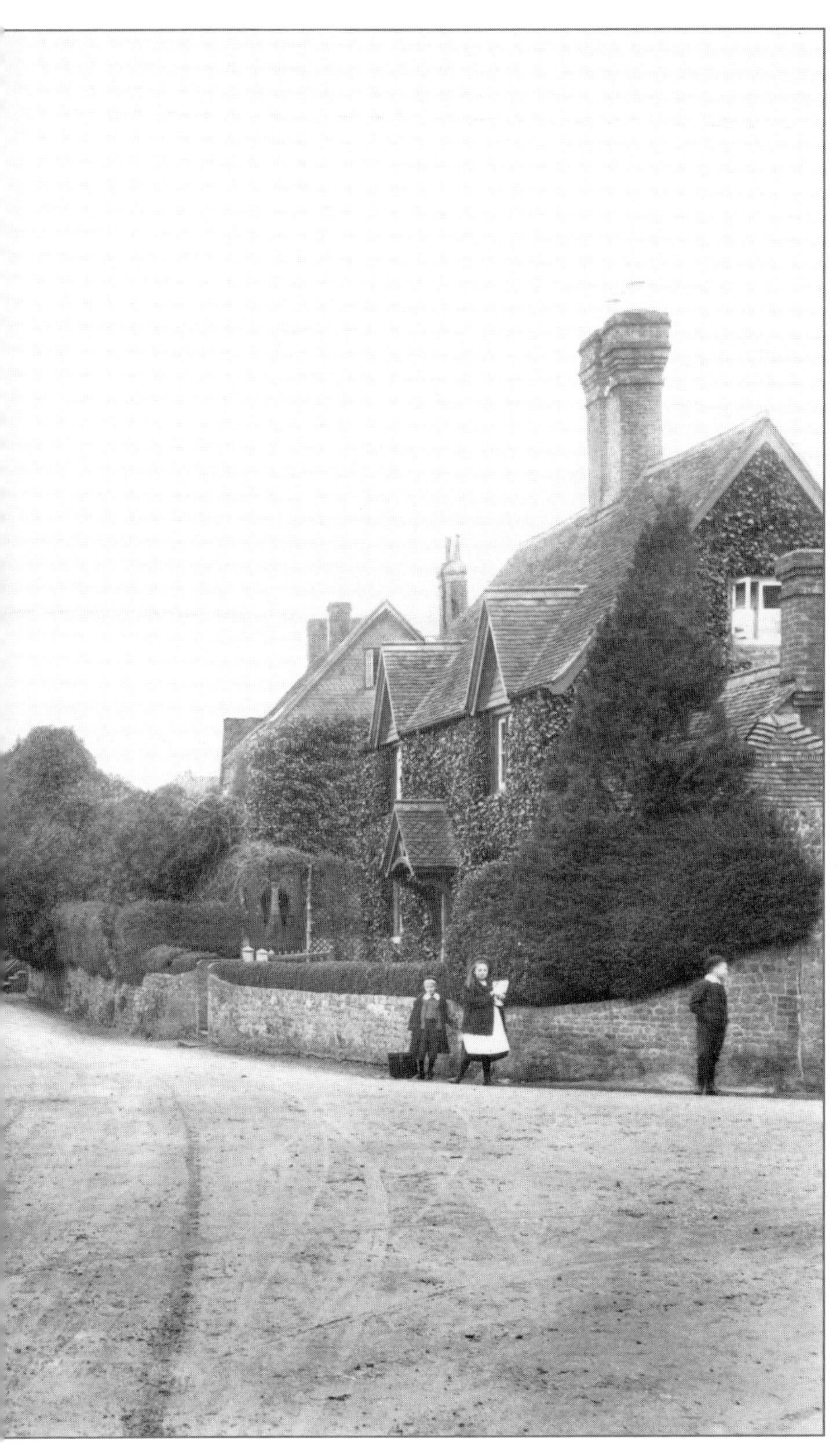

**Easebourne
The Village 1906**
55444
This is the same street as in view 54380 but we are looking in the opposite direction. There are cart tracks in the loose, unsealed road surface. Children wait at the roadside, perhaps for transport to school. There are no vehicles in sight; it was a quiet village.

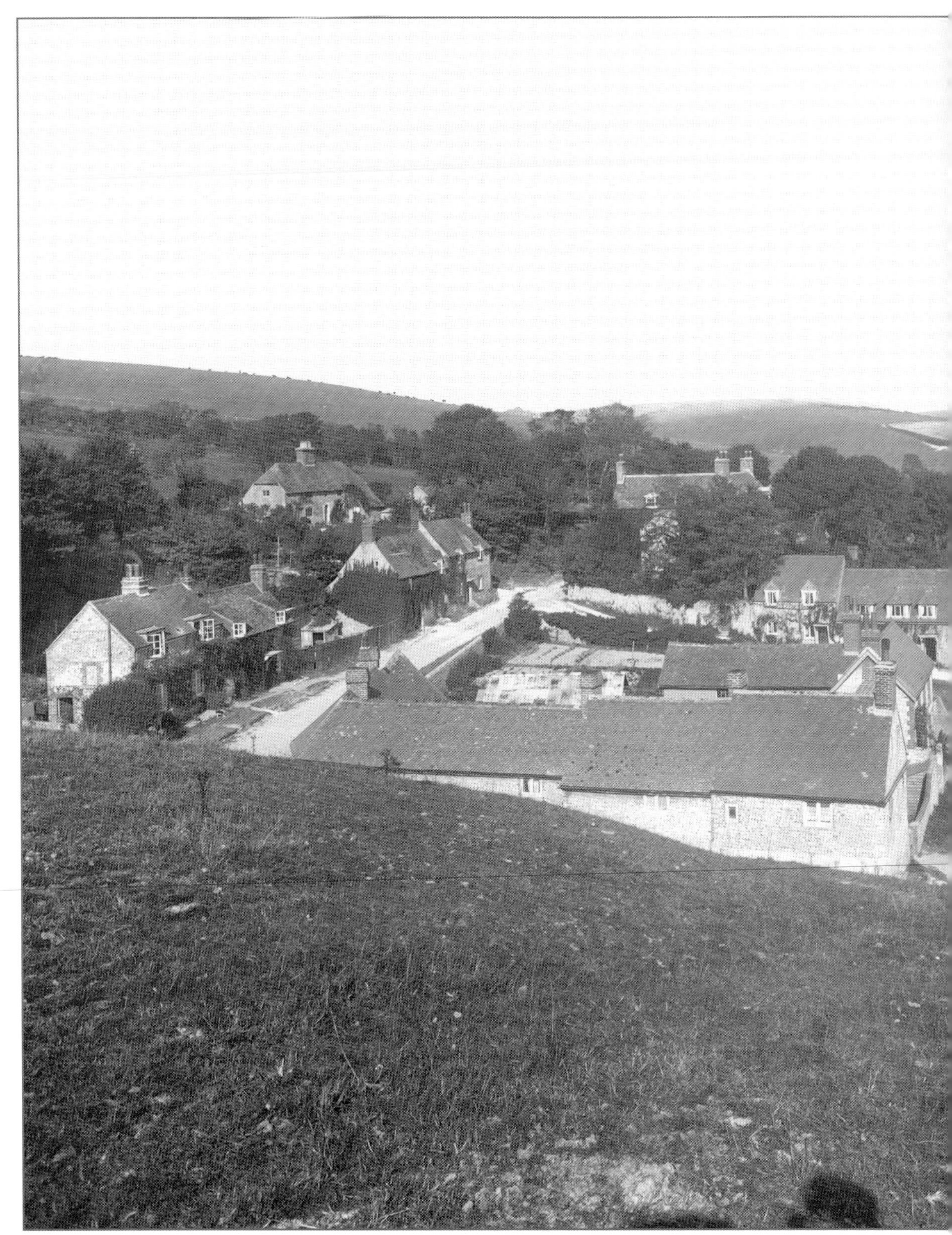

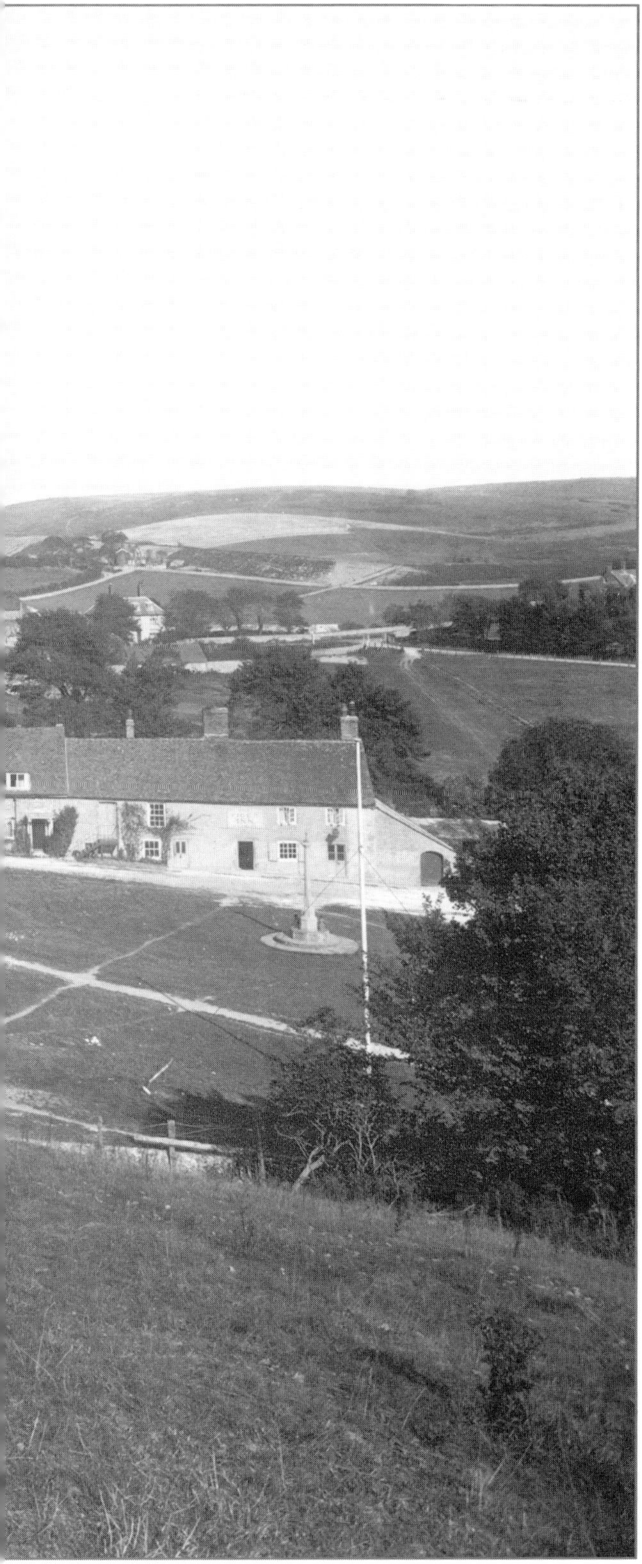

The Downs

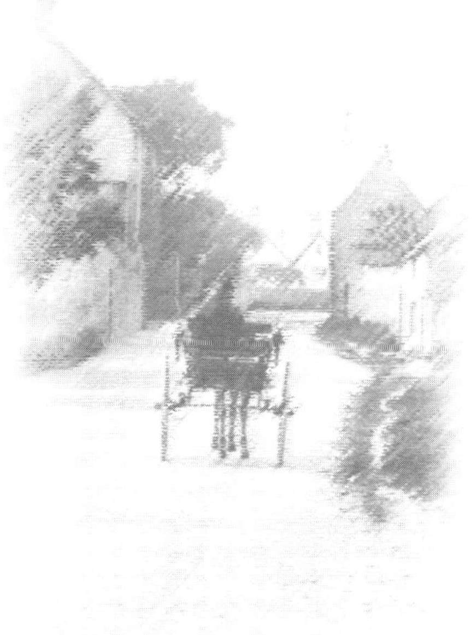

Eastdean, The Village 1921 71404
We are in a valley of the Downs near Beachy Head.
The Tiger Inn is a fine building that was a barracks
during the Napoleonic wars. The village church of
St Simon and St Jude's has a semi-detached
Norman tower and a sepulchral cross slab bearing
the arms of the Bardolf family, who were Lords of
the Manor of Birling. The road southwards leads to
Birling Gap, a coastline hamlet with spectacular
scenery and chalk cliffs. The scene is similar today,
but with more trees and buildings in the foreground.
The inn has been extended at the right-hand end.

▼ Eastdean, The Old Forge 1921 71405
Here we see a workplace with an open-air view; the craftsmen are taking a breather. Apparatus for wheelwrighting is nearby; there is an iron cone for forging circular iron rings, and a flat circular area for laying out wheels. The yoke hung on the front wall was used for draught animals, probably oxen. A tall white flagpole stands in the garden.

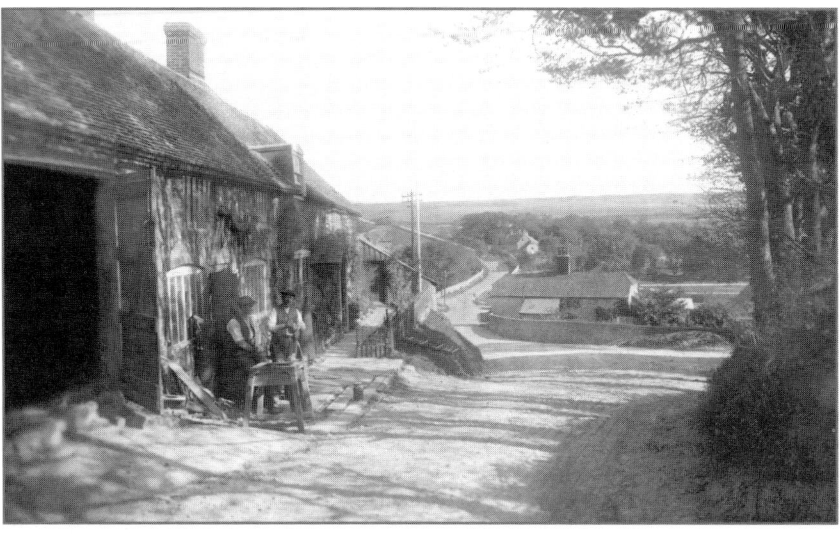

▼ Belmont, From the Downs 1903 50296
We are on a high, sandy hillside on the outskirts of Hastings. Nearby, Minnis Rock Hermitage has three rock cells cut out of a sandstone cliff face; it is well conserved. The whole area is now much more developed with housing. The beauty spots of Fairlight Glen and Ecclesbourne Glen are nearby. It is washing day; we can see linen hanging from the lines.

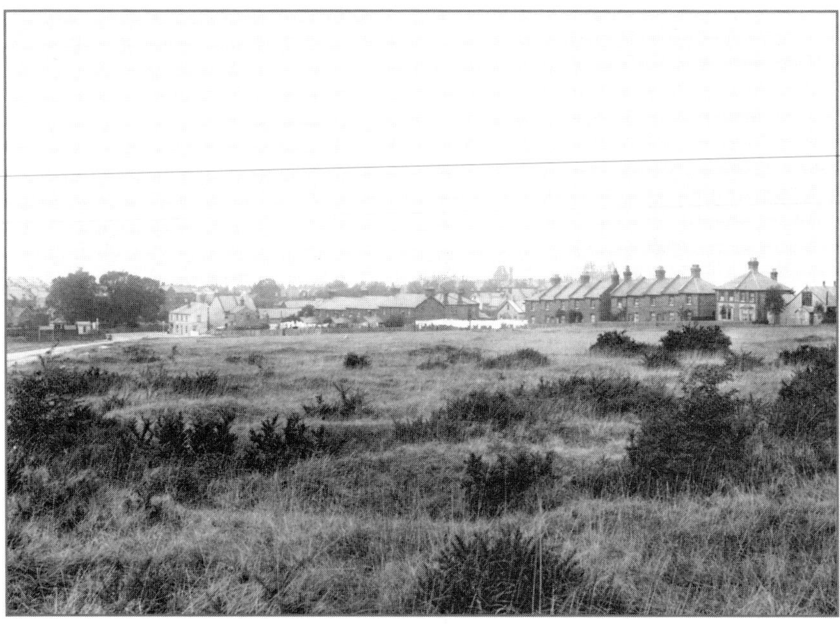

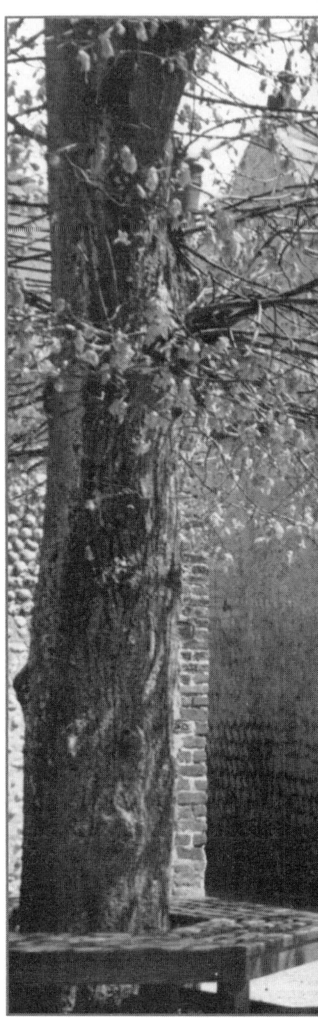

▲ Willingdon, The Post Office c1950 W446007
We are on the slope of the Downs between Eastbourne and Polegate. A nearby vantage point at Combe hill is 638 feet high. The village church of St Mary's is an Early English building with an ancient chest and coffin. Opposite the church is the Hoo, a large rambling house built in 1902. The Post Office proprietor was R F Brierley; alongside is the entrance to the builders' and decorators' yard, F J French & Sons.

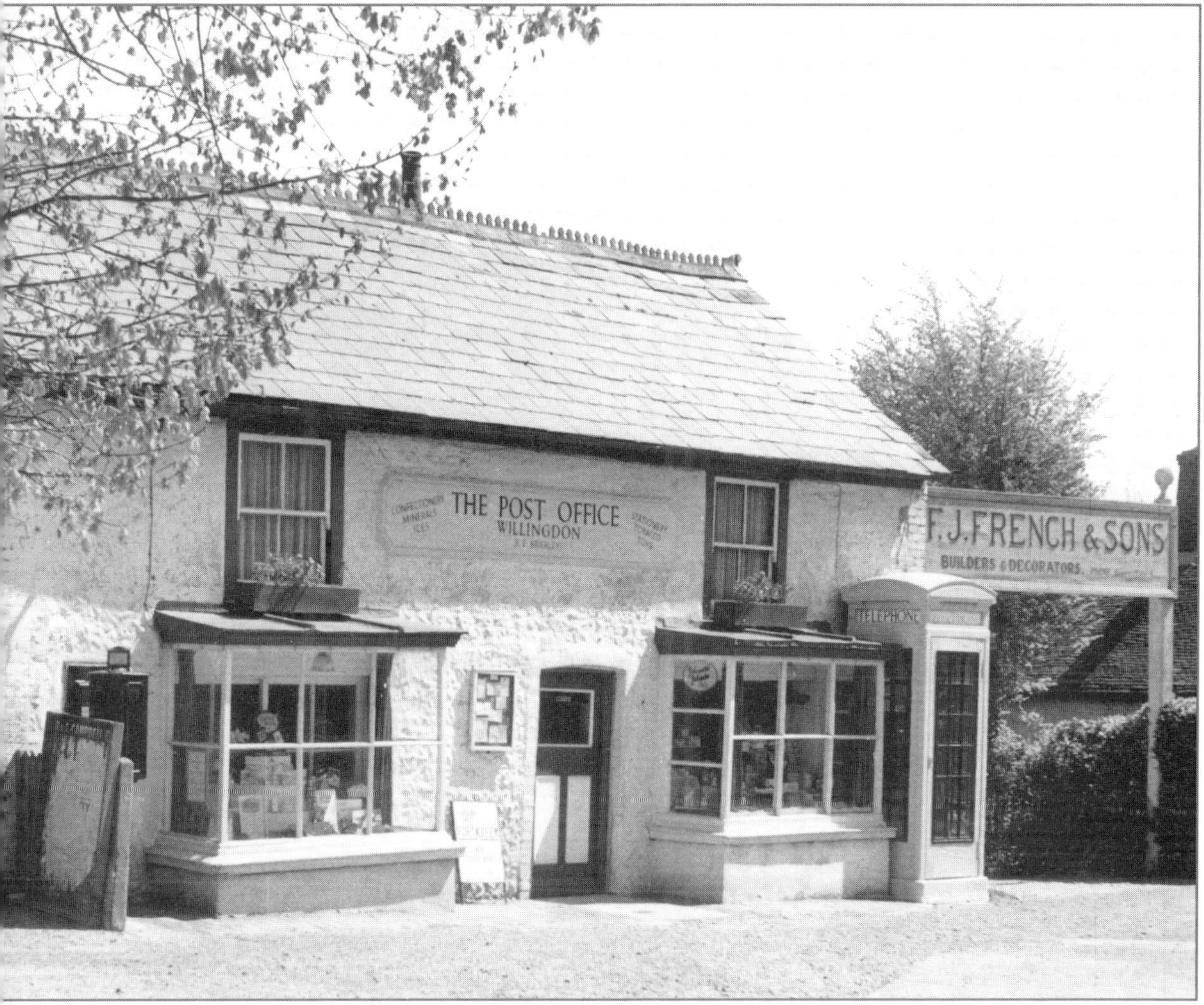

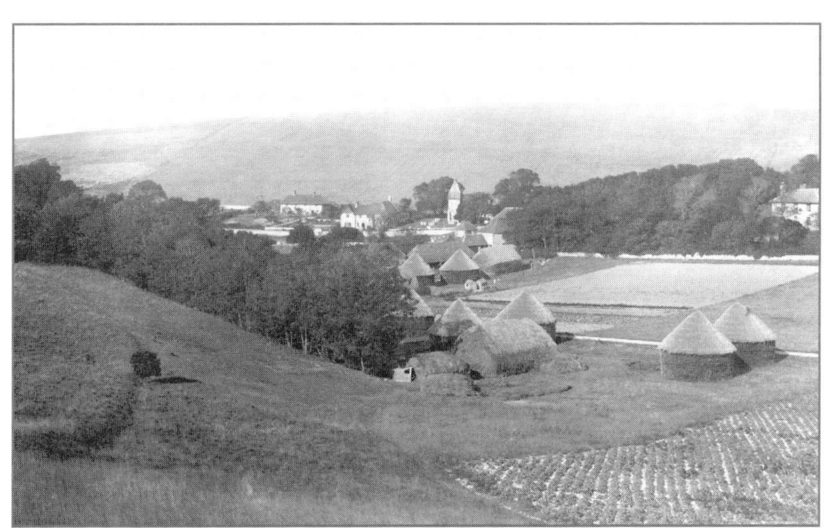

◄ Westdean
General View 1921 71401
Here we see a rural scene in a fold of the Downs - now much more wooded and obscured by trees. A stack yard is in the foreground, with round and rectangular corn ricks. All Saints church has an uncommon half-hipped spire. An old story says that King Alfred came here to build a palace, but instead he built a shipyard on the estuary of the Cuckmere nearby. Not far away is Charleston Manor, the remains of a late 12th-century hall house. There is also a tithe barn and a dovecote still housing pigeons.

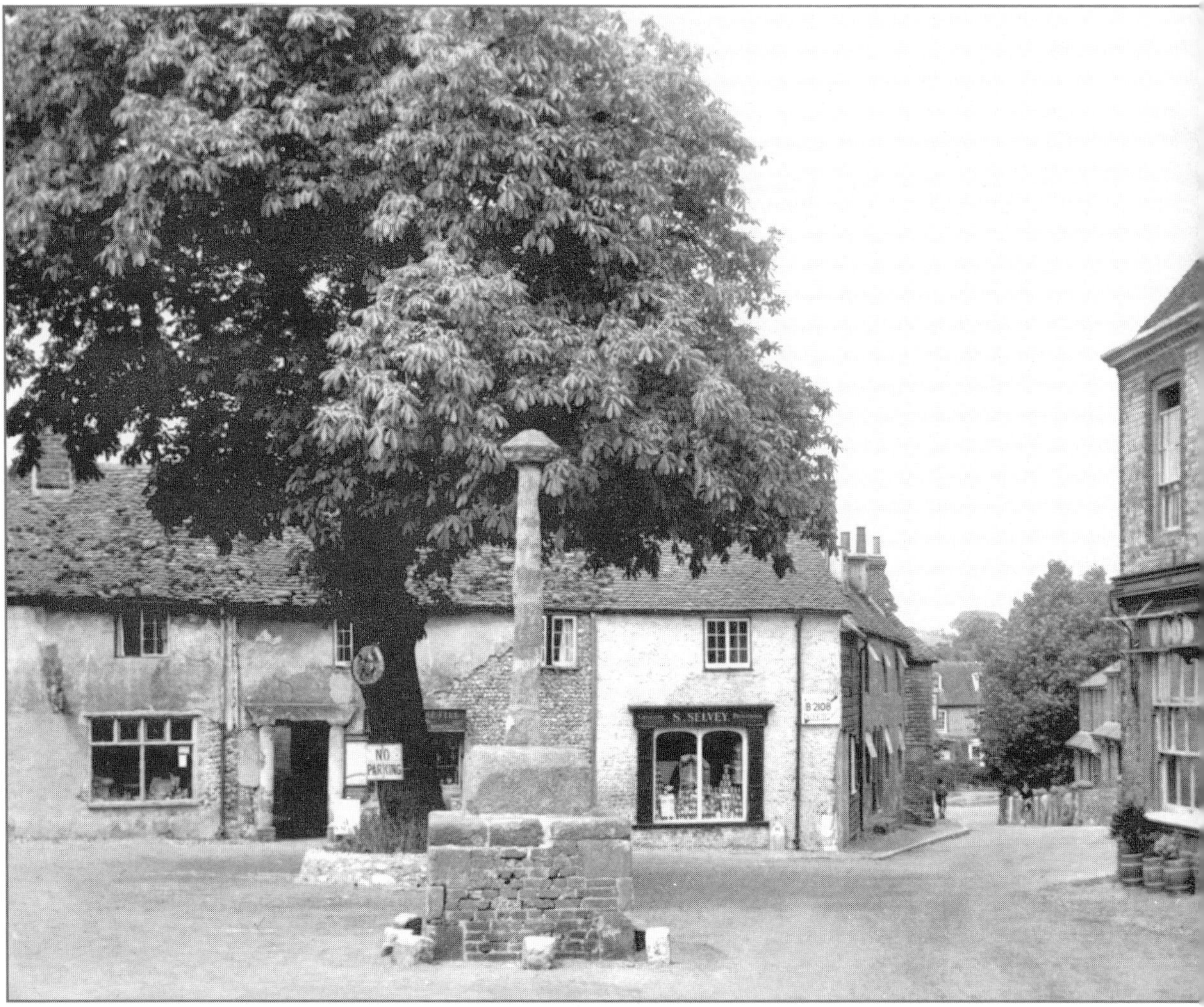

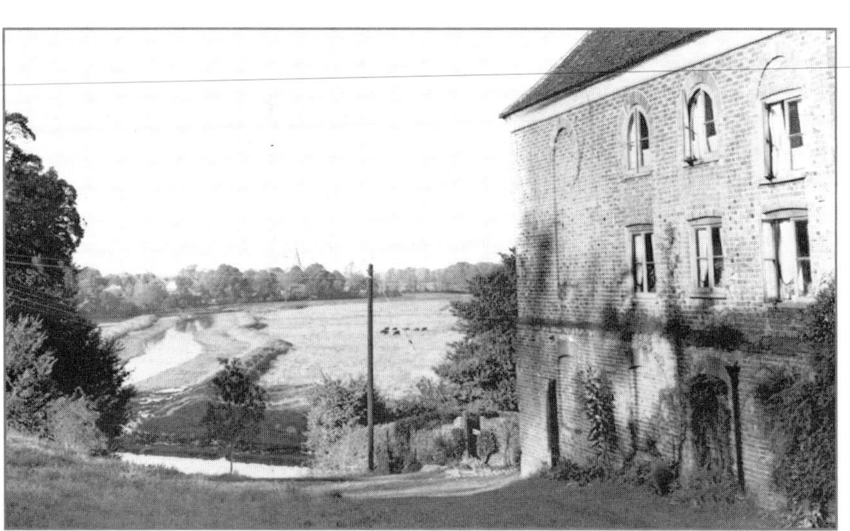

◀ Alfriston, Burnt House and the River Cuckmere c1960

A33024

Burnt Farmhouse is isolated; it incorporates the remains of Field Place, which burned down in 1765. The tower of Litlington church can be seen in the distance. The farmhouse is still inhabited and well conserved.

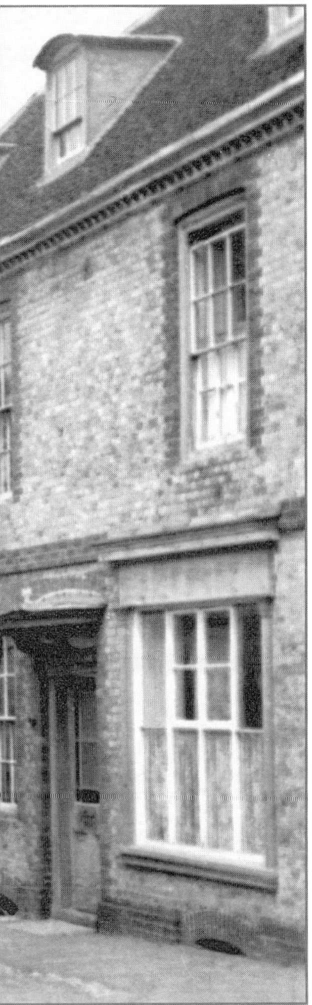

Alfriston, Market Square c1955 A33017
A Saxon settlement beside the River Cuckmere, Alfriston was a centre for smuggling. The 14th-century church of St Andrew is built on a mound on the large village green. The Clergy House, a 14th-century timber-framed and thatched hall house, is in the care of the National Trust and is open to visitors. The 16th-century Star Inn was a hostel for pilgrims and the exterior is decorated with woodcarvings of beasts. The George Inn has Tudor wall paintings. We can see old shops in the photograph - S Selvey, the grocer, and Wood, the butcher. The ancient market cross has been knocked down by vehicles and restored several times. The scene is similar today, and well conserved, but all the shops are now engaged in tourist-related trading.

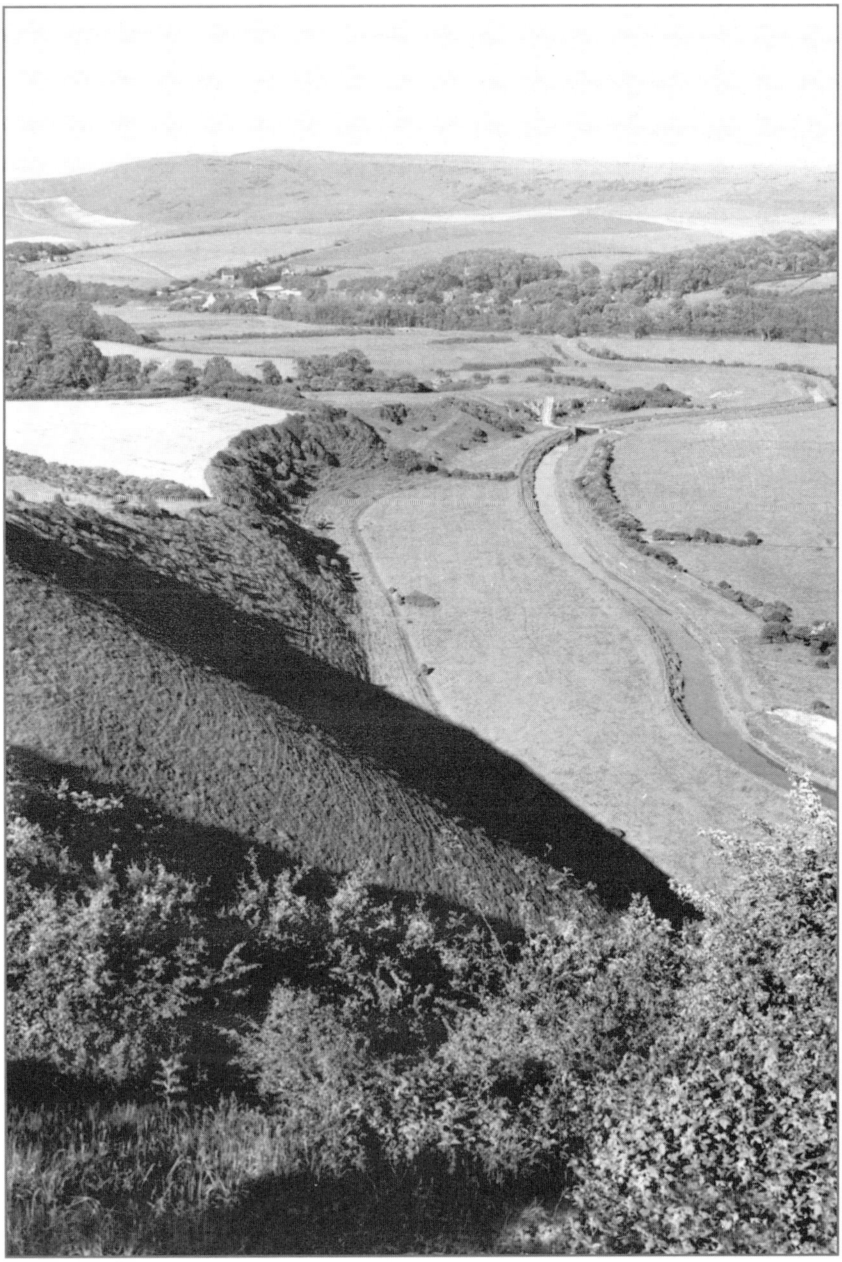

Alfriston, View from High and Over c1960 A33044
High and Over, or Hindover, is a vantage point on the South Downs, overlooking the Cuckmere river valley. A hill figure of a white horse was re-cut in the escarpment in 1924; it is visible from Cuckmere Haven. Many villages in the Cuckmere valley have medieval dovecotes. This is a relic of the past, when the Lord of the Manor was entitled to keep a pigeon house, and the birds could feed off his tenants' crops.

▼ Litlington, The Village c1960 L480010
This leafy flint village is situated in the Cuckmere valley near Alfriston. Nearby is one of the smallest Neolithic long barrows in Sussex. In the picture the Stores has a sign offering 'Morning coffee and light refreshments, Teas'. There is still a very good tea garden here.

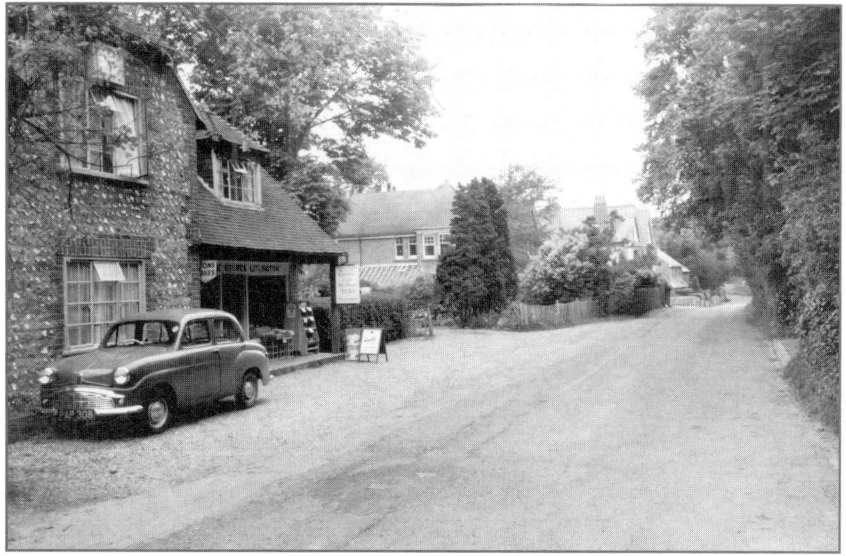

▼ Polegate, The Horse and Groom c1965 P259023
This public house stands beside the main London to Eastbourne road. It was built in 1936, and is a popular stopping place for day-trippers to the Downs and the coastal resorts. It was usual to have a drink on the outward and homeward journeys.

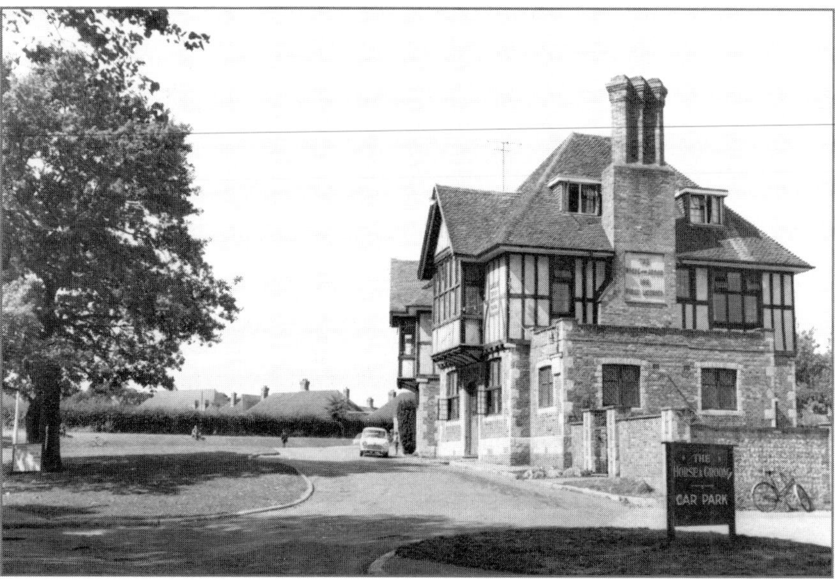

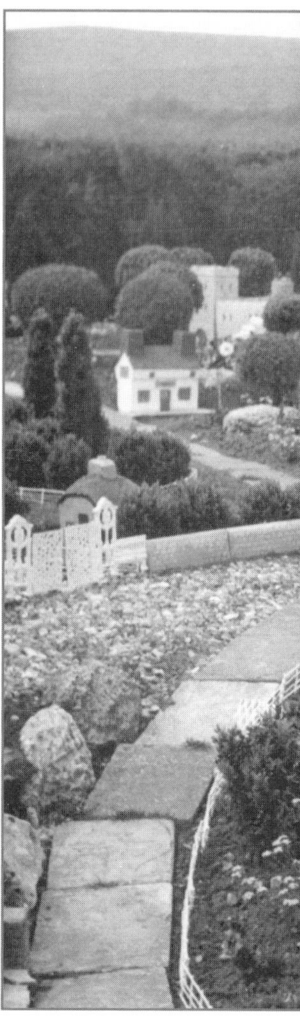

▲ Wannock, The Gardens c1960 W372084
Wannock gardens were created in the 1930s on the site of a watermill. The model village was a popular tripper attraction. We see it just before the site was developed for full-size housing.

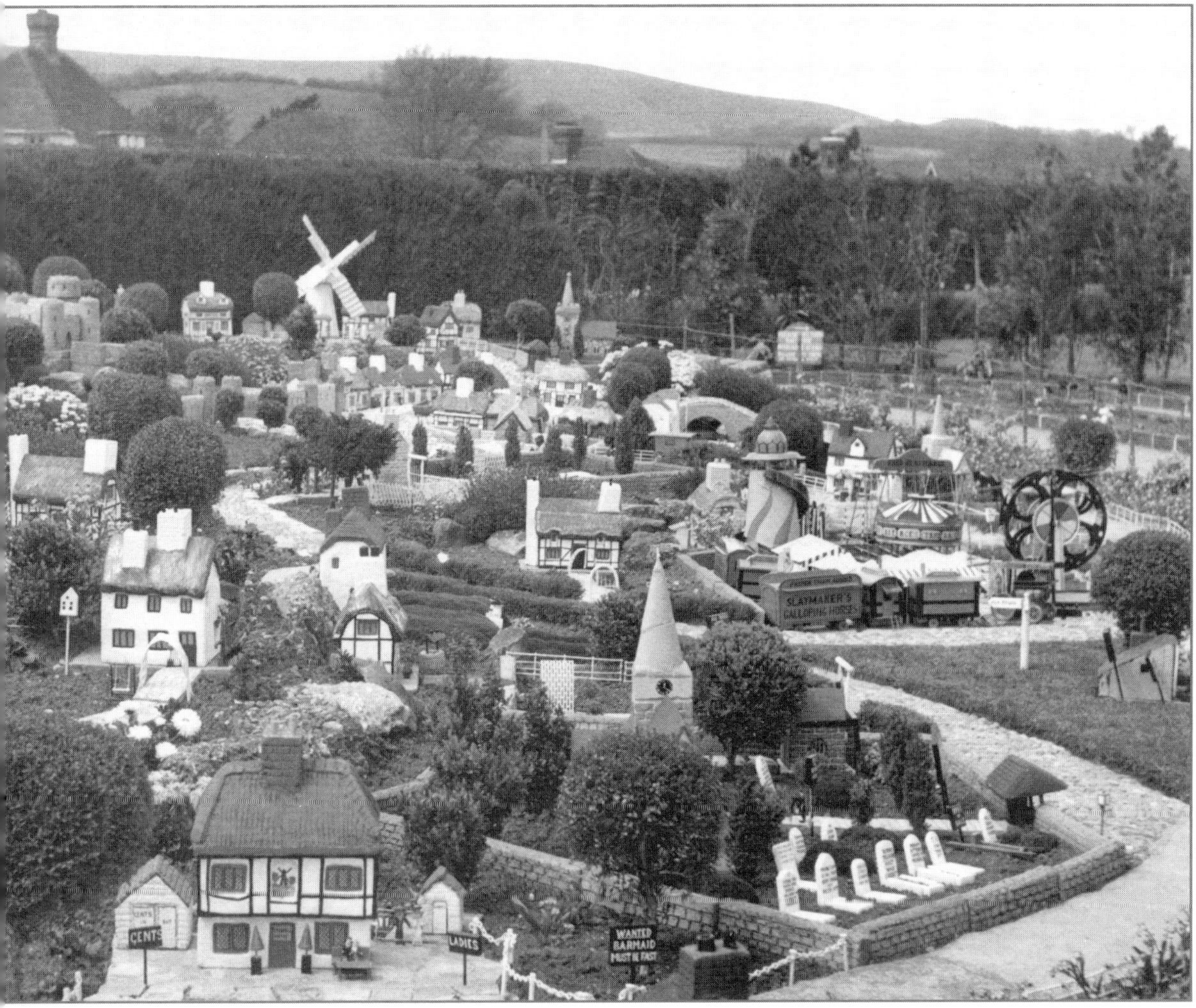

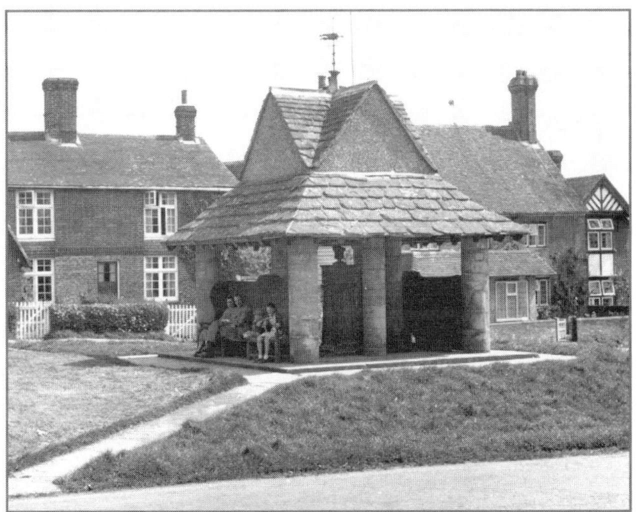

◄ Sedlescombe, The Village Pump c1955

S494009

Sedlescombe is a hillside village near Battle, with a large green. A local mill made the best gunpowder in Europe. An iron pot containing a large number of coins of Edward the Confessor was found in 1876. They were thought to have belonged to King Harold, and hidden during the Battle of Hastings. Some are displayed in Hastings Museum. Durhamford Manor is a large 15th-century half-timbered house. Manor House is a 17th-century half-timbered house that has been converted into cottages. The nearby Pestalozzi village is a development of the Oaklands Estate; it is a sociological experiment where children of all nations are brought up together. The pump house, dated 1900, was a centre of village life before piped mains water supplies. An iron cage protects the ornate lead pump head.

**East Hoathly ▶
South Street c1950**
E177006
This area was connected with the iron industry. The church has a Tudor doorway and a Norman piscina on a carved pillar. Thomas Turner, who lived in the village in the mid-18th century, left an important diary spanning eleven years of his life. The Pelham family were influential local landowners, and their emblem was the Pelham Buckle; cast iron milestones in the area have the Pelham Buckle carved on them. Belmont is a Georgian house, and the gatehouse is an early Victorian house sited to the rear of Belmont. The village is noted for trug manufacture at a local steamed wood works.

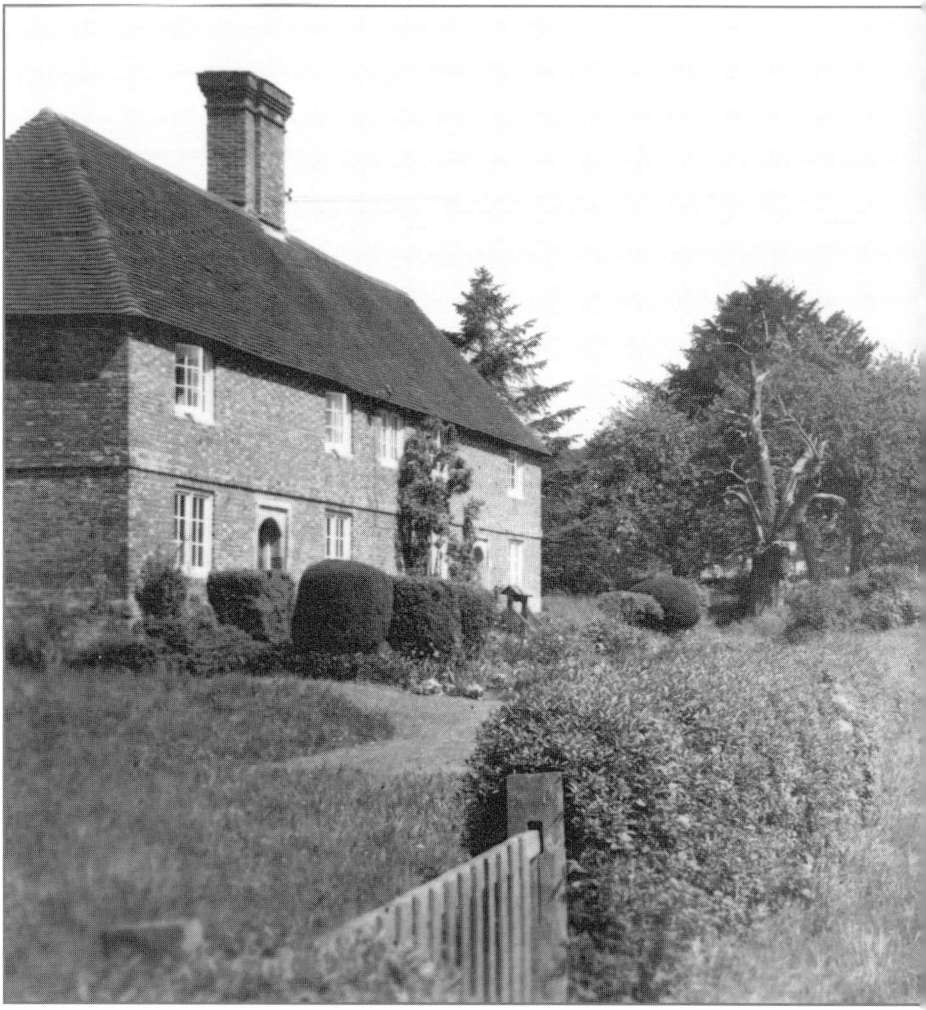

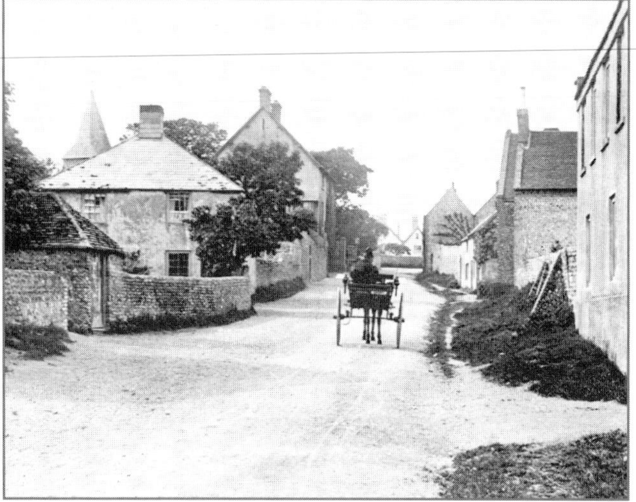

◀ East Blatchington, The Village 1891 28388
We are on the Downs, just north of Seaford. The church of St Peter has a fine Norman font. Admiral Walker, who fought with Nelson, is buried here. T A Guthrie (1856-1953), known as F Anstey, novelist and contributor to 'Punch' magazine, is buried in the churchyard. In 1862 Henry Coxwell, a local aviation pioneer who soared to the height of 26,000 feet in a balloon in 1862, is also buried here. In 1794 a very large barracks was built just north of the village; it was used to house militia during the Napoleonic Wars. After the First World War, the barracks were closed and demolished. The village is now a part of Seaford; it is surrounded by recent housing estates, although the scene is still recognisable.

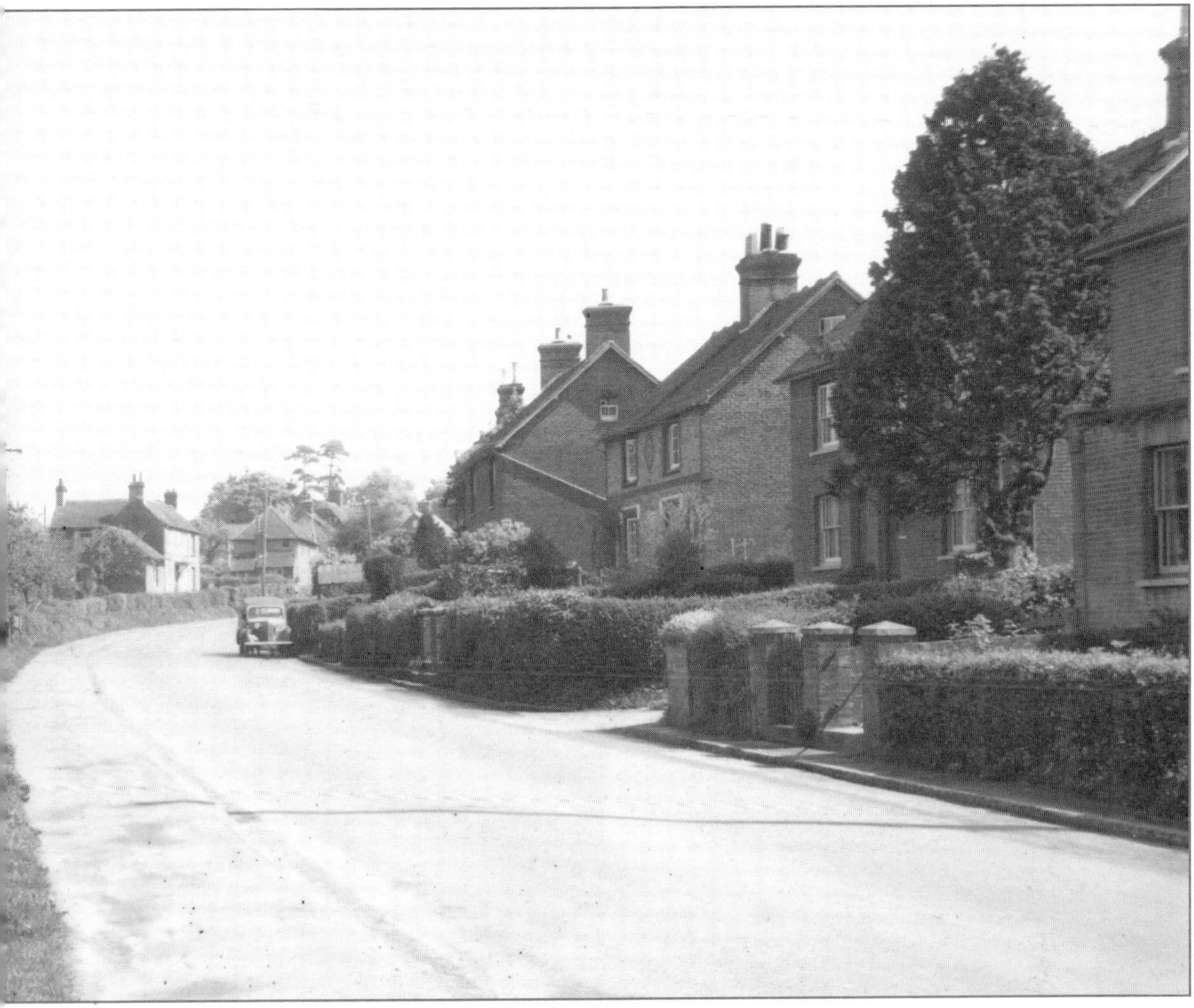

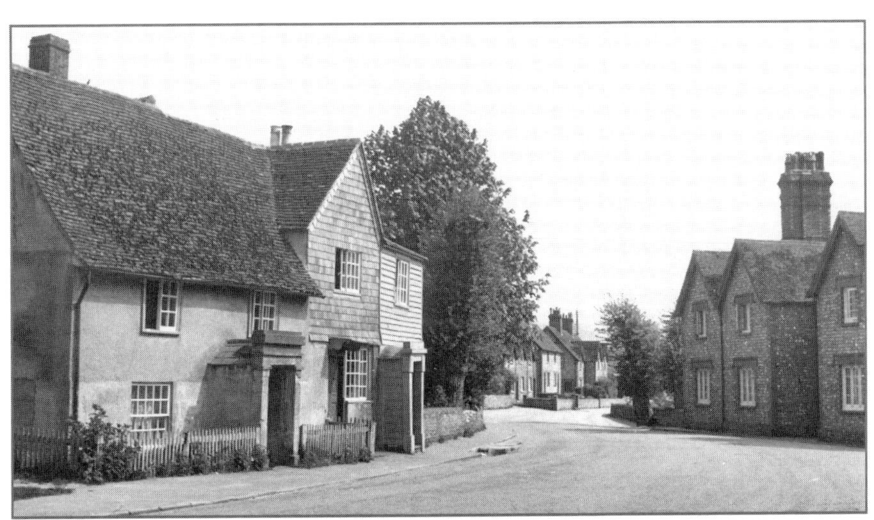

◀ Glynde, The Square c1955 G202010
Glynde is most famous for its internationaly renowned opera house built in the grounds of Glyndbourne. In this view of the village the old building on the left is timber-framed with a false façade. It has been rendered, tile-hung and weatherboarded, and substantial porches have been added. Horizontally sliding lights are fitted in some of the windows. On the right-hand side of the street stand flint-walled houses with brick dressings.

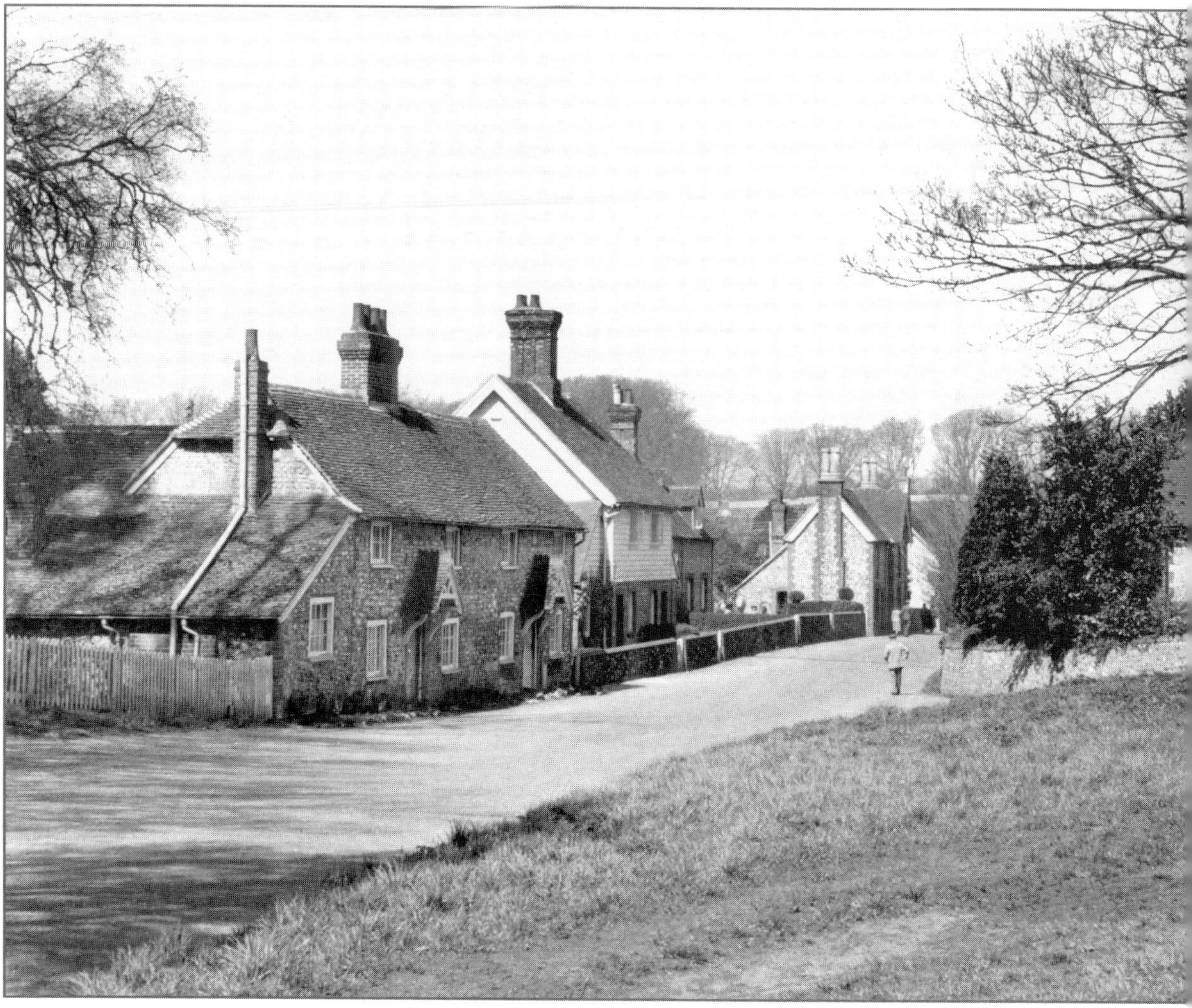

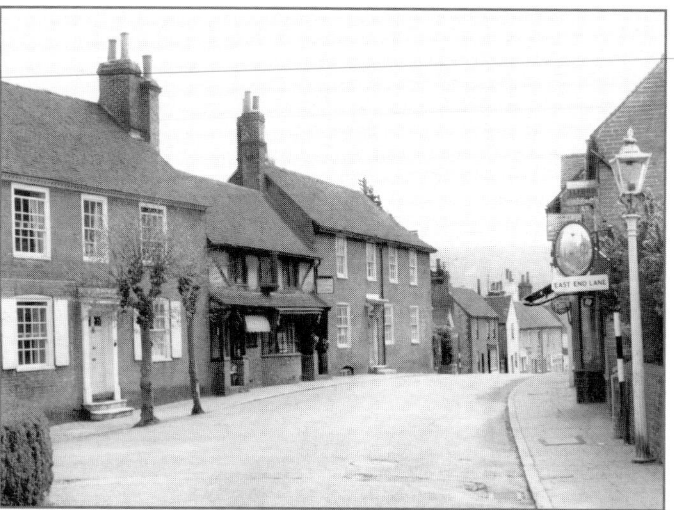

◀ **Ditchling, High Street c1960** D158097
A range of 16th-century houses and cottages descends the hill towards a central crossroads, notably Old Forge, Bowries and Ricksteddle. St Margaret's church has a 13th-century oak chest and 14th-century glass. Wing's Place, a fine 16th-century timber-framed house that was used as a pilgrim's rest house, is now known as Anne of Cleves House, but in reality it has no connection with her. The Old Meeting House was founded in 1698 and is used by Baptists from a wide area. The village is now noted as an art and craft centre. Ditchling Beacon is a famous vantagepoint 813 feet up on the Downs with panoramic views. There are dewponds alongside the road by the Beacon.

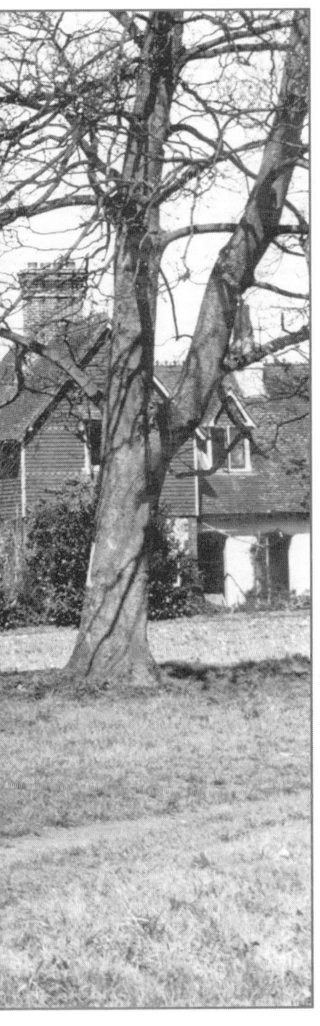

◀ Falmer, The Village c1955 F170001
We are on the Downs between Brighton and Lewes. Near the rebuilt church there is a thatched barn and an early dewpond. Dewponds were depressions in the chalk ground, lined with puddled clay; they were used to collect rainfall for watering farm livestock. There is another example of a dewpond nearby at Balmer. The picture shows Downland cottages with flint walling and tiled roofs. The village is now cut in two by a very busy dual carriageway, and is the location of the University of Sussex campus. The scene is similar today, but most properties are now used by the university.

▼ Clayton, The Village c1960
C419001
We are at the foot of the Downs by the route of the London to Brighton main line railway. St John the Baptist's church has a wooden bell turret, and the interior is decorated with a series of 12th-century wall paintings. A railway tunnel near the village has an ornate northern entrance. Two windmills, Jack and Jill, are located on the top of the Downs overlooking the village far below. The black smock mill Jack is conserved, while the white post mill Jill is in full working order and open to visitors.

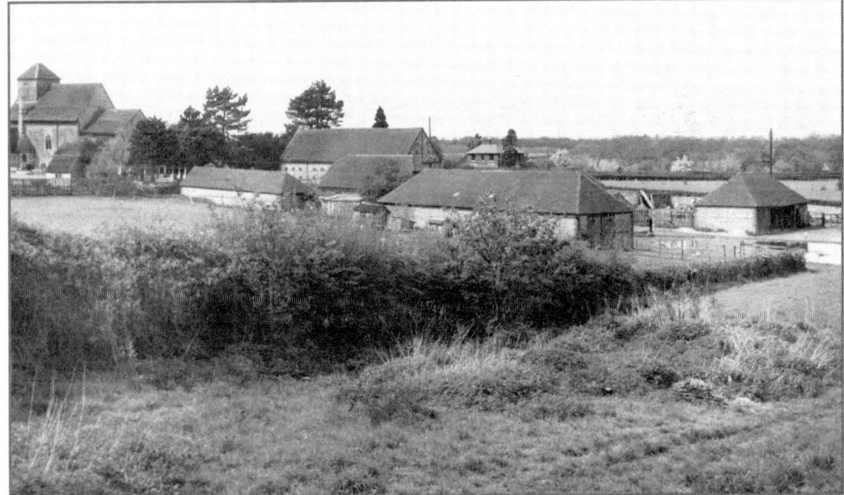

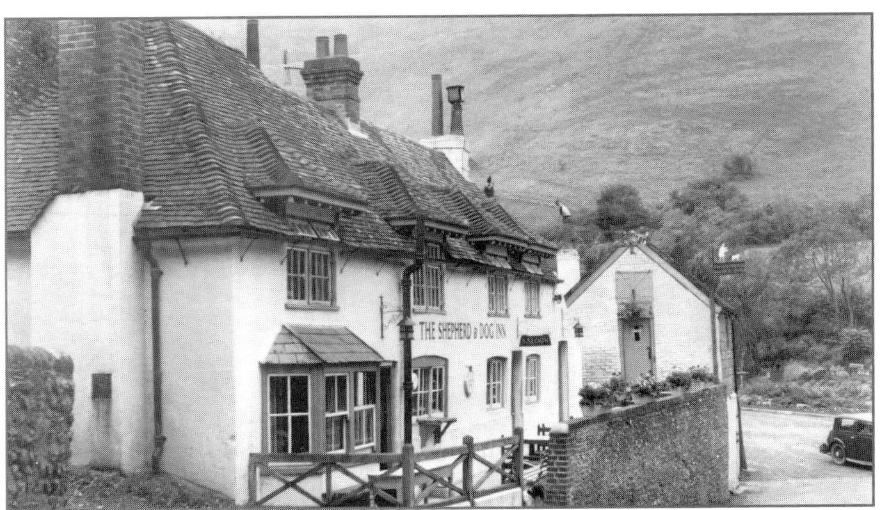

**◀ Fulking
The Shepherd
and Dog c1950** F133001
This well-known public house stands at the foot of the Downs. The area was noted for grazing sheep. There is a spring-fed well by the roadside next to the pub. There are great views of the scarp side of the Downs. There is now a scheme to encourage more livestock farming on the South Downs.

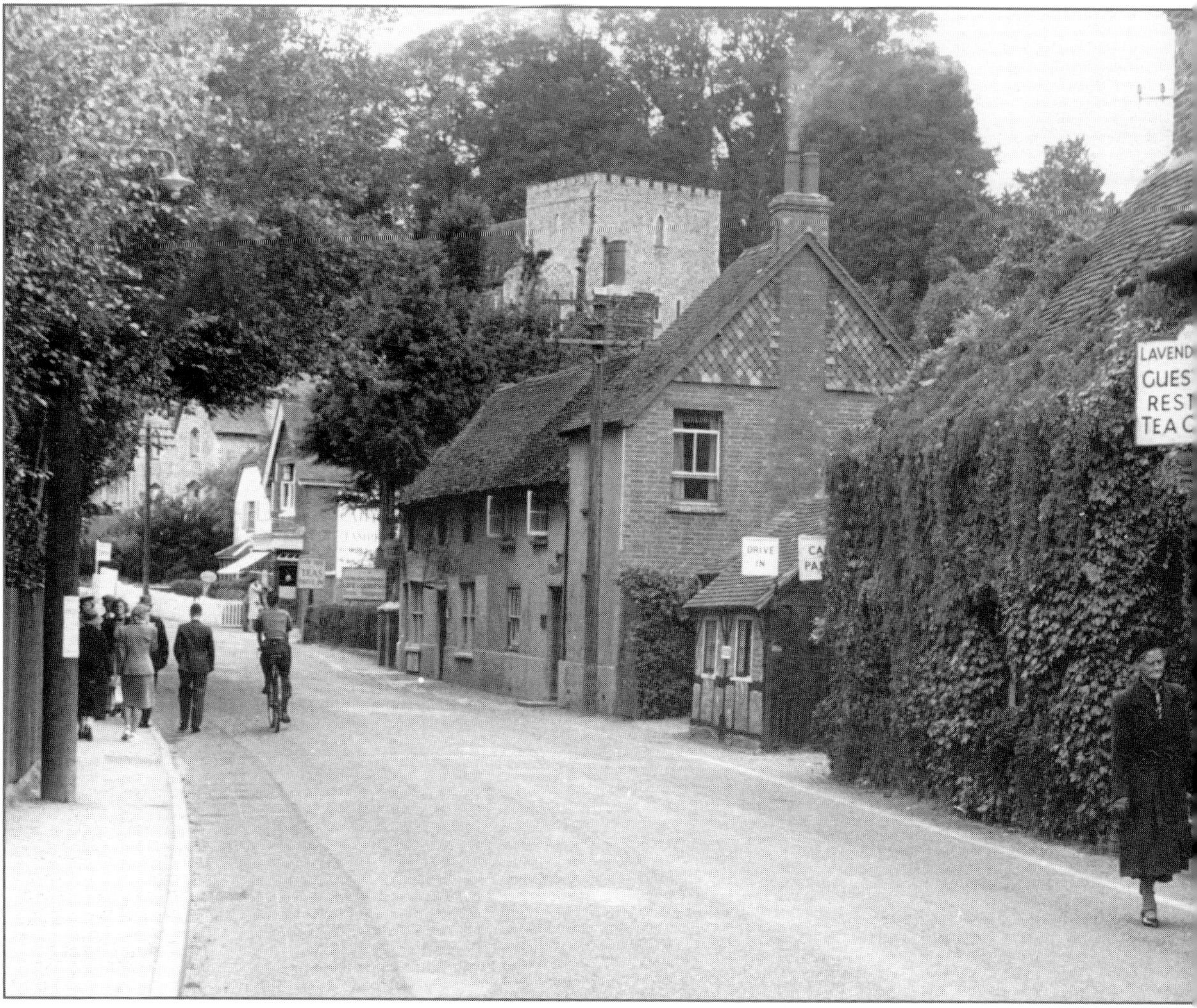

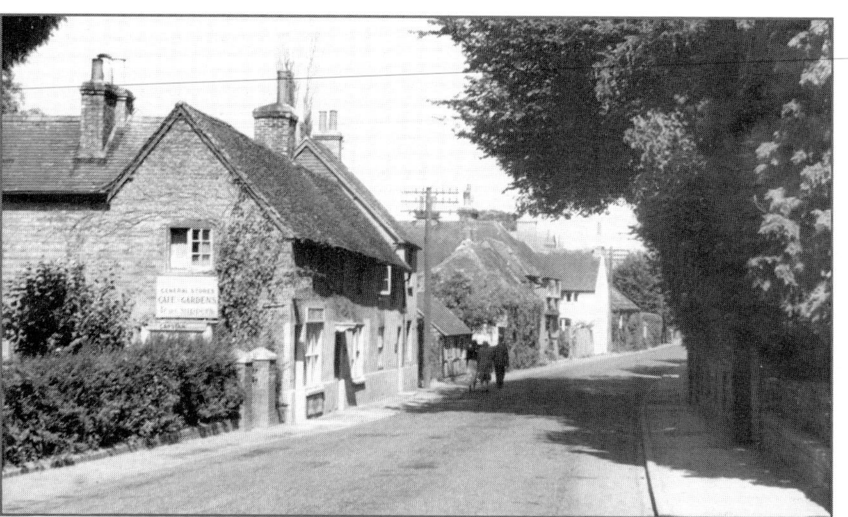

Bramber, The Village c1950 B179002
Bramber is located at the foot of a Norman castle guarding the tidal River Adur. The castle was stormed and wrecked by the Parliamentarians in the Civil War, in 1641. St Mary's House is a medieval timber-framed house open to visitors.

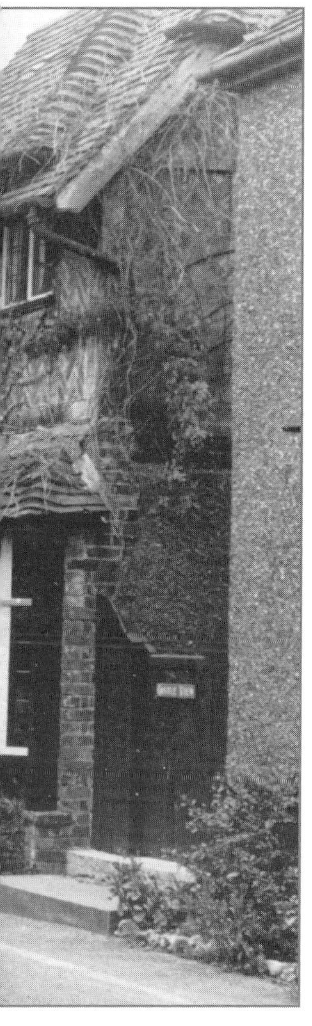

Bramber, The Village Street c1950 B179007

The Norman church of St Nicholas is perched on a small hill near the castle ruins. There was a railway station nearby, but the line is now closed. Lavender Cottage dates back to the 15th century. In those days the sea came much closer, and it used to be a fisherman's home. It is reputed to have a tunnel between the grounds and a nearby castle; it was used by an amorous couple to visit each other.

Bramber, Yew Tree Tea Gardens c1950 B179006

Here we see a tea garden with a variety of seating, benches and tables - plenty of space is needed for serving coach parties. The garden pond is deep, but little water is visible. The village was a popular coach trip destination from the coastal resorts; now visitors travel in their cars. It is now largely residential with pubs and restaurants.

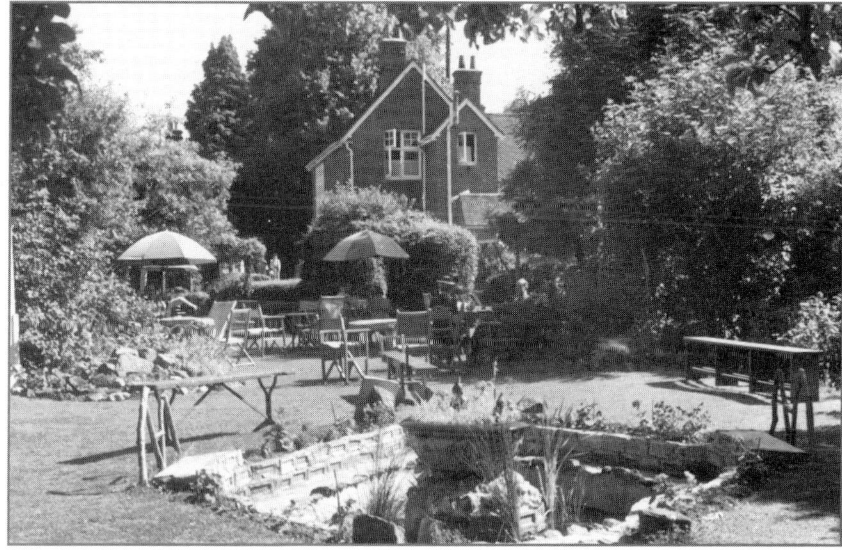

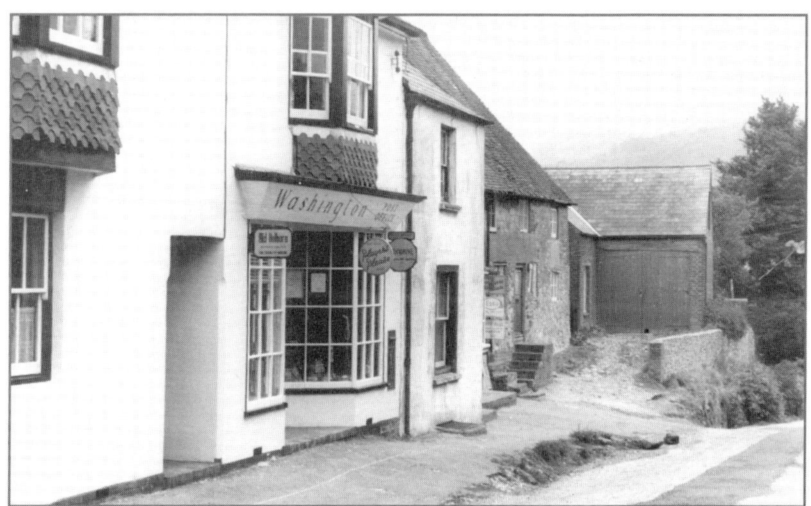

Washington, The Post Office c1960 W359019

Washington is on the main London to Worthing Road at the foot of the Downs. There are fine views of Chanctonbury Ring, a ring of beech trees planted on the site of an Iron Age hill fort 800 feet up on the top of the Downs. A crock of Anglo-Saxon coins was found at Chancton Farm in 1866; they are now in the British Museum. In the picture the Post Office has signs advertising tobacco and cigarettes fixed to the shop front, with an Esso paraffin sign further along. The large door of the outbuilding has a cat hole.

▼ **Findon, Post Office Corner c1960** F131091

Findon is on the top of the Downs, just north of Worthing, and was noted for an annual sheep fair. Now horse breeding and training is an important local activity. Findon Place is a manor house built in the 13th century and extended around the year 1740, with extensive stables added in 1800. Cissbury Ring is an Iron Age fort, with flint mines, 602 feet up on the Downs to the east. The Post Office has a pillar-box with a sign on top with an arrow pointing to the entrance a few feet away.

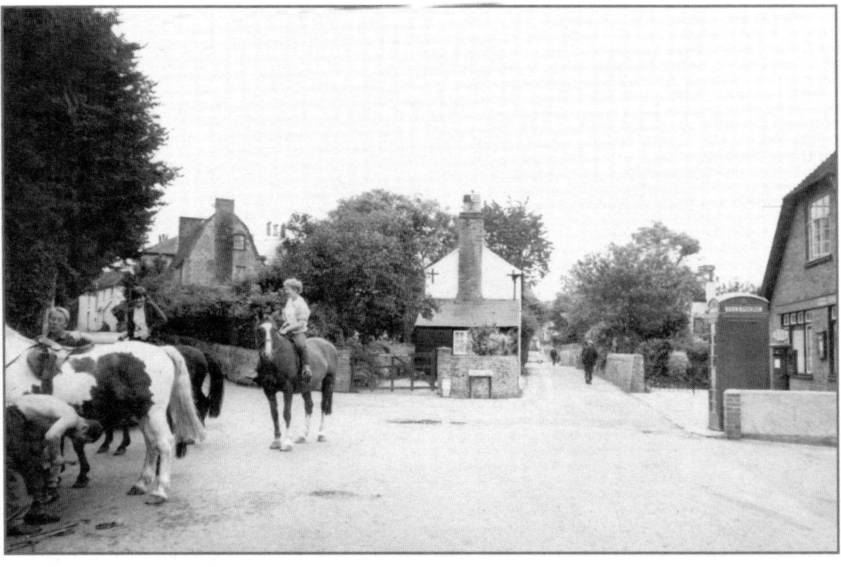

▼ **High Salvington, The Village 1919** 68993

Here we see newer housing in a location on top of the Downs, amongst gorse bushes. Wooden sheds stand in the gardens.

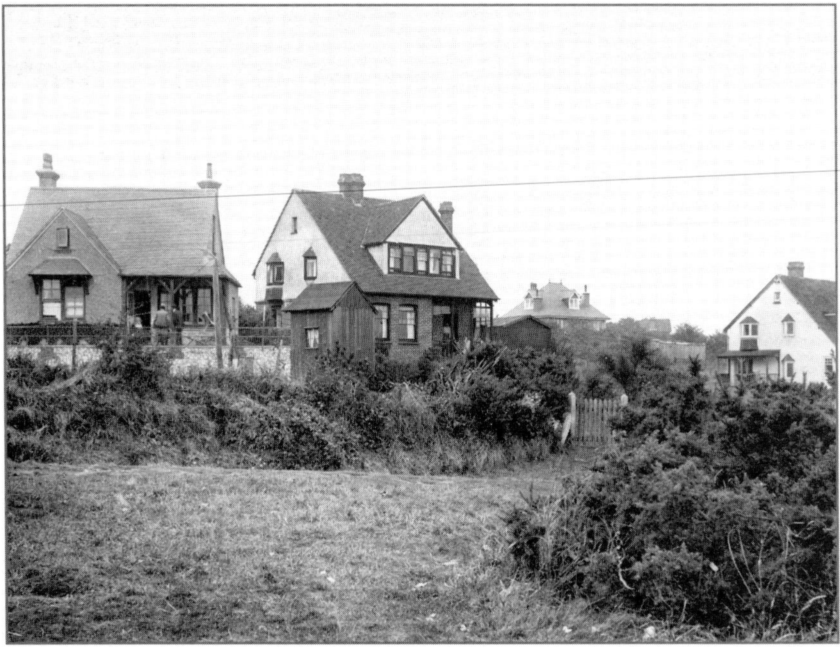

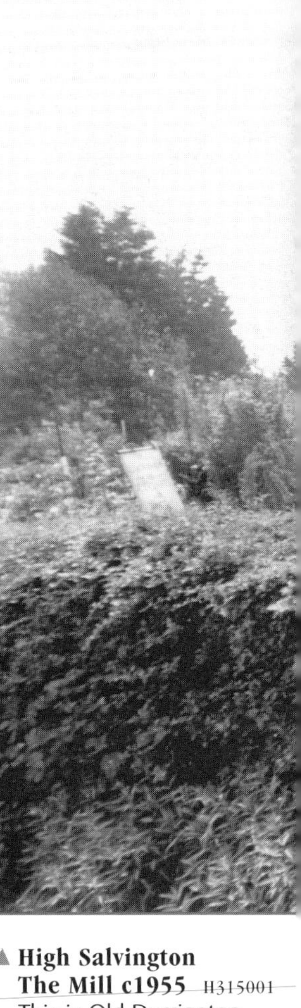

▲ **High Salvington The Mill c1955** H315001

This is Old Durrington windmill, photographed at a time when the site was used as a tea garden. Only two sails were on the mill at this time. The white tailpole was used to turn the body of the mill so that the sails pointed into the wind. It was built about 1720, and ceased work in 1897. The mill is now fully restored and opens to visitors on Sunday afternoons during the summer months.

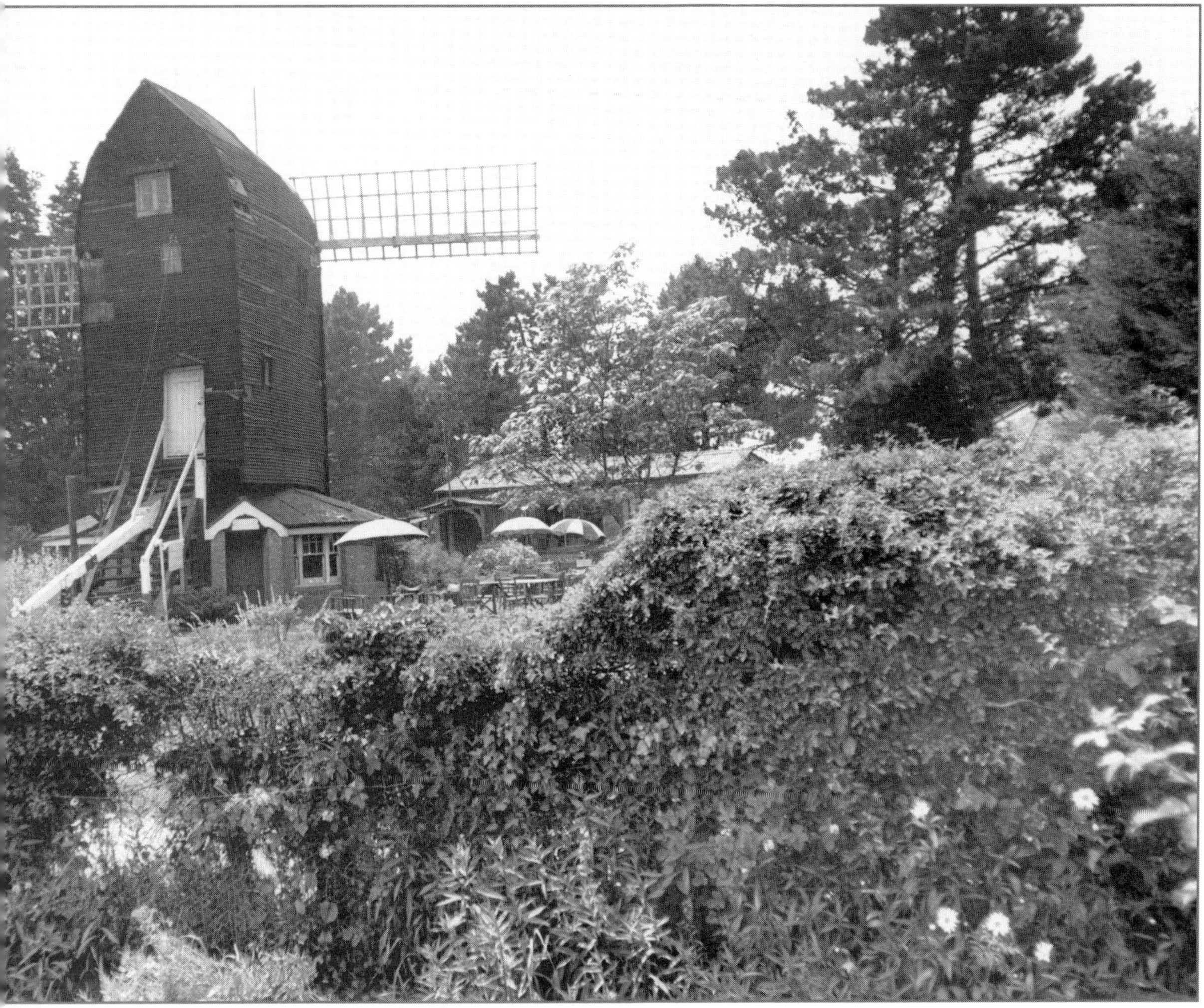

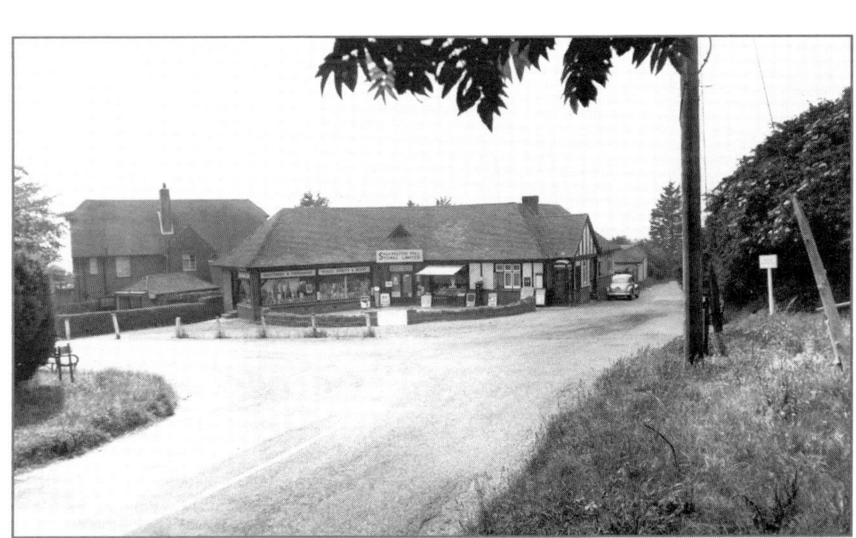

**High Salvington
The Post Office c1955**
H315002
A modern stores serves an
expanding residential area.

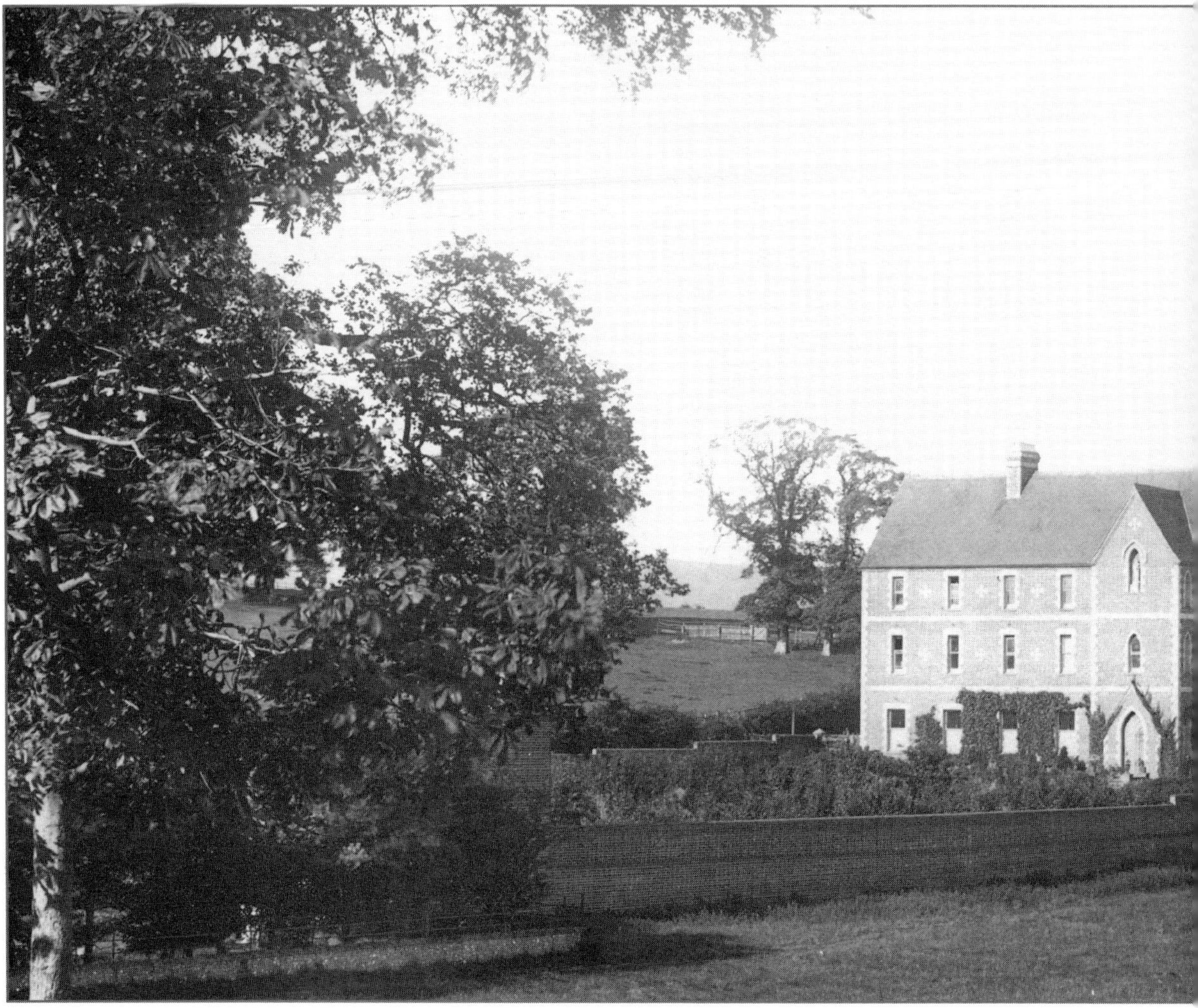

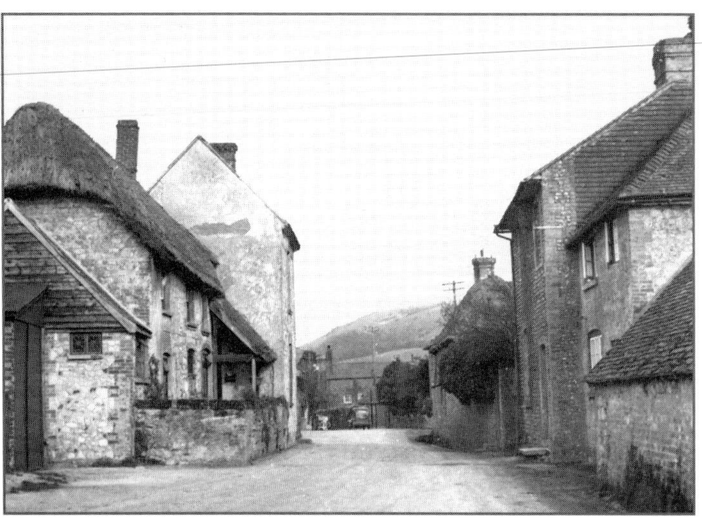

Amberley, The Village c1960 A44008
We are in a marshy area - Amberley Wild Brooks, beside the tidal and navigable River Arun. The castle was a fortified manor of the Bishops of Chichester; it was crenellated c1377 to defend the coastal area and the river estuary. The manor was granted long before the Norman Conquest. During the civil war King Charles II sheltered here after the Battle of Worcester en route to Shoreham to embark for France. The Norman church of St Michael adjoins the castle. The varying height of the old houses built of flint and stone with thatch and tile, contrasts with the varying width of the roadway. It is now a village where artists like to work.

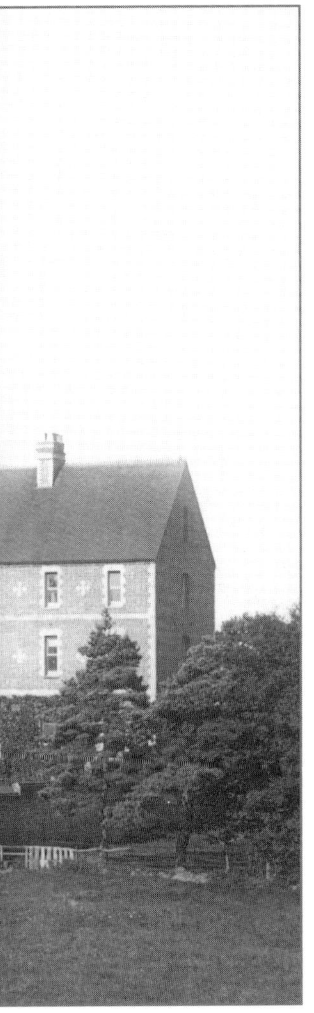

Storrington, The Monastery 1894 34414

We are in a large village at the foot of the Downs, which has several commons. The Premonstratensian monastery of Our Lady of England is still in use. The poet Francis Thompson (1859-1907) wrote some of his poems here. The site is very little changed today, although the roof space has been converted to additional rooms and dormer windows added. The parish church is nearby.

Houghton, The George and Dragon c1960 H515048

Houghton is a hamlet with a long stone bridge across the tidal River Arun. In 1292 the Earl of Arundel submitted to the Bishop of Chichester, who had excommunicated him for walking his dog in the bishop's forest. The inn is a 13th-century timber-framed brick and flint building. King Charles II is said to have taken refreshments here in 1651 while fleeing from the Battle of Worcester. A Watney's Red Barrel illuminated sign (a much-advertised keg beer of the time) hangs below the main sign.

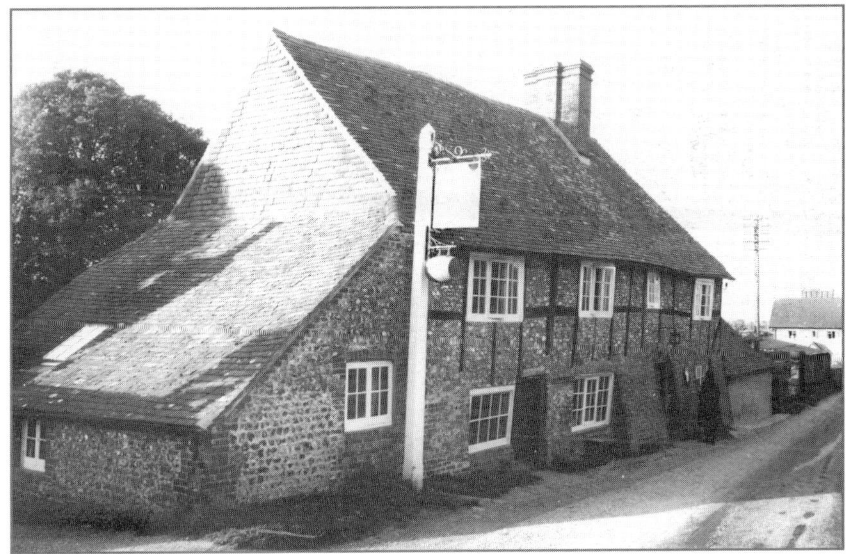

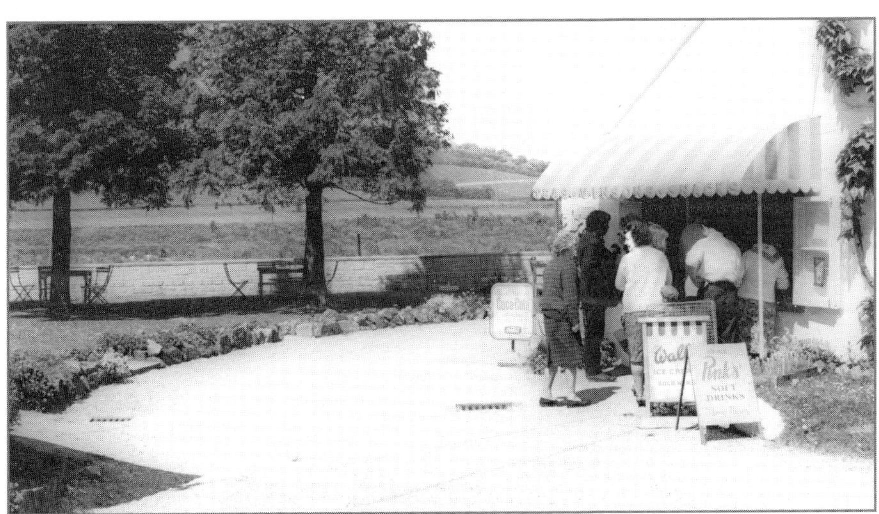

Houghton, Vinson's Tea Lawns c1960

H515058

We are near the long stone road bridge to Houghton, built in 1875 and crossing the tidal River Arun. Vinson's was a popular riverside tea rooms and garden. There is still a tea garden on the site. The Chalk Pits industrial and historical museum is nearby, next to the main line railway station.

▼ Bury, The Church from the River 1898 42556

We are on the navigable and tidal River Arun. The church of St John the Evangelist has a shingled broach spire; flint and stone are used for walling and buildings. A ferry with landing steps connected with a footpath to Amberley on the opposite bank. Novelist and poet John Galsworthy lived in Bury House from 1926 until 1933. The 'Forsyte Saga' was completed here. A visitor to the house was Sir James Barrie, the creator of Peter Pan. The area is now known as Bury Wharf, and the converted farm buildings are used for residential purposes.

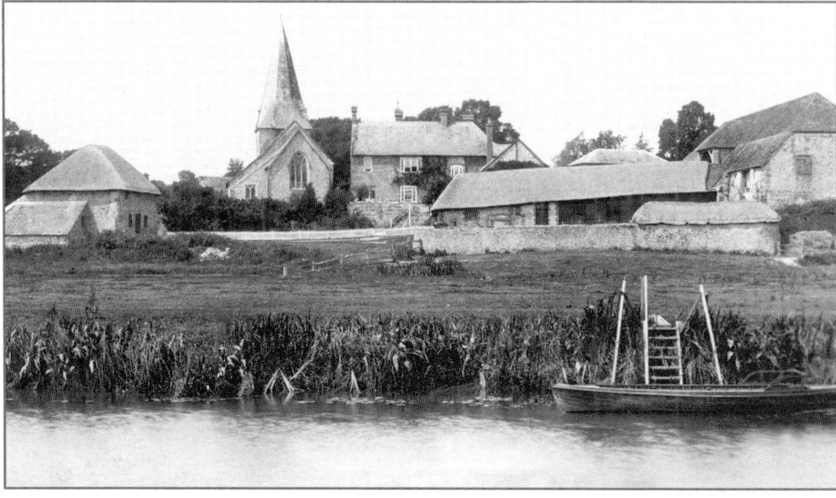

▼ Compton, The Post Office c1955 C421049

A secluded village in the middle of the Downs near the Hampshire border, south of Harting. There is a fine Neolithic long barrow on Telegraph Hill, which is 534 feet high. The Norman church of St Mary was rebuilt in 1849, with a timber bell turret and a shingled spire. The Post Office, here with advertising signs for Senior Service cigarettes fixed to the shopfront, is now a house.

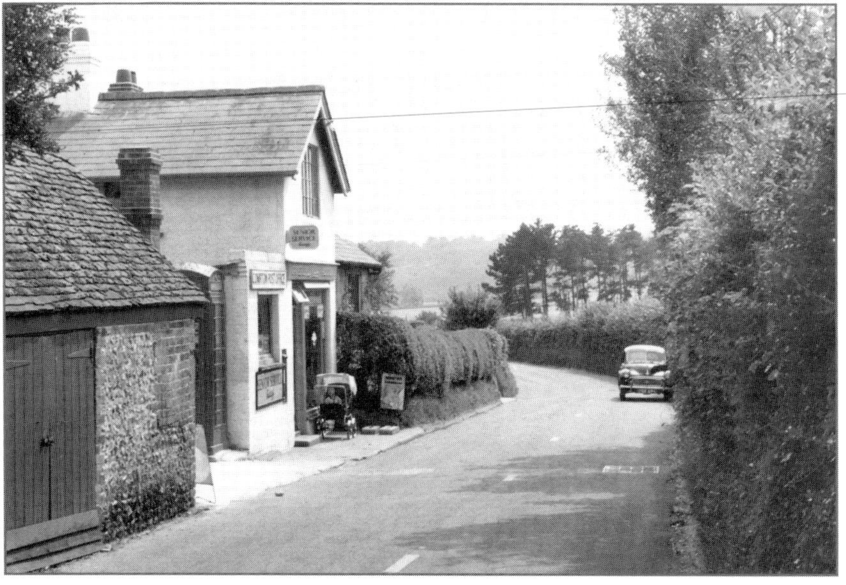

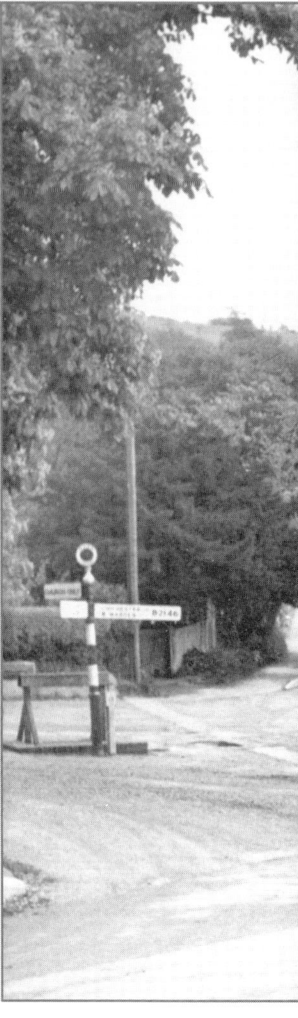

▲ Compton, The Coach and Horses c1950

C421018

An old coaching inn on the Emsworth to Harting road, which sold Henty and Constable's ales at the time of the photograph. The Inn is still trading. The scene today is little changed.

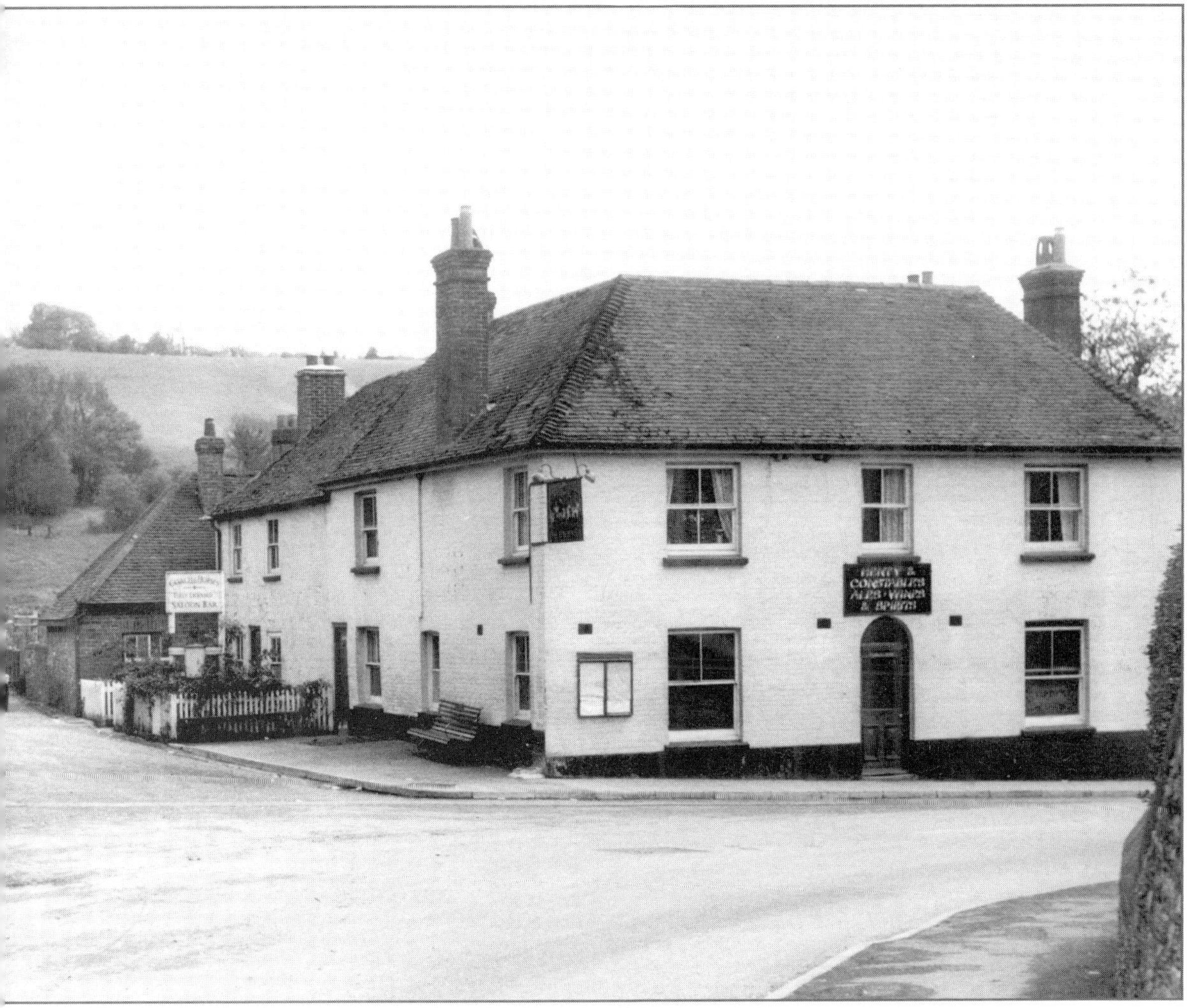

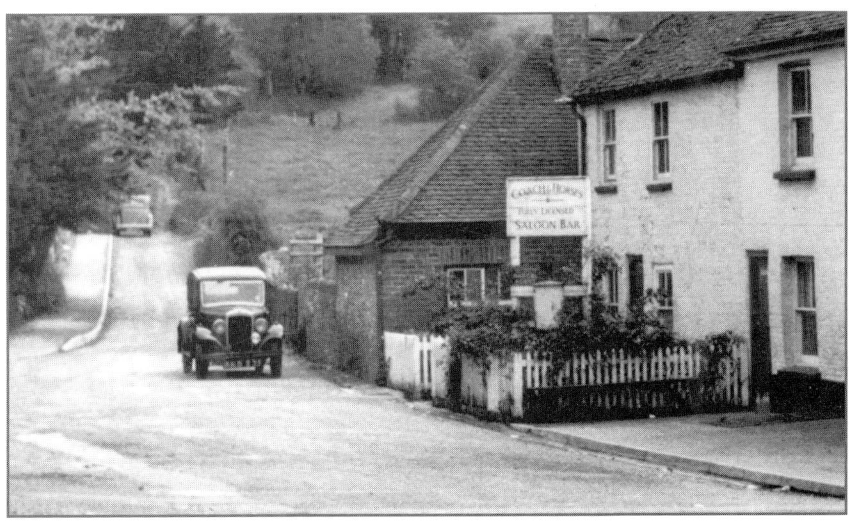

**Detail From:
Compton, The Coach
and Horses c1950**

▼ East Harting, The Village 1906 54414

A random collection of cottages around a pair of lanes forms an oval.
The thatch-roofed house has a well-clipped hedge and a Chilean pine
- or monkey-puzzle tree - grows in a garden further down the hill. The
roadway is of stone; motor transport has not yet arrived. The scene is
still recognisable.

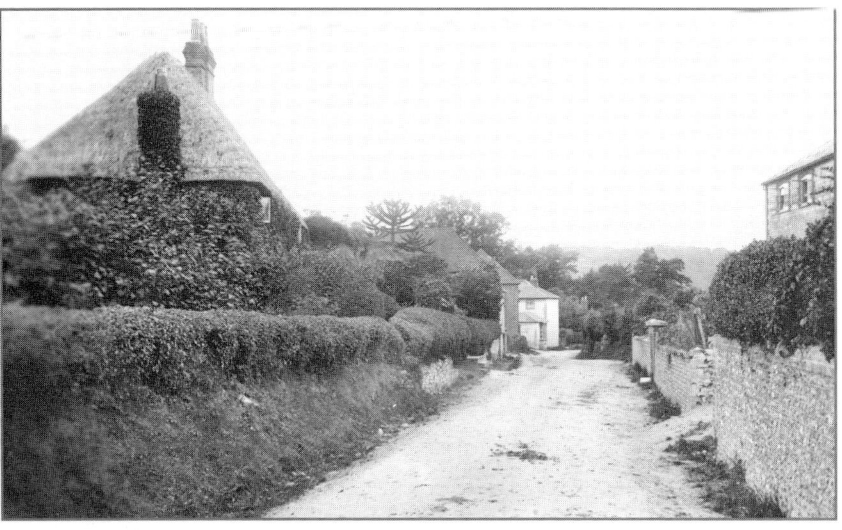

▼ South Harting, The Church and Village 1906 54413

We are in the main part of the Hartings, nestling in the northern slopes of the
Downs, on the pilgrims' route to Chichester. The church of St Mary and St Gabriel
has a shingled broach-spire on a central tower. The Caryl Chapel was desecrated
by the Royalists in 1643 and later by the Parliamentarians, and left in ruins. A
variety of houses of all shapes and sizes are seen in the foreground. Anthony
Trollope, the Victorian novelist, lived in the village for many years and is
buried here.

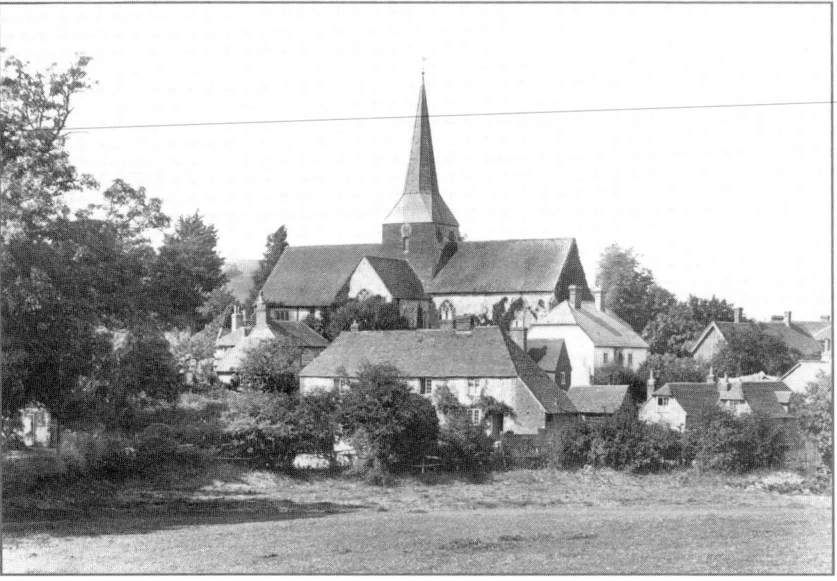

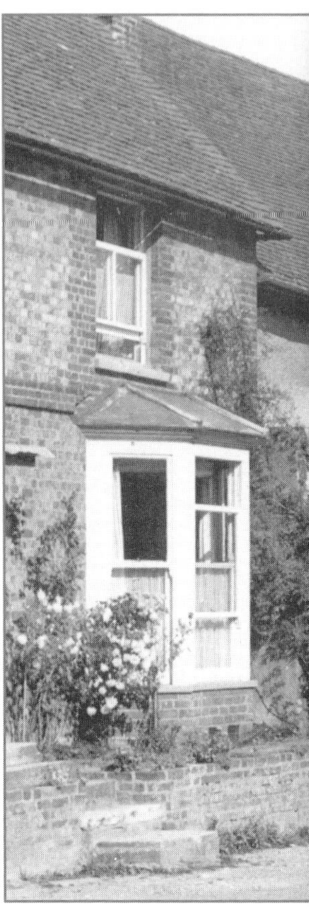

**▲ South Harting, High
Street c1955** S820005
A brick extension to the
front of the terrace of
older houses contains the
shop; small cigarette
advertising signs are fixed
to the shopfront. The
White Hart Inn is next
door with an old type of
telephone box outside. At
the road junction we see
the Ship Inn. Nearby
Harting Down, 747 feet is
a local vantage point with
great views. Uppark is a
17th-century mansion at
the top of the Downs with
a deer park. It is in the
care of the National Trust,
and has recently been
completely restored after
a disastrous fire. It is once
again open to visitors.
The scene is little
different now.

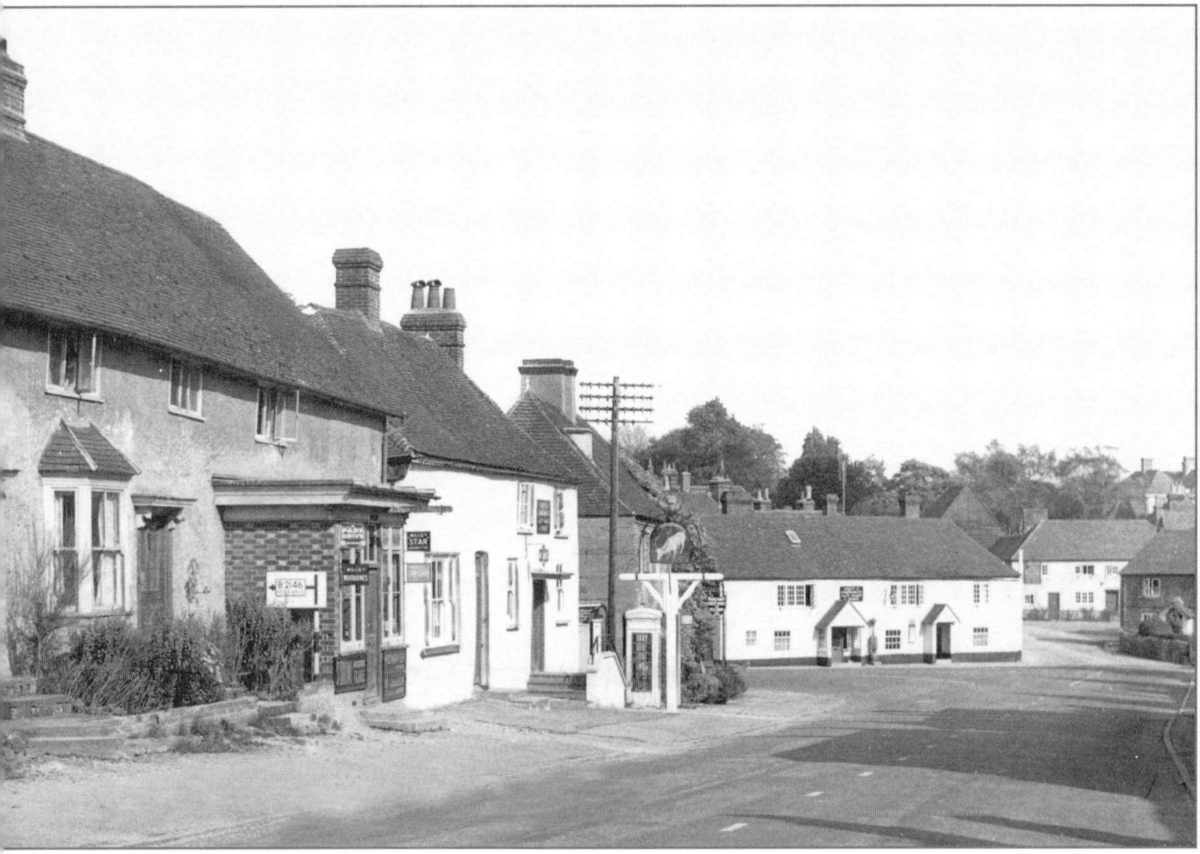

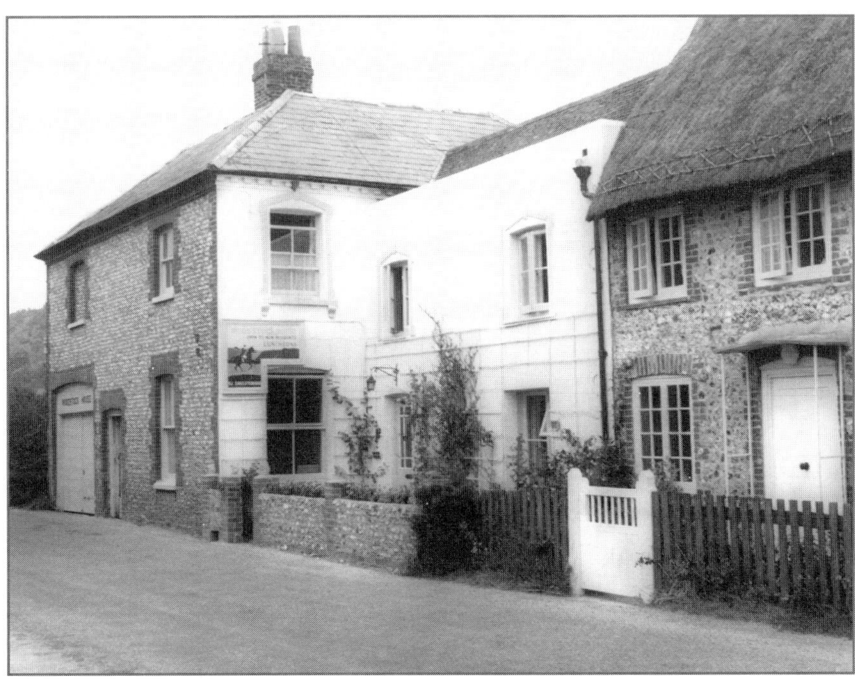

◄ Charlton, Woodstock House c1955 C418002
Woodstock House is a country house hotel nestling in the Downs below the heights of Charlton Forest. We are near Goodwood racecourse, hence the racing scene on the hotel restaurant signboard. The buildings have flint walls and thatched, tiled and slate roofing. The rendered and painted façade in the central building probably conceals an older building. Nearby are Goodwood House and Park, built in 1660 and greatly extended in 1760. It is The Duke of Richmond's estate, and has fine art collections. The park is noted for trees and views and is open to visitors.

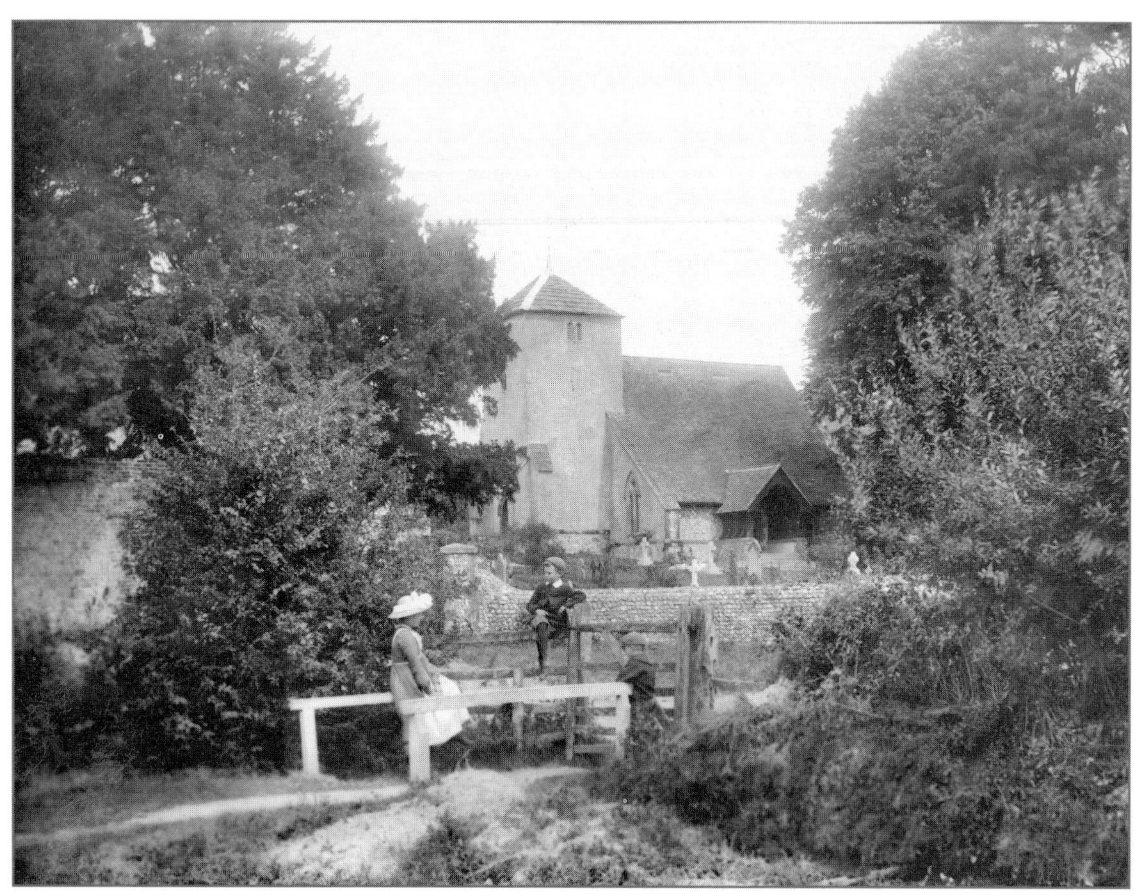

Cocking
The Church 1906 54384
We are just below the Downs on the main road between Midhurst and
Chichester. The church has a 14th-century tower, and a mural painting in the
nave dated 1220. The rebuilt Manor House is nearby. The locality is excellent
for rambling over the Downs. In the picture three children are dressed up in
their best clothes and keep still for the photographer.

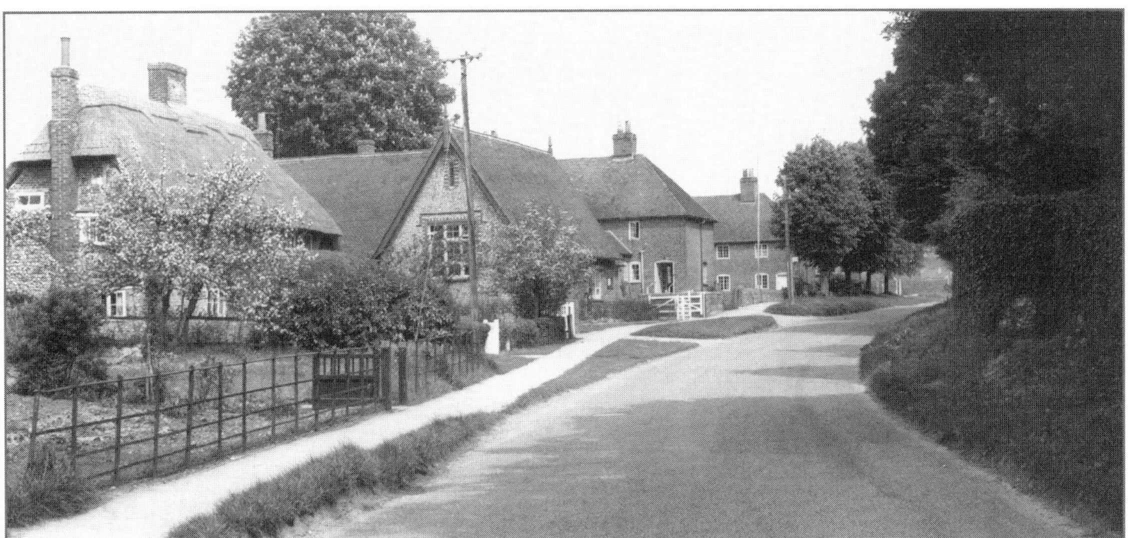

Boxgrove, The Village c1960 B167027
We are on the southern slope of the Downs, north of Chichester. Boxgrove Priory, of the Benedictine Order, was founded in 1105. At its dissolution in 1537, the priory church became the parish church dedicated to St Mary and St Blaise. The remainder of the monastic buildings were ruined, but some parts survive and are conserved. The De La Warr Chantry is a building within a building; here, priests prayed for the soul of its builder. Chantry chapels were declared illegal in 1547, and although the statues have long gone much carved stonework survives. The picture shows the road past the school with the Priory on the right. The scene today is little changed.

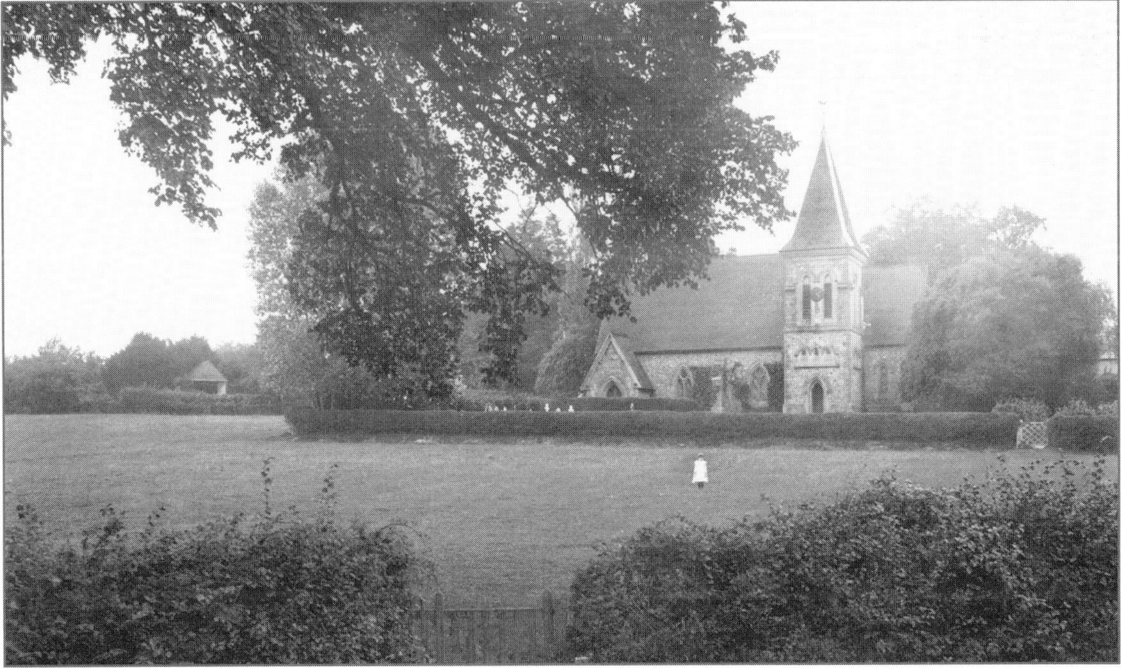

Duncton, The Church 1912 64896
We are at the foot of the Downs, with fine views nearby. Holy Trinity Church was built in 1866 in the Decorated style, on the site of a medieval church. It has the oldest dated bell in Sussex, 1369, which is of Dutch origin. A young girl waits patiently in the field for photographer to finish.

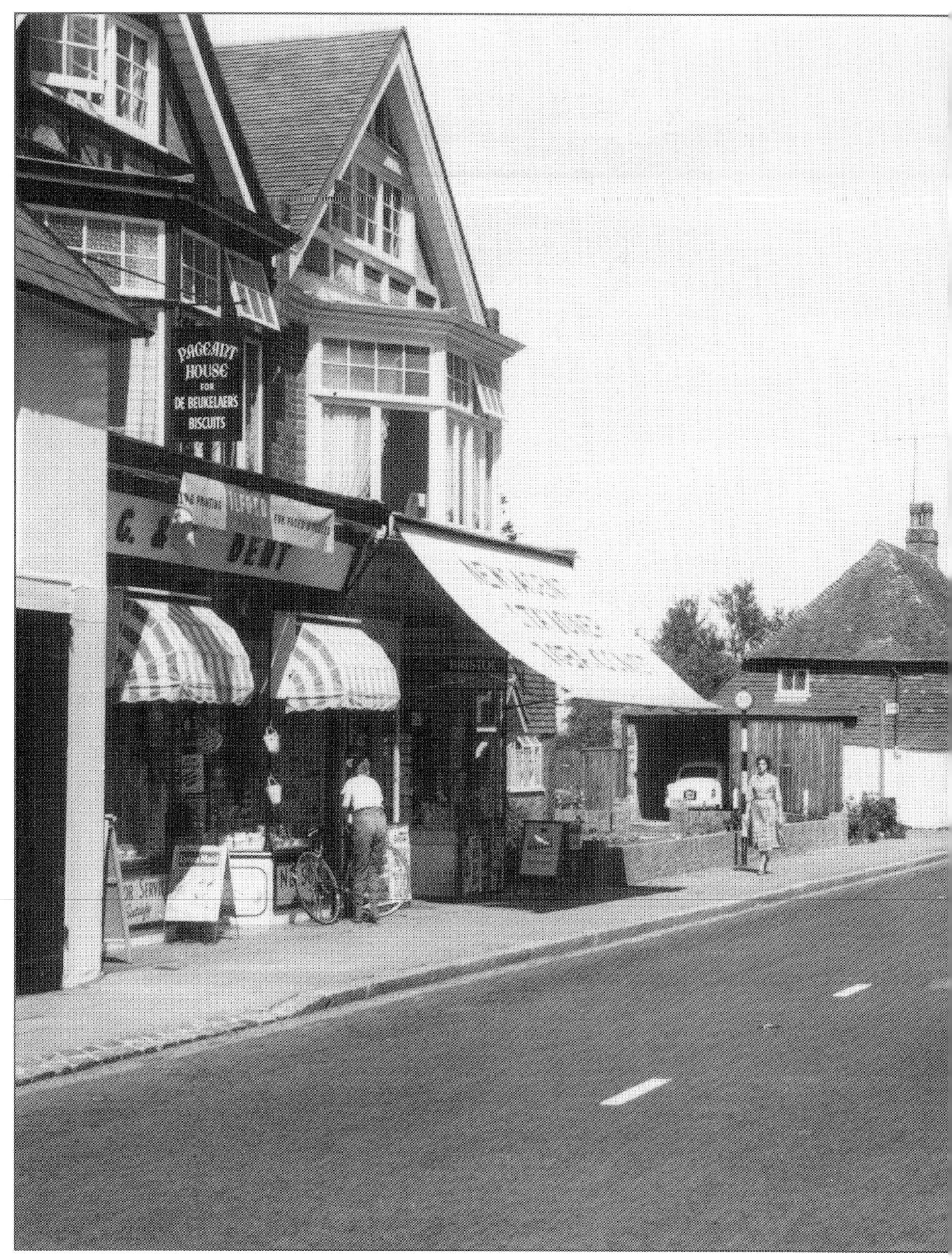
PAGEANT
HOUSE
FOR
DE BEUKELAERS
BISCUITS
ILFORD
BRISTOL

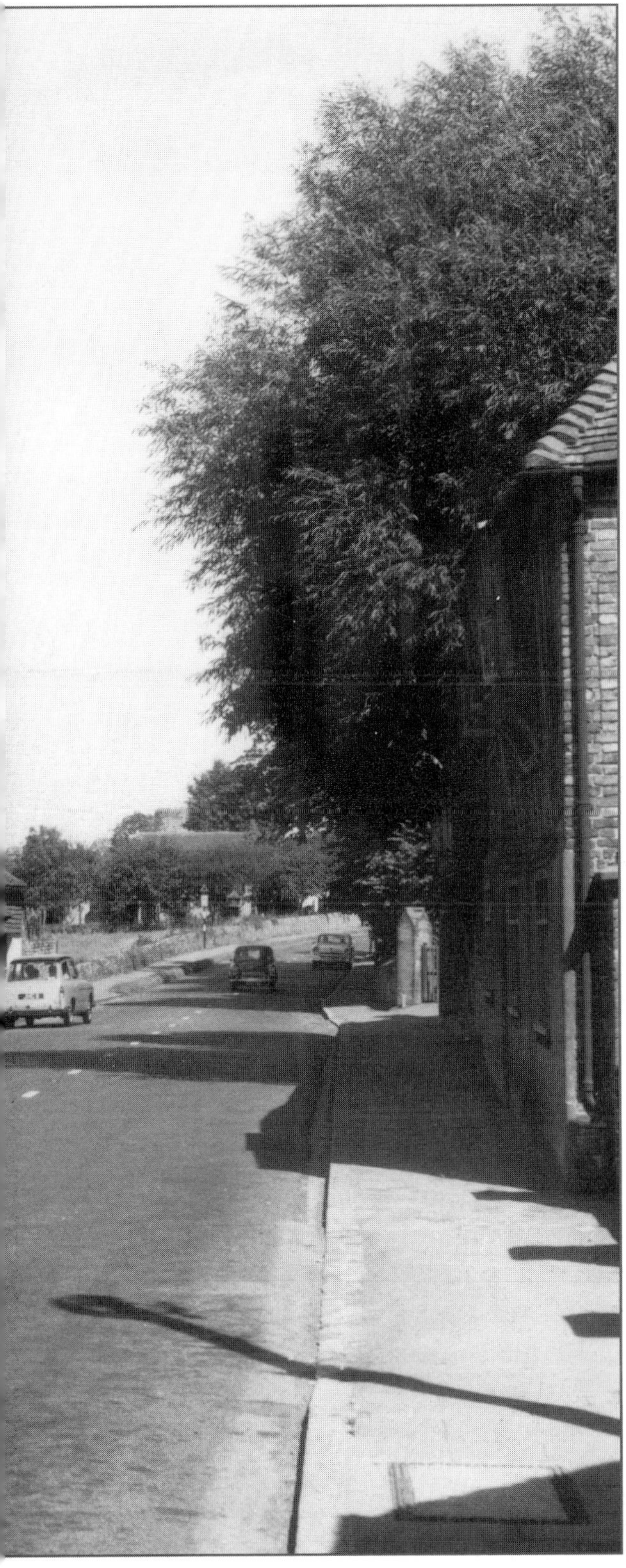

The Coast

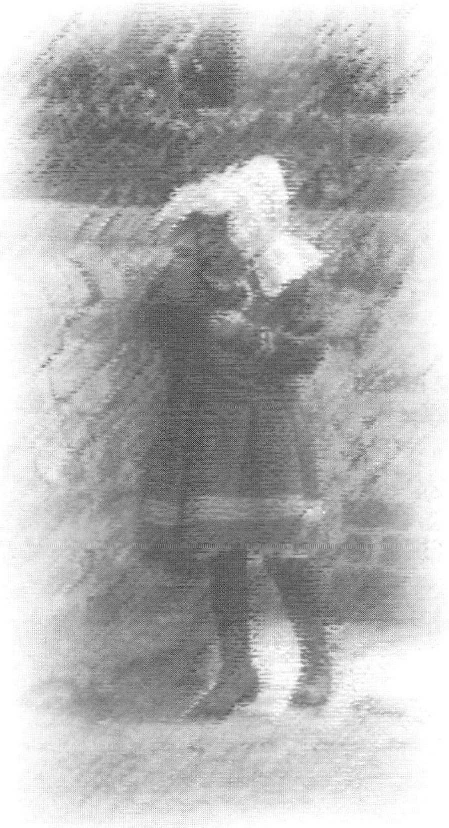

Westham, The Village c1965 W373009
The Normans built a church in Westham after the
Conqueror had landed nearby. Priesthawes House
was built from stone taken from nearby Pevensey
Castle. The local coastline is noted for Martello
coastal defence towers, dating from the Napoleonic
Wars. In the photograph we can see Dent's, Pageant
House, selling food and fancy goods; the other
shop is a newsagent, stationer and tobacconist. The
main road is busy with traffic - here an Austin A40
car heads out along the coast road. The scene has
now changed a little: the newsagents are still
trading, and the other shop has been converted to a
house.

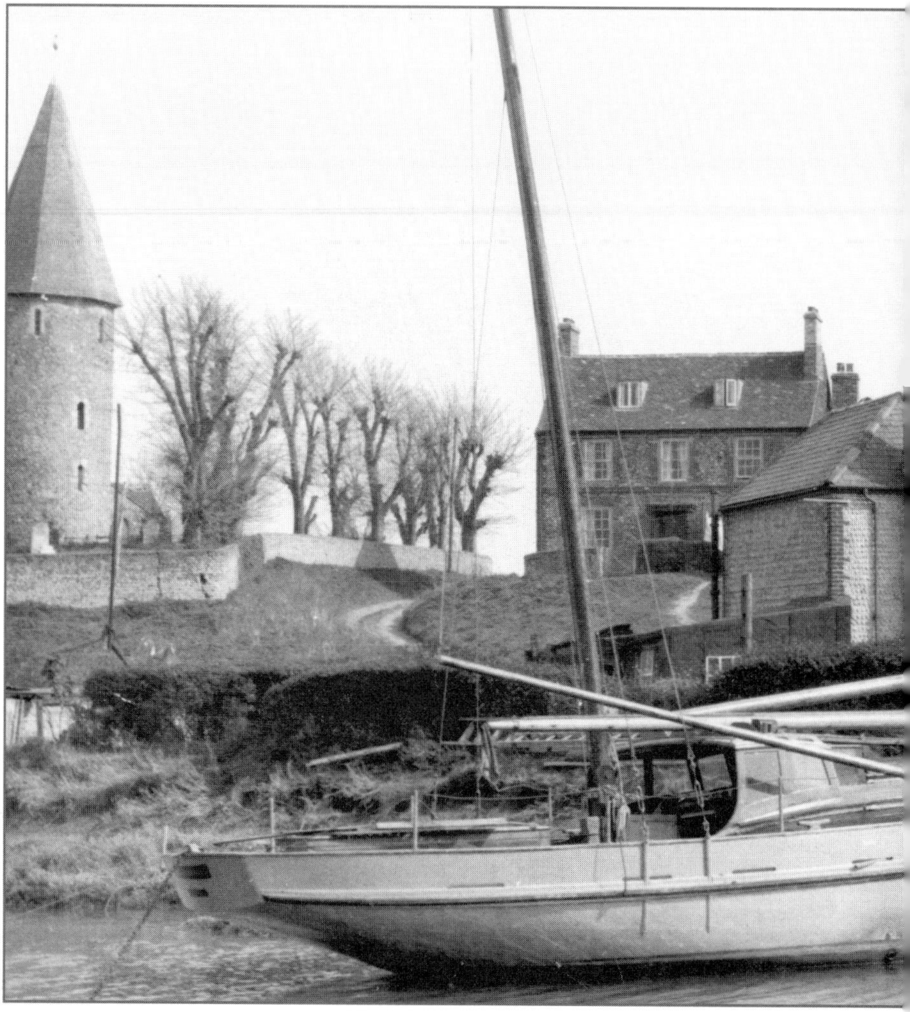

Piddinghoe ▶
The Village c1955

P343003

We are in the Ouse valley just north of Newhaven. St John's church is on high ground overlooking the tidal river. It has a Norman flint-built round tower, and a shingled octagonal spire. It is one of the three Norman round towers of Sussex. The weather vane is a sea-trout not the 'begilded dolphin' mentioned in the poetry of Rudyard Kipling - 'Where Piddinghoe's begilded dolphin veers'. Pottery was a local industry; a conical kiln has been rebuilt and conserved. The sailing cruiser is moored in a mud berth, and local people look on curiously. The village was notorious for smuggling. The scene is more wooded now.

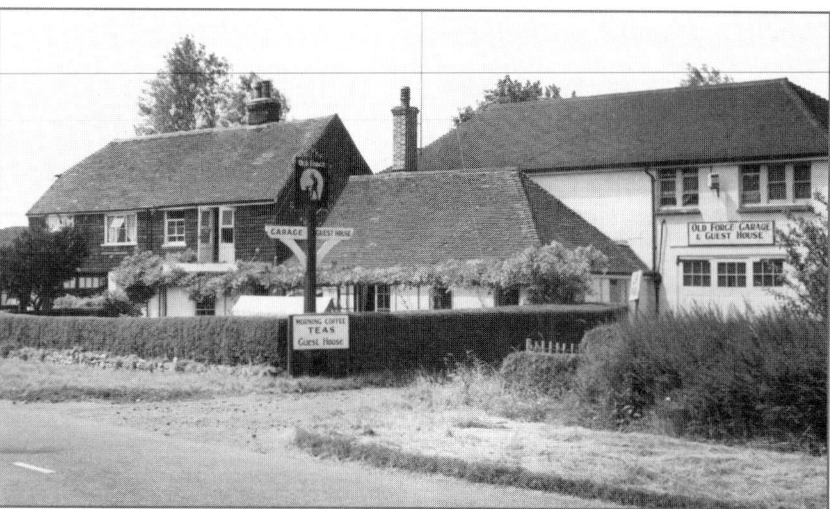

◀ **Magham Down**
The Old Forge Guest House c1960 M274004
Magham Down is a hamlet on a crossroads between Hailsham and Herstmonceux. The main road tourist route has great views of the Downs. The site of the old village blacksmith's has been developed for the modern needs of visitors to the area with a filling station, motor repairs, teas and guest-house.

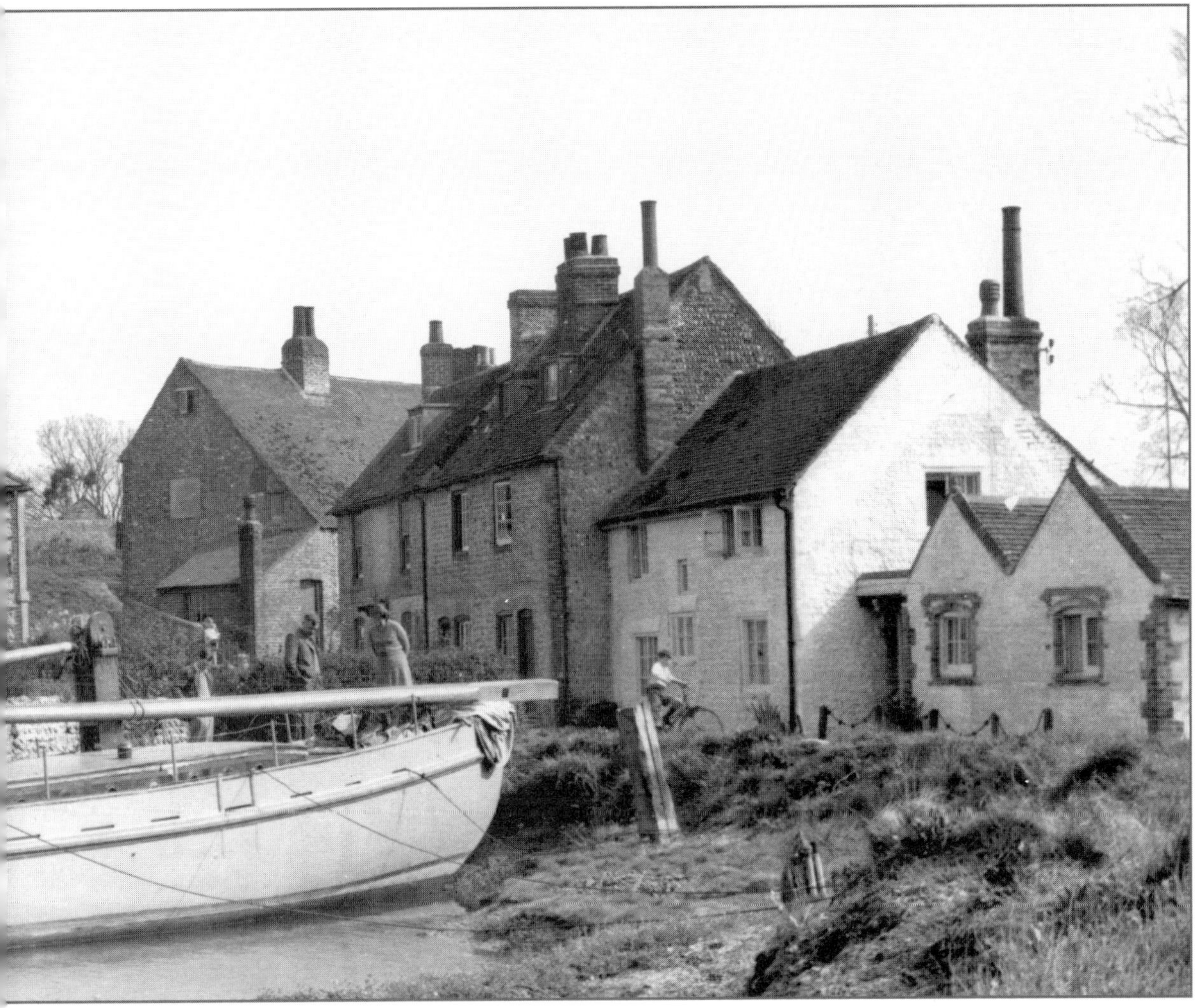

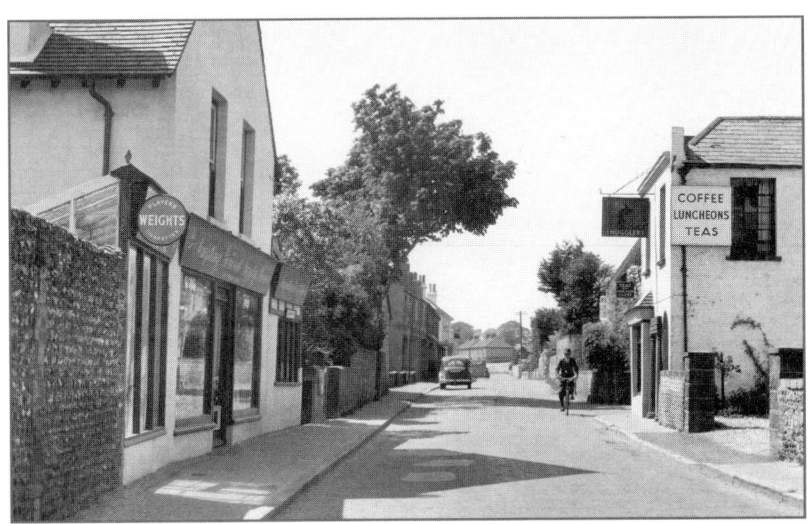

◄ Sompting, West Street c1955
S148004
We are very near to Worthing, where the downland has been inhabited ever since pre-historic times. The Norman church of St Mary has many Saxon features including a tower with a Rhenish helm roof, which is unique in Britain. The picture shows Sompting General Supply Stores with a sign fixed to the shopfront advertising Players Weights cigarettes, a popular budget brand. On the opposite side of the road, Smugglers has signs offering teas and homemade cakes - no fast food yet.

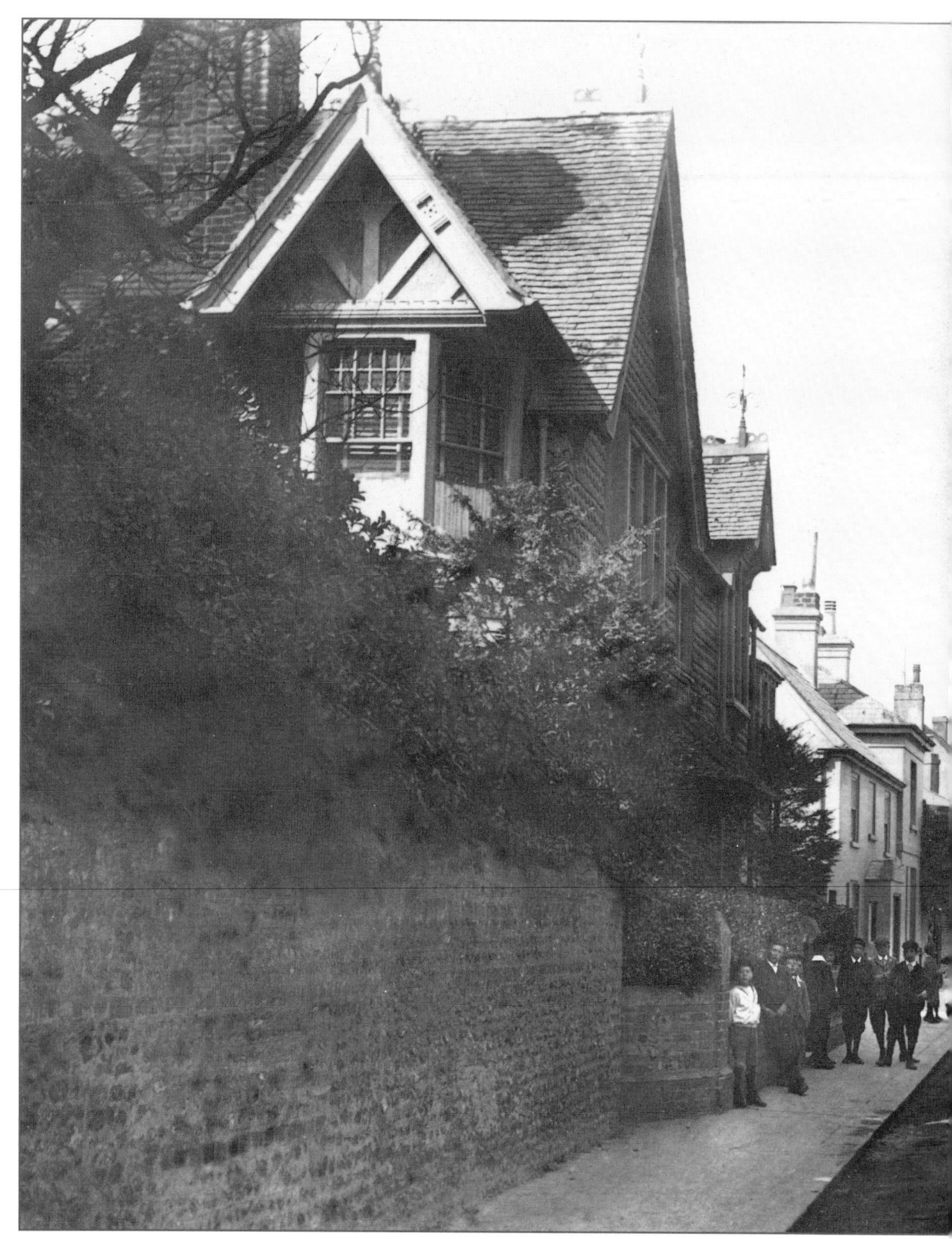

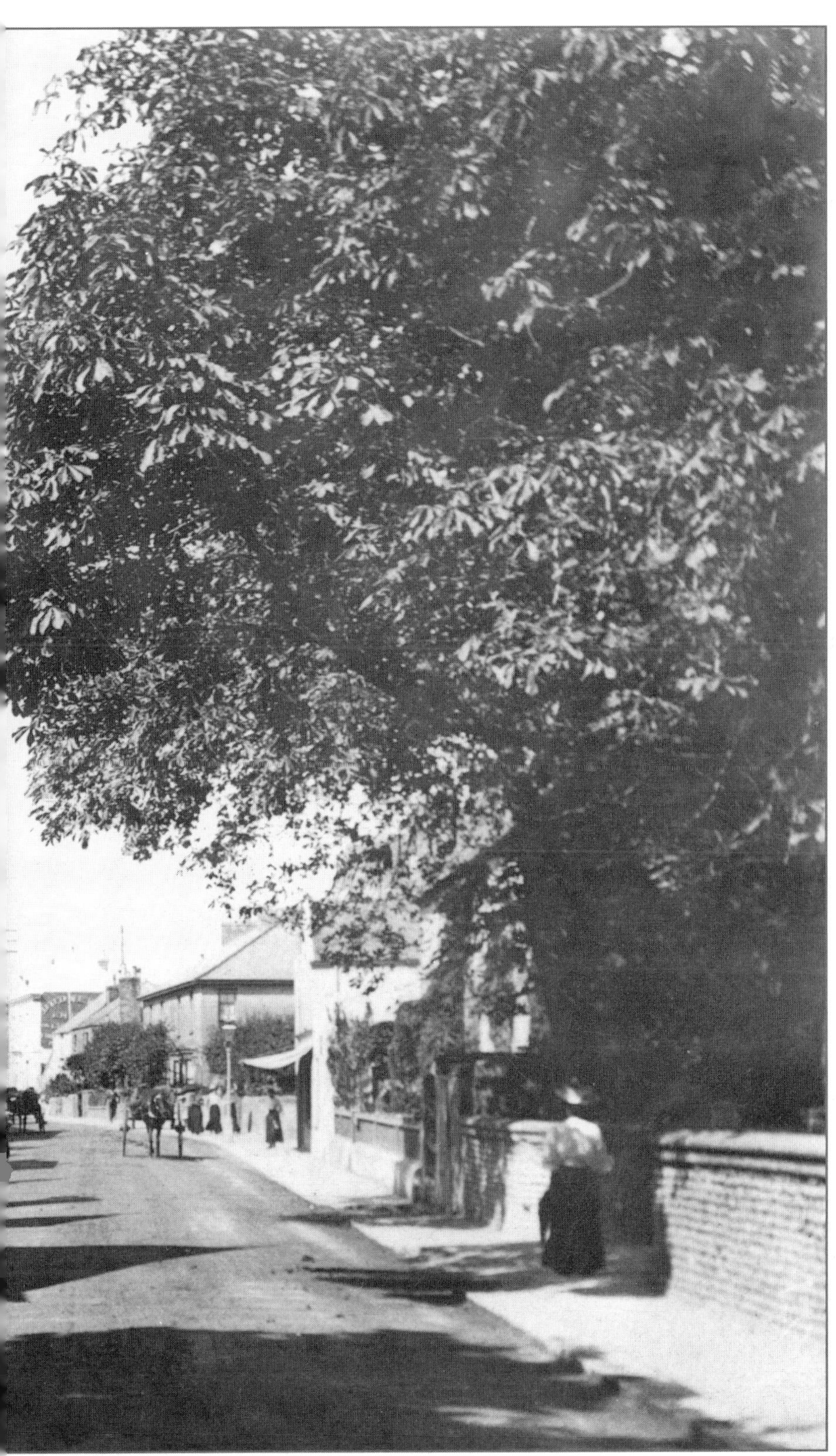

Broadwater
The Village 1906

56721

Broadwater is the old parish on which Worthing was built; its church is the mother church of the town. It was an old market under the Camois family, and is now a district of Worthing. In the picture we see large houses with garden walls of flint. Children wait on the pavement and road edge to be included in the photograph. Women in long skirts walk along, or wait on the opposite pavement. Two horse-drawn vehicles travel along the road. There are proper pavements with kerbstones, and the road surface is fairly smooth.

Broadwater, c1950 ▶
B221005
This is a much more recent view of this district of Worthing. Nearby there is a large old cemetery and chapel, with many graves of the wealthy. In the picture we can see that the motor age is beginning. The small trees planted near the kerb edge have not been allowed much exposed soil to grow in.

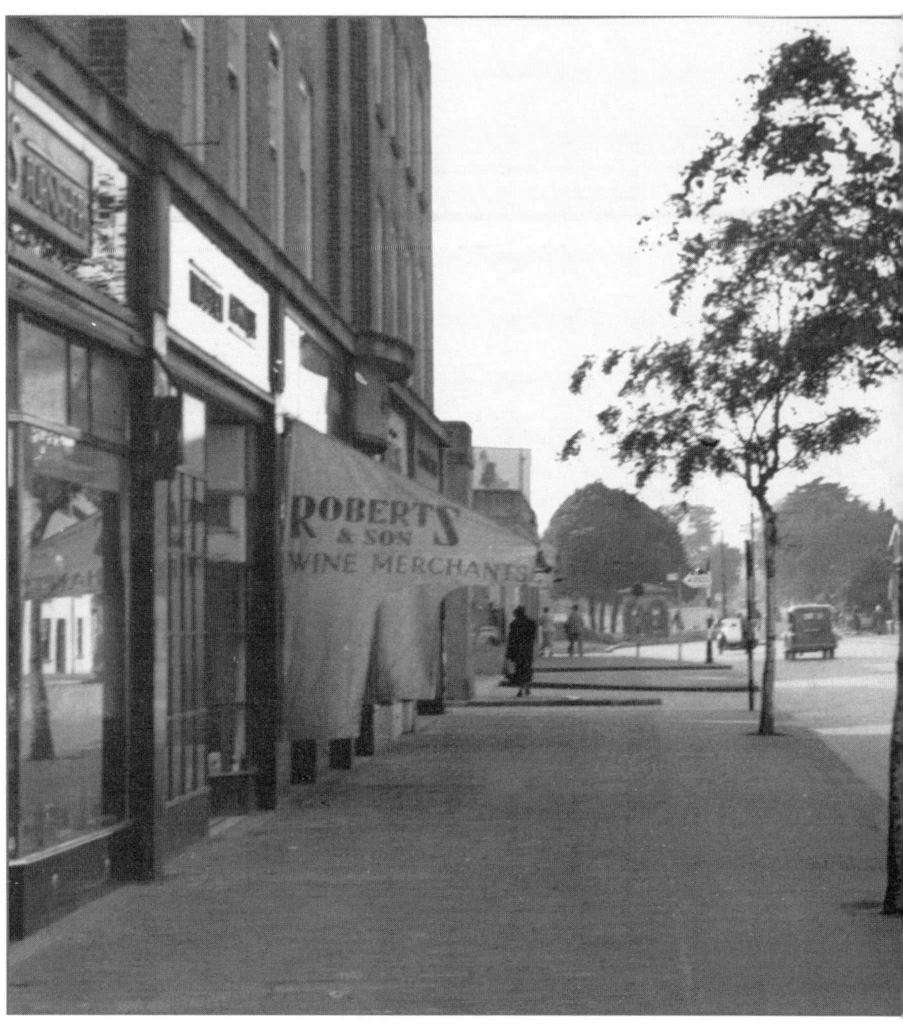

◀ **West Tarring, The Church 1890** 22721
The church of St Andrew was restored in 1885 and has a shingled broach spire. In the days of Queen Elizabeth I, the Admiralty commandeered the church tower as a lookout and signal station to watch the coast for defence against the Spanish Armada. The Old Palace was used as a stopover point for the archbishops of Canterbury. It is now the assembly hall of the Thomas A'Becket School. West Tarring is now part of the town of Worthing.

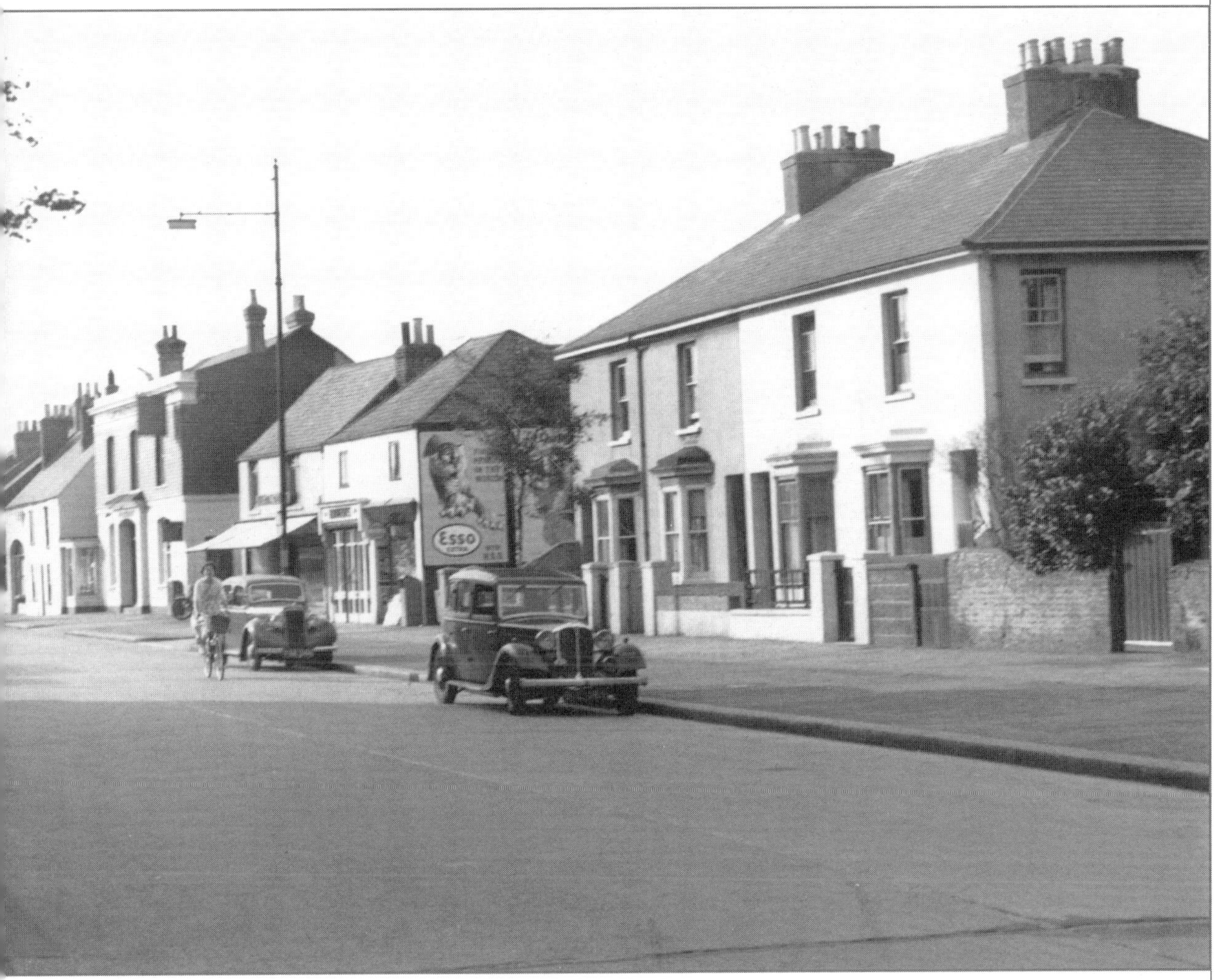

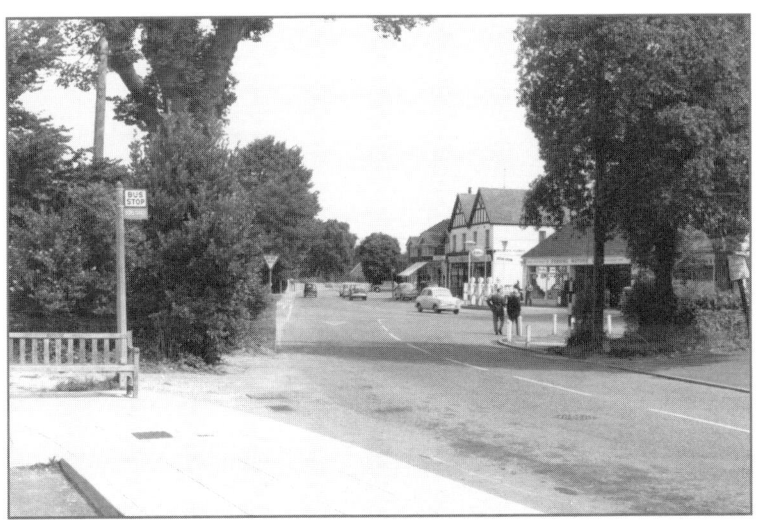

◀ **Ferring, The Village c1955** F130051
Ferring is a residential village near the sea. The Norman church keeps the registers of Kingston, a village long lost due to coastal erosion. Highdown Hill, 269 feet high, was a Roman dwelling place and Saxon burial ground. Here, too, is the Miller's Tomb. Local wind miller John Oliver built himself an inscribed tomb and a summerhouse close to his mill in 1766; he died in 1793, and was interred in his tomb. In the picture: In the picture we can see a bus stop sign on a concrete post, for Southdown route 106 only, Worthing to South Ferring. Marsh's stores and Ferring Motors' garage are on the opposite side of the road.

▼ **Ferring, Sea Lane c1960** F130016
On this road leading to the sea front, the cottage on the left has flint walls and a thatched roof. The front garden is decorated with staddle stones. These were formerly used to support small granary buildings off the ground, to help to keep vermin out. Wattle fencing panels are being used for garden screening.

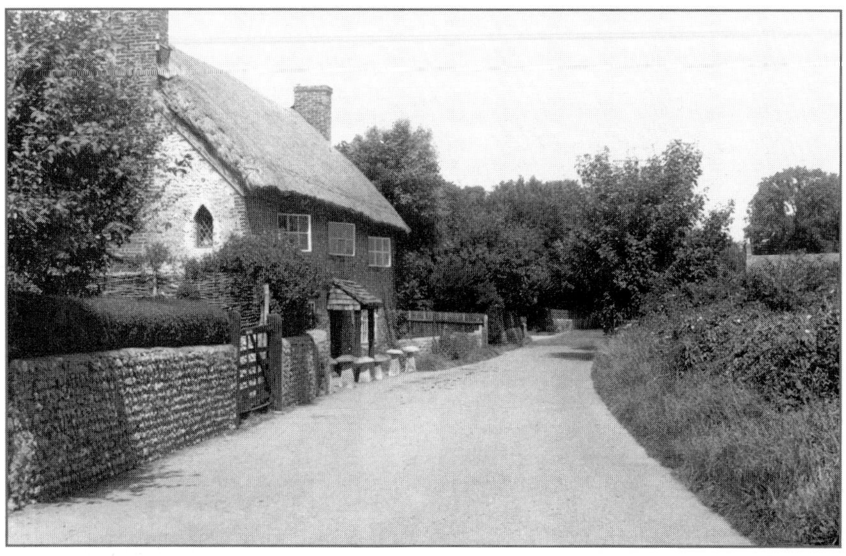

▼ **Ferring, The Greystoke Manor Hotel c1960** F130003
This hotel near the sea front has brick walls with flint gables and garden walling. The tall chimney pots are all the same size. A flint walled outbuilding has a corrugated steel roof.

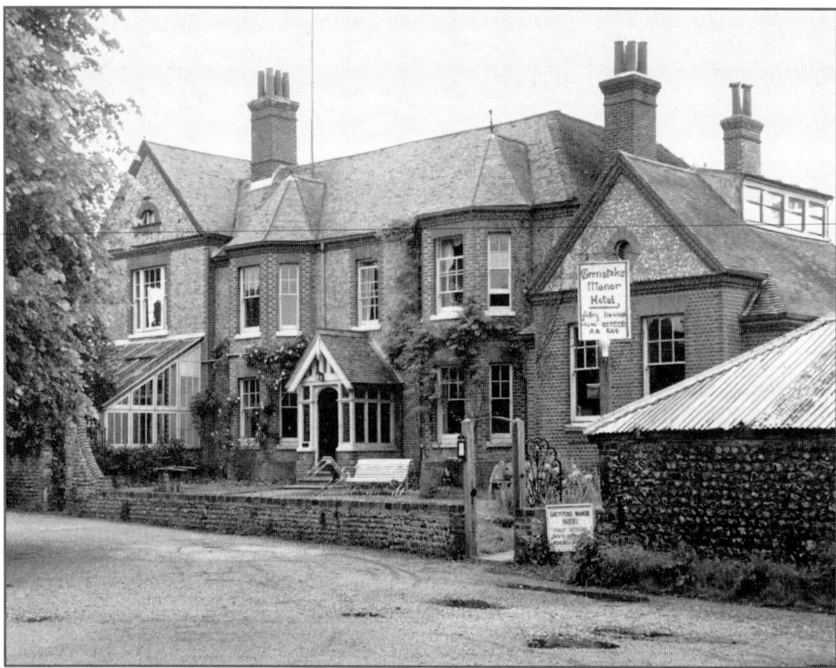

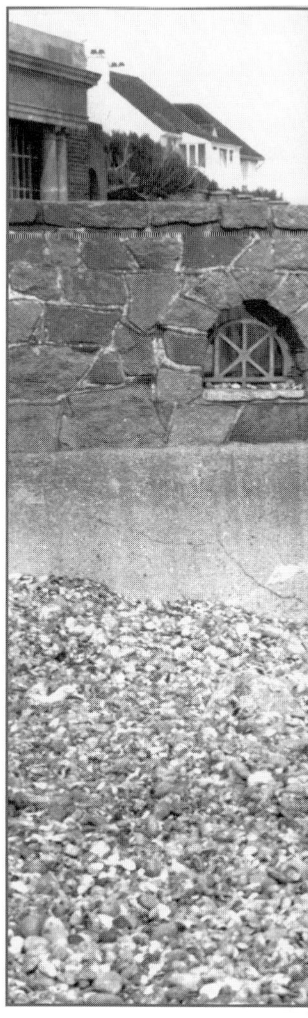

▲ **Angmering-on-Sea The Beach c1955**
A327039
Angmering-on-Sea is a modern residential area with a quiet beach. The photograph shows a typical shingle beach of large flint pebbles, wooden groyne sea defences and a concrete sea wall. The railway station is midway between Angmering and Angmering on Sea.

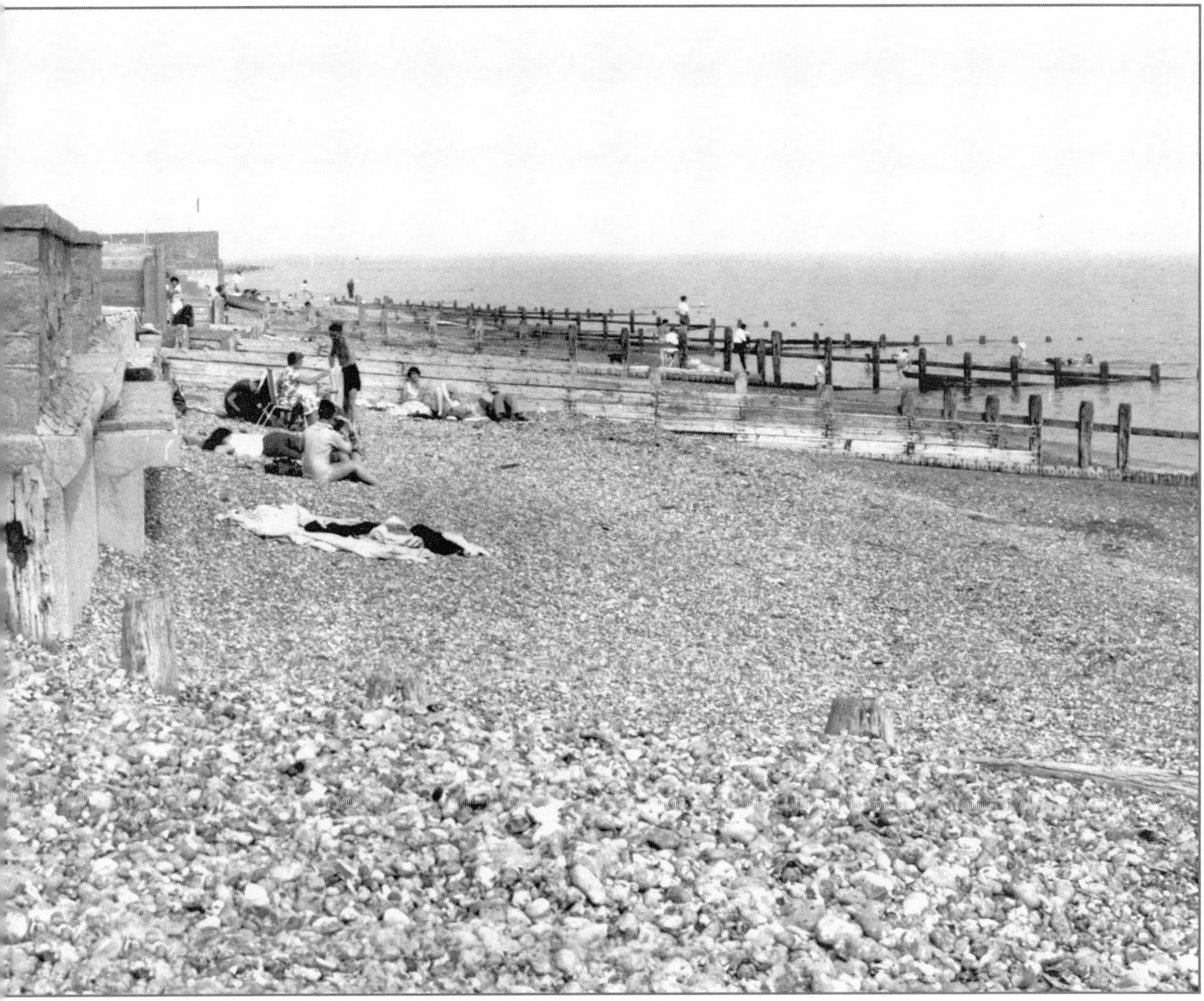

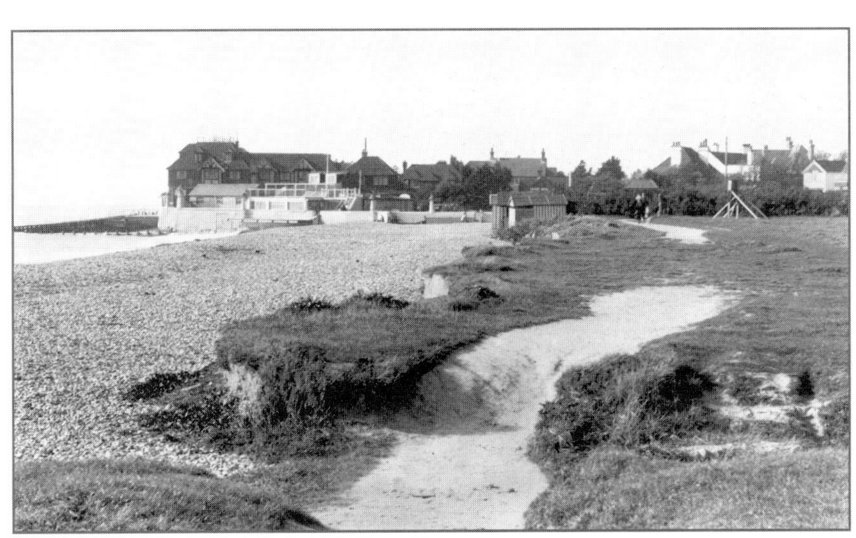

**◄ Angmering-on-Sea
The Foreshore c1960**

A327064

A shingle beach with sandy soil and grass forming the shoreline. The seawall and wooden groynes are in the distance. Beach huts await bathers and picnickers. The land in the background has been developed with many houses.

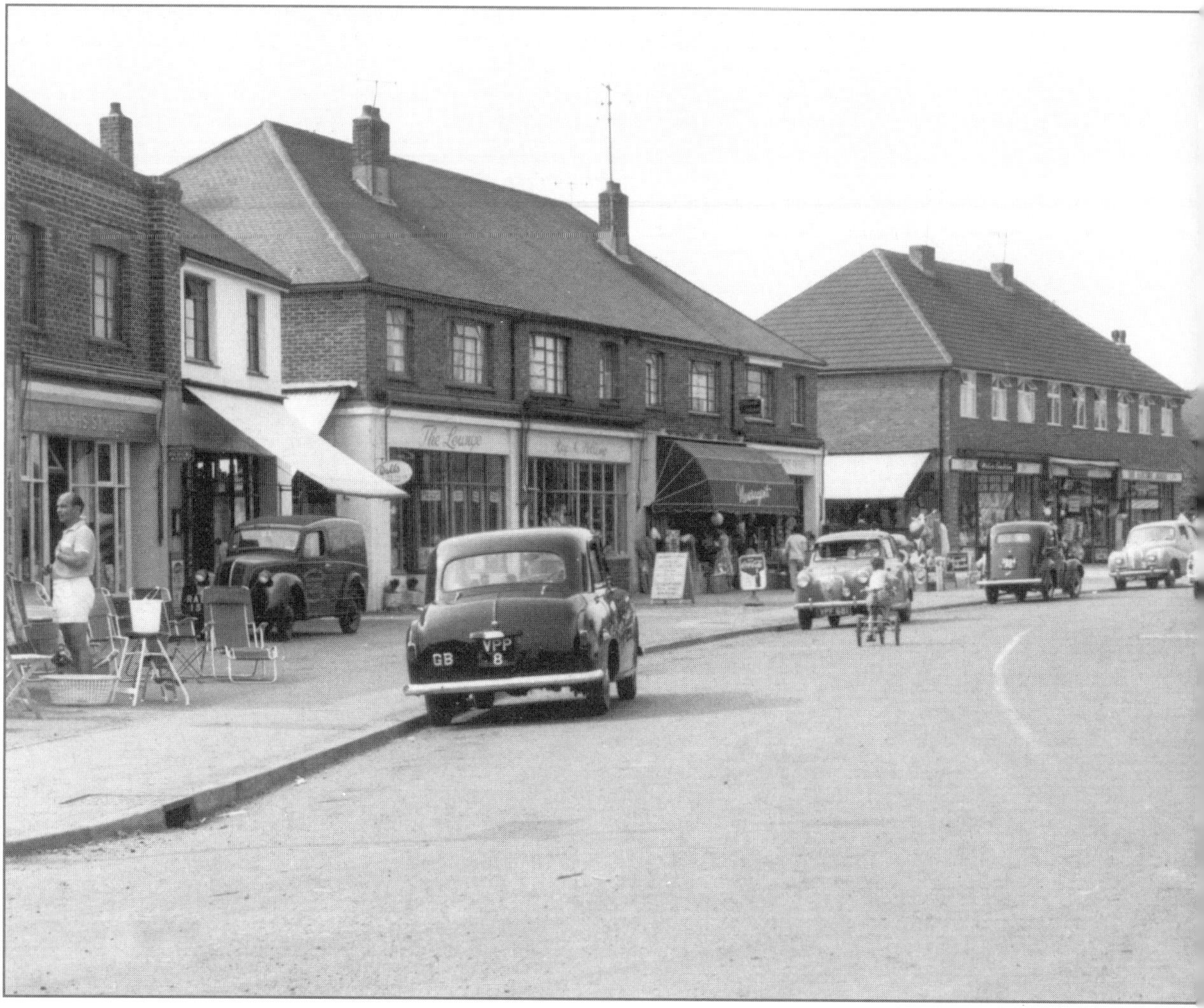

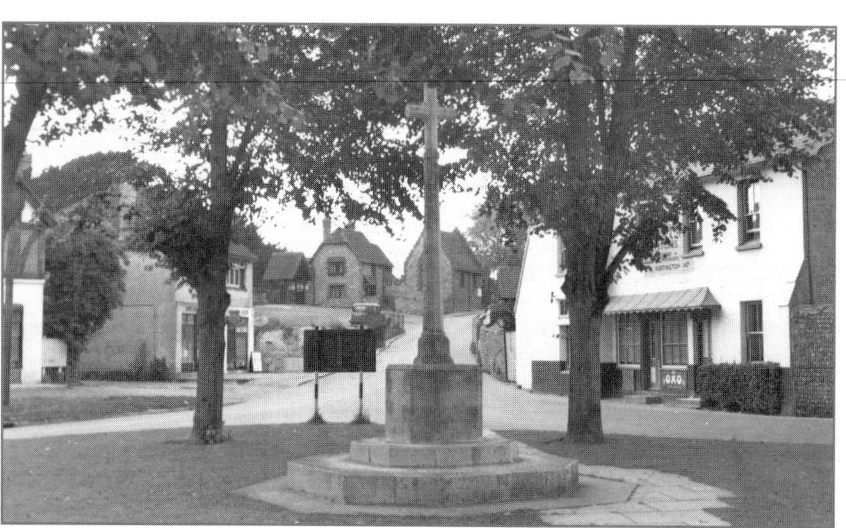

◀ **Angmering, The Village Green c1955** A52004
The great house was New Place; it has now been converted into cottages. It was the home of the Palmer family in the time of Henry VIII. Ecclesden Manor is a long, low Tudor-style house built in 1634. We are at the hub of the village, with the war memorial in the foreground. The Village Stores has a sign advertising Oxo on the shopfront. The scene is little different today.

◀ Angmering-on-Sea The Village c1955 A327036

A rapidly expanding village, just inland from the coastline. Here we see a parade of modern shops - on the left outdoor furniture is displayed outside a shop. The street scene has a range of 1950s vehicles, including a Morris van, and Hillman, Austin and Ford cars.

▼ Angmering, The Village c1960 A52008

The church of St Margaret was rebuilt in 1852 and has a tower dating from 1507, which is just visible through the trees. The Pigeon House is a medieval yeoman's house. A Roman villa and bath building, about one mile east of the church, were first excavated in 1819 and again more recently. Harrow Hill is an archaeological site with traces of an Iron Age hill-fort, a group of Neolithic flint mines and a Bronze Age farm enclosure. The scene today is little changed.

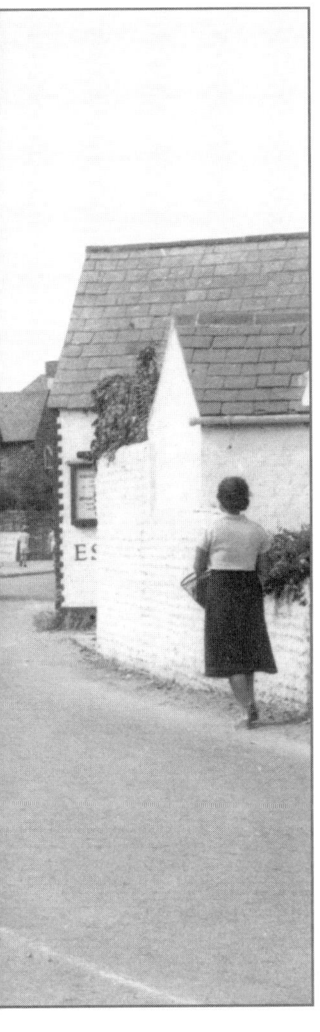

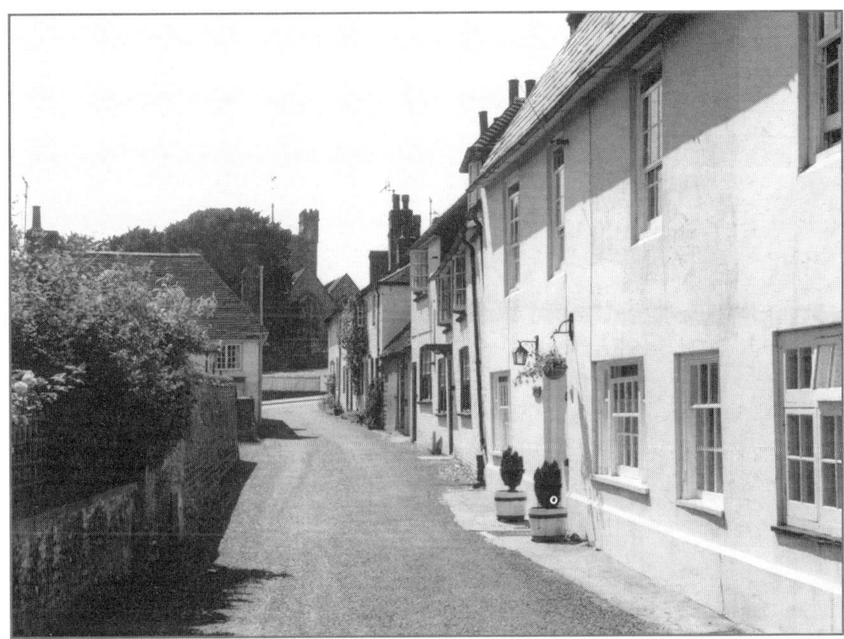

◀ Funtington The Village c1960

F160014

An isolated village of flint and brick cottages, to the west of Chichester. In the village are Adsdean, a gabled Tudor style house of around 1850, and the church of St Mary, built in 1859. Northbrook Watermill is in very flat country nearby. The Stores is seen next door to a thatched house and restaurant. The shop is now a house, although Halliday's restaurant is still trading.

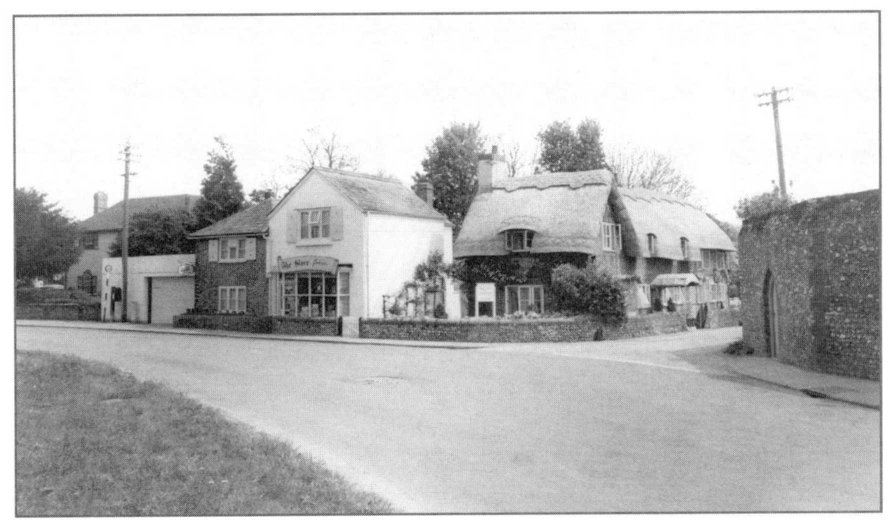

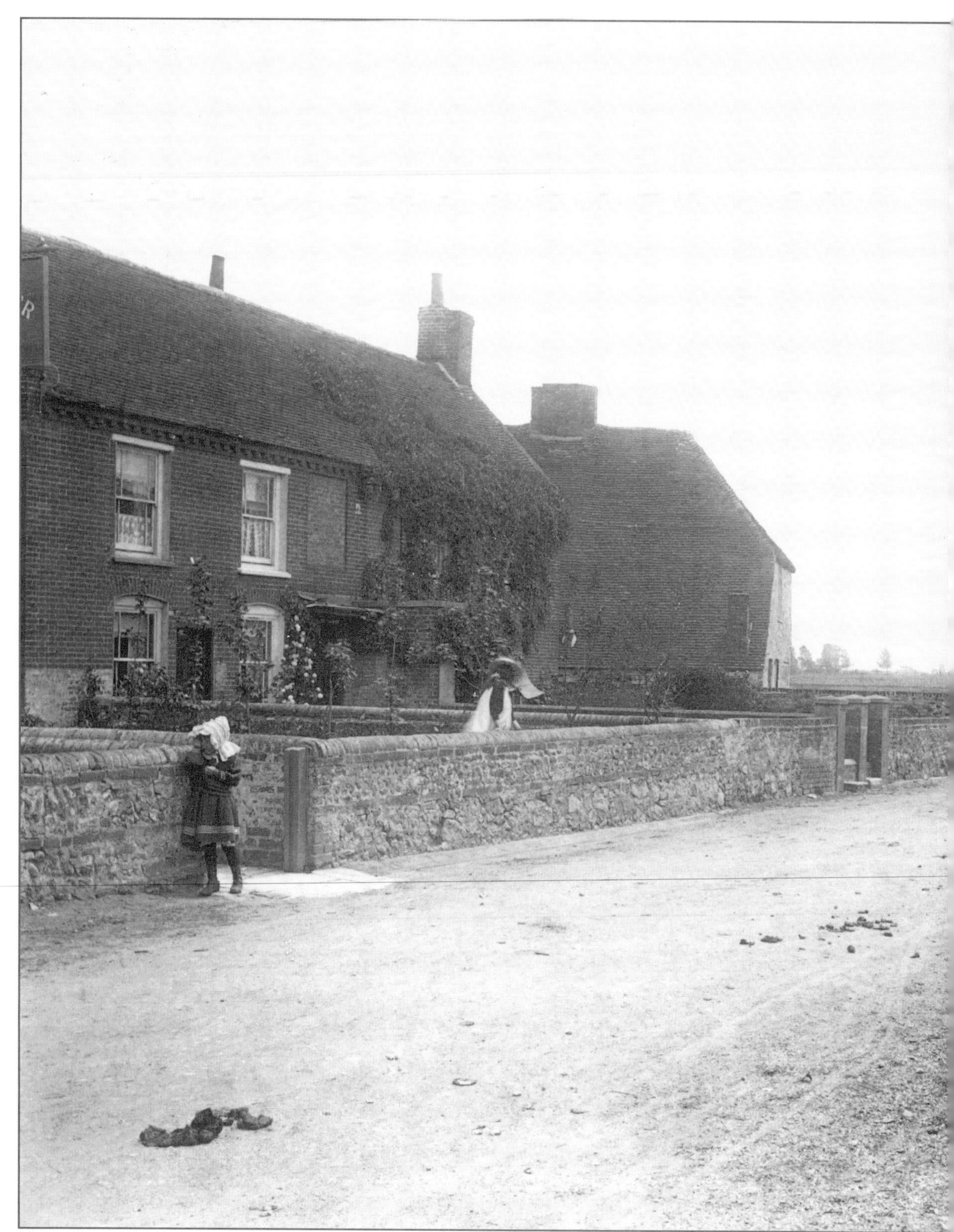

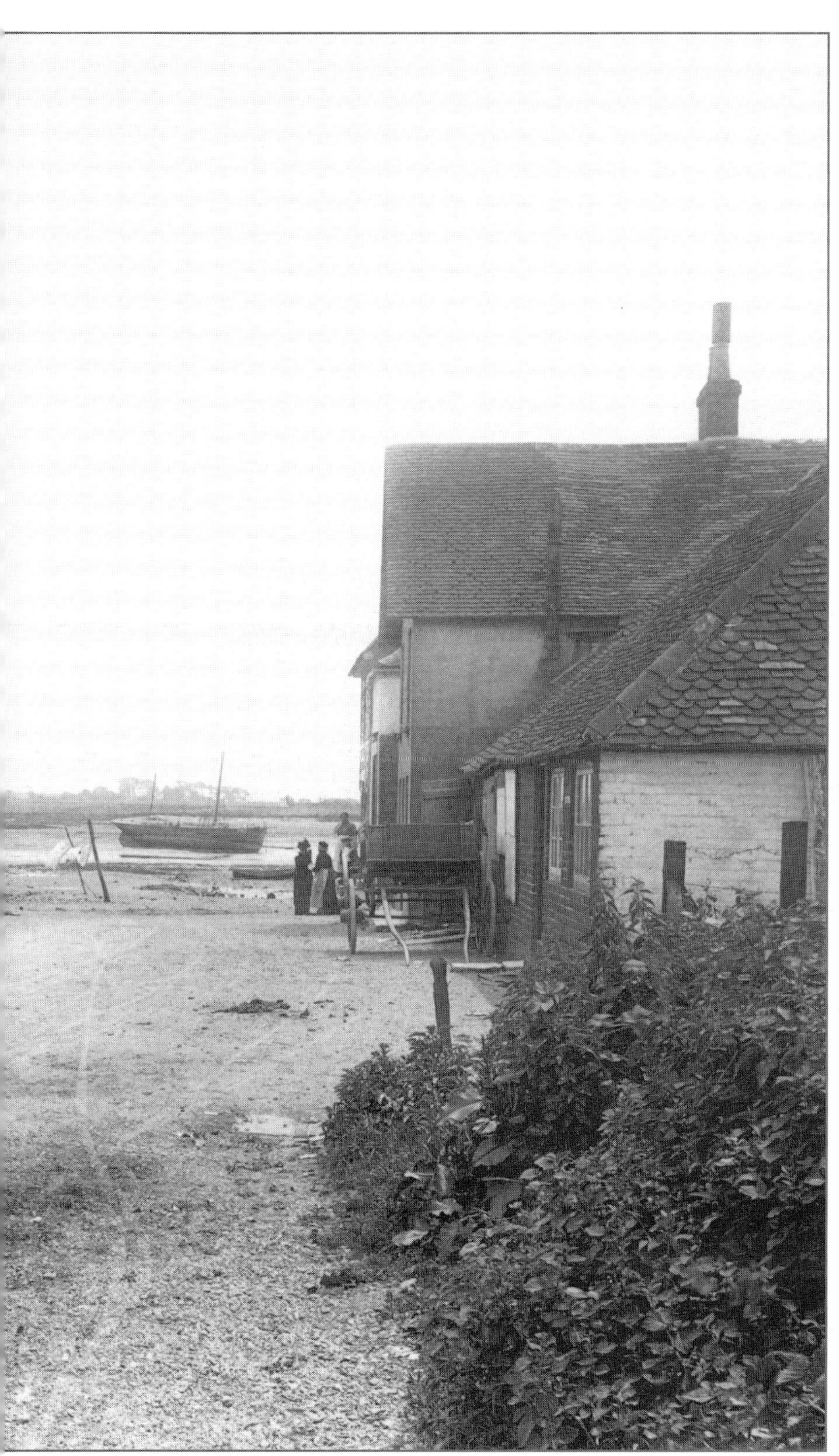

Bosham, The Village 1902 48336
A fishing village and yachting centre located on a creek of Chichester Harbour. A straight and wide road leading to the quay creates an impression of past importance. The Romans, the Saxons and the Vikings used the area for invasion. In later centuries fishing was an important industry. The roadway can flood at very high tides. A two-masted sailing ship lies in a mud berth, a washing line post leans on the beach and women in long skirts stand and look towards the harbour.

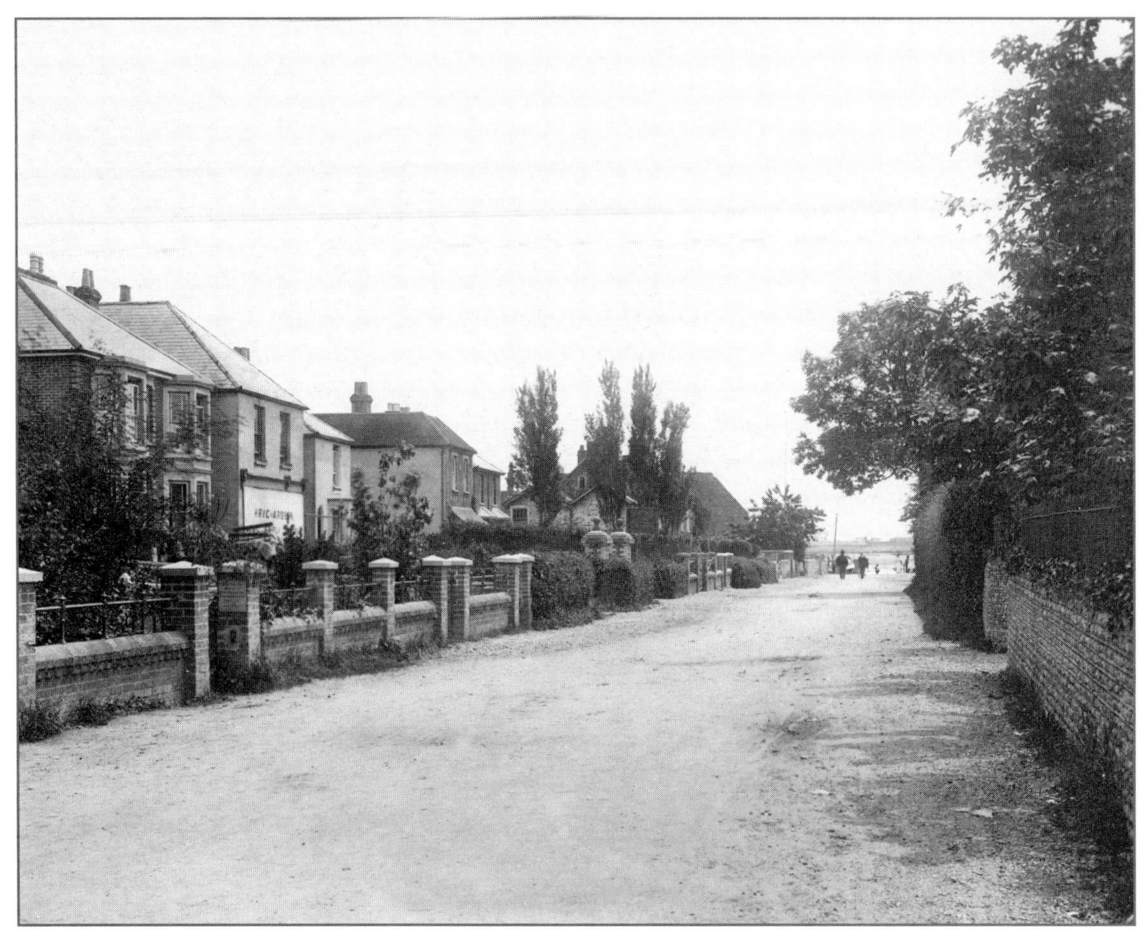

Bosham
The Village 1902 48335
Bosham was occupied by the Romans and invaded by the Danes,
who stole the church bells. King Canute had a palace here and
legend has it that this is where he attempted to command the
waves. In the photograph we are looking towards the quay, further
back along the same road we saw in 48336. The name
'Richardson' is on a sunblind over a shop front. The scene is still
recognisable today; the shops now cater to the tourist trade.

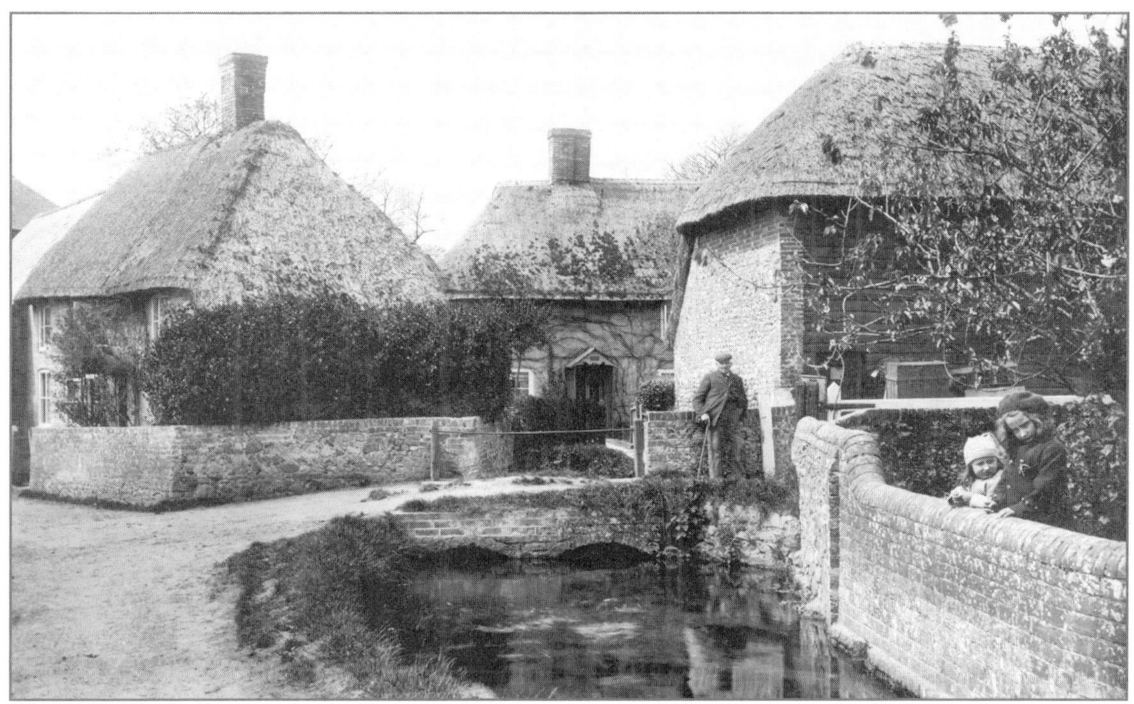

Bosham, The Village 1903 50908
This group of thatched cottages by the millstream are still recognisable today.

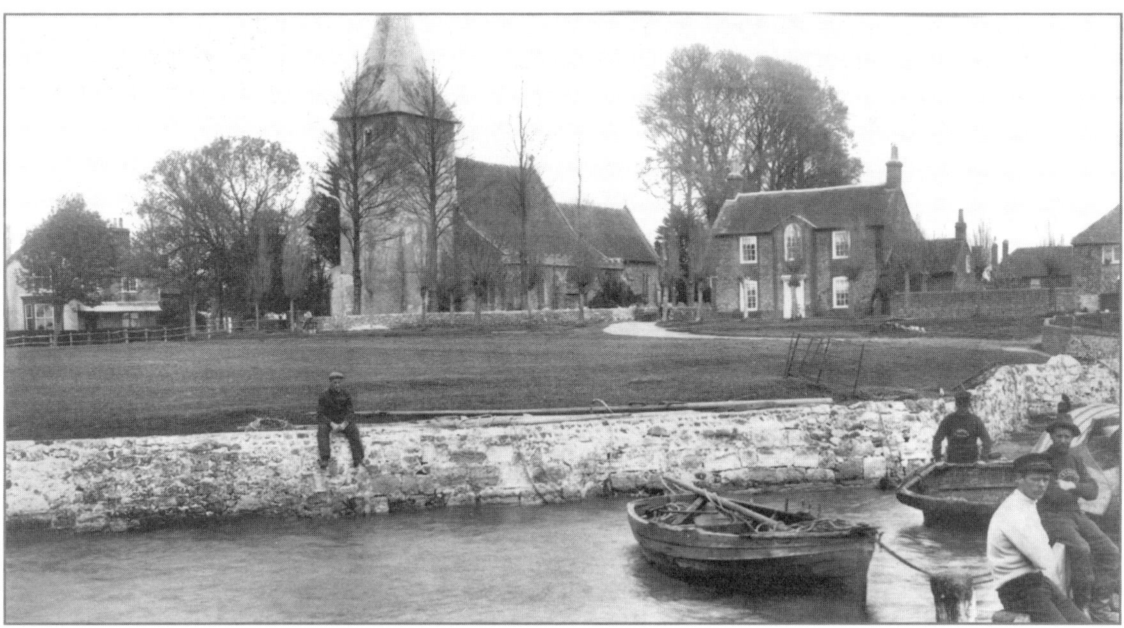

Bosham, The Church and the Green 1903 50919
A Roman basilica once occupied the site of the Green. The quay is in the foreground, with fishermen sitting around and tending their boats. Behind Quay Meadow stands the Saxon church of Holy Trinity with a wooden shingled broach spire. The original church is pictured on the Bayeux tapestry. Bosham was an important harbour in Anglo-Saxon times; King Harold II sailed from here on his way to Normandy.

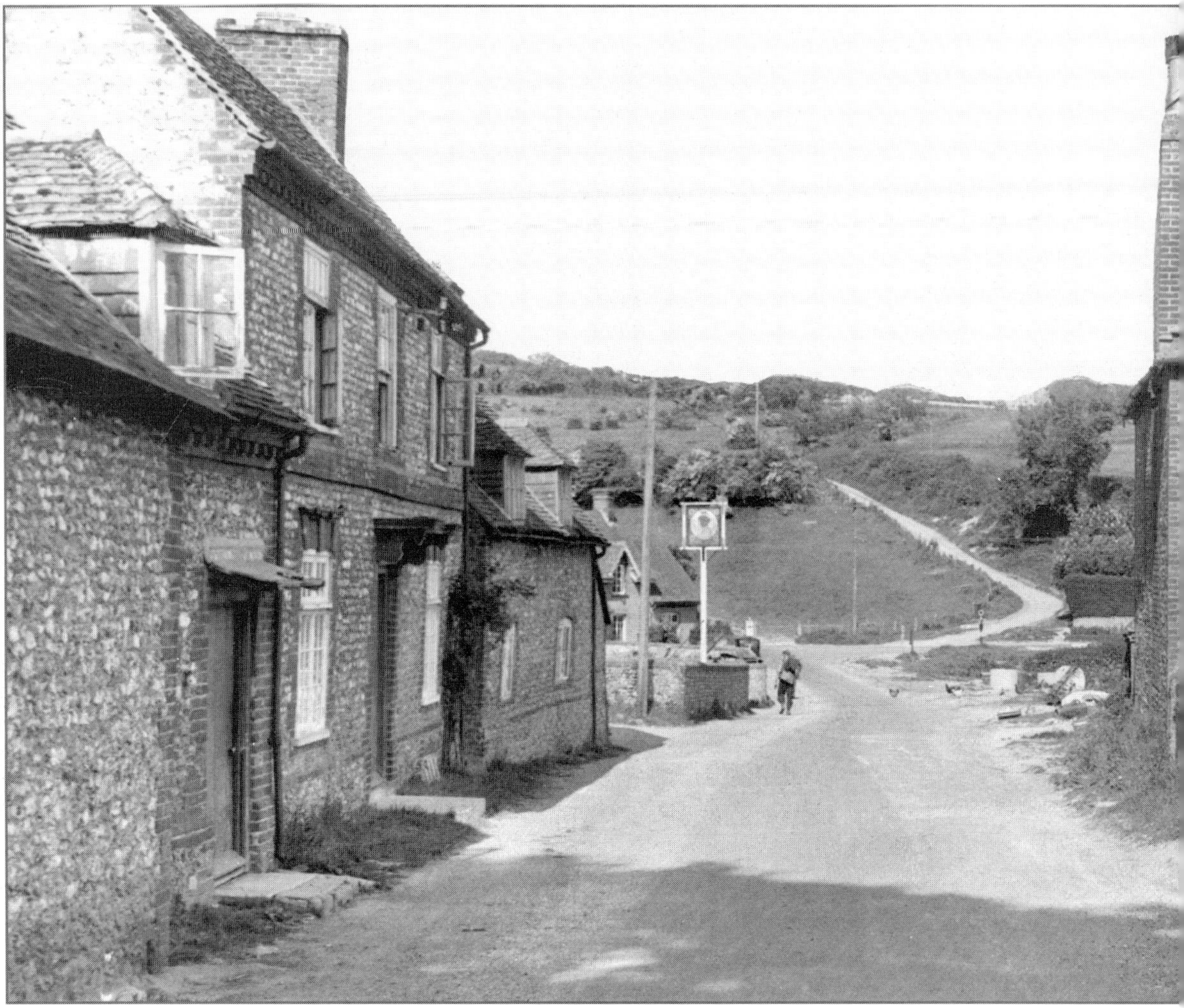

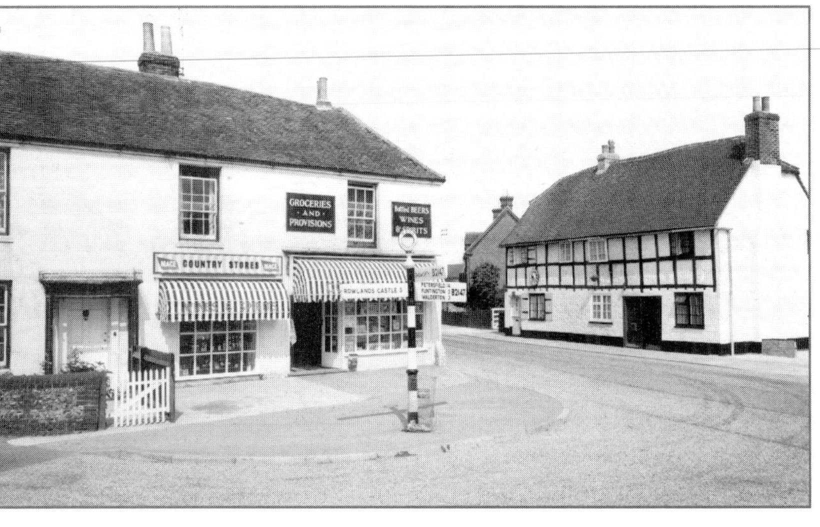

◄ Westbourne, The Square c1960 W613034

An old centre for the district that had a market close to the Hampshire border and the coast. The church of St John the Baptist has an avenue of yew trees. The Country Stores, a Mace shop complete with modern sunblinds, offers a wide range of supplies. A fine example of a West Sussex County Council signpost with cast iron post and circular ornamentation on the top stands on the pavement. The scene is still similar today, but the shop is a house agent's and the old signpost has been reduced.

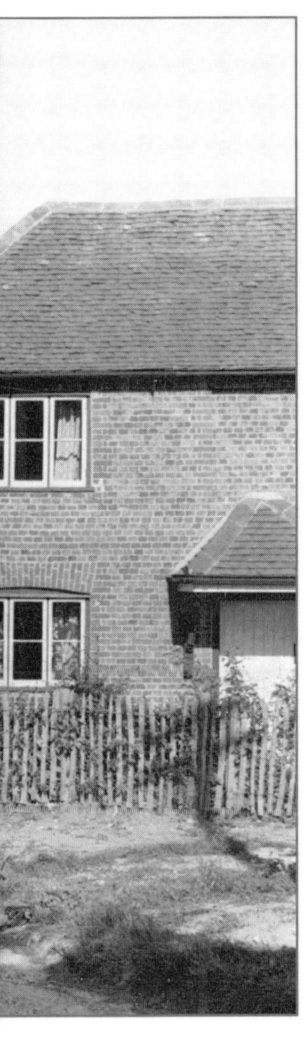

West Marden, The Village c1955 W614002

This sizeable hamlet on the Downs south of Harting has no church, but boasts some attractive flint cottages and fine scenery. There is plenty of history here: Bow Hill was a great Stone Age centre on the Downs and there is the site of a Roman villa nearby. A local mansion, Watergate House, is now demolished. The signboard of the Victoria Inn is visible to the left of the picture. The scene today is little changed.

Felpham, The Village 1903 50211

We are east of Bognor Regis. The poet and biographer William Hayley lived in the Turret. In 1800 he invited his poet friend William Blake to come and live in the village, where he stayed for four years. The medieval church of St Mary can be seen in the background of the picture. A four-wheeled cart is pulled by two horses in tandem and appears to be loaded with brushwood faggots; all of the action is halted whilst waiting patiently for the photographer. There is a fine flint garden wall in the foreground.

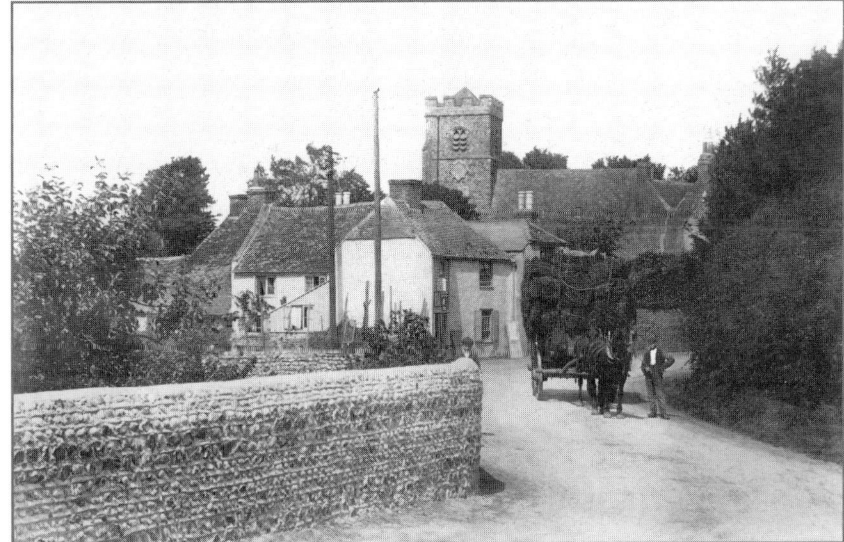

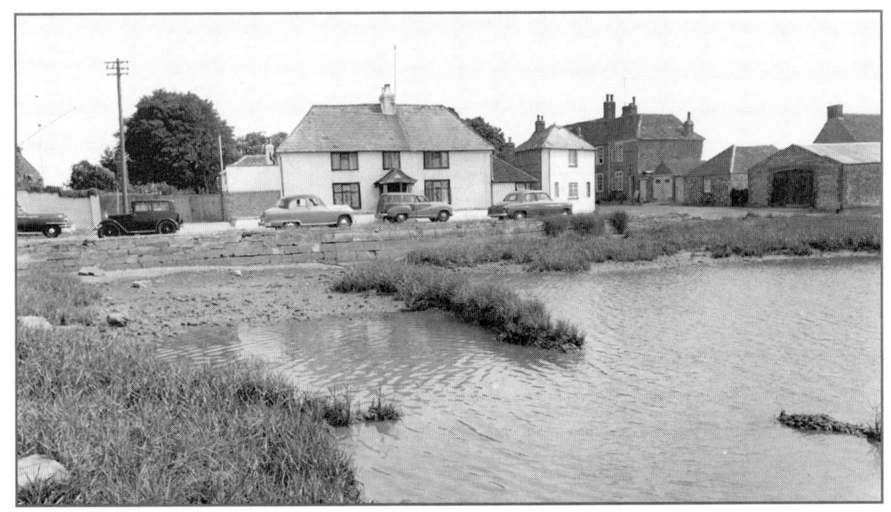

Sidlesham, The Quay c1960 S589162

Sidlesham is a hamlet near Pagham Harbour. The 13th-century church of St Mary is built of stone rubble, not the usual flint of the area. Mapson's Farm was built in 1796. At high tides the sea comes very close to the fronts of the buildings. A range of cars waits on the roadway - let us hope they are above the high water line.

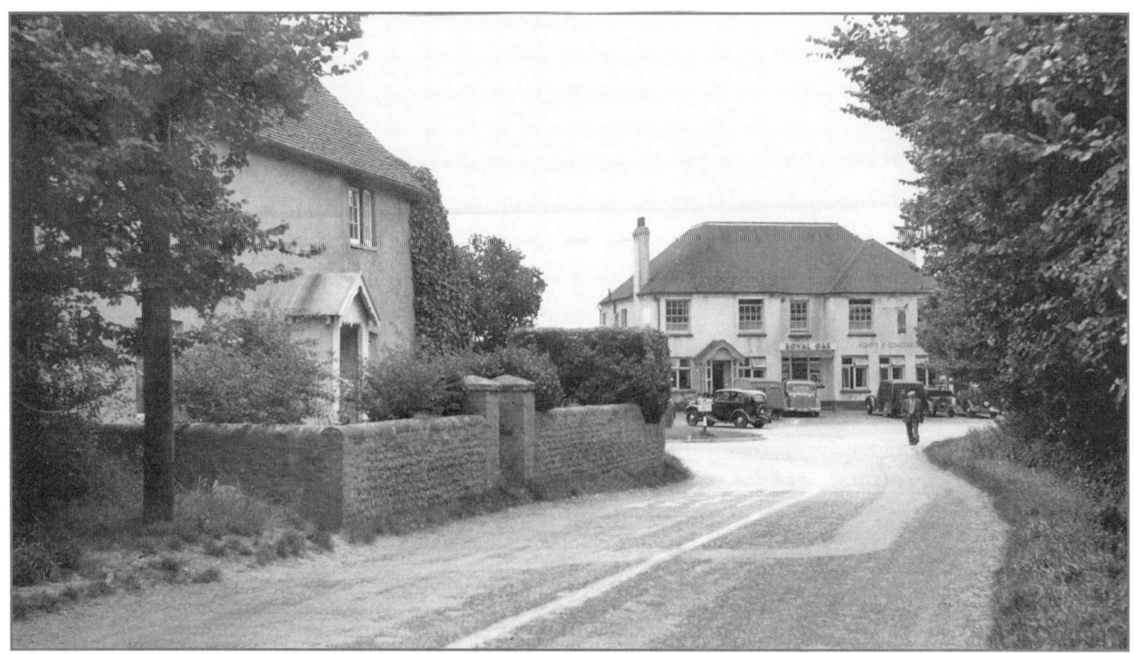

East Wittering, Church Road Corner c1950 E13010
The Witterings are seaside villages of bungalows, chalets and caravans on the Selsey peninsula, a flat area south of Chichester. The Norman church of the Assumption was rebuilt in 1875. The Royal Oak public house sold Henty and Constable ales. An interesting range of cars and vans occupy the car park.

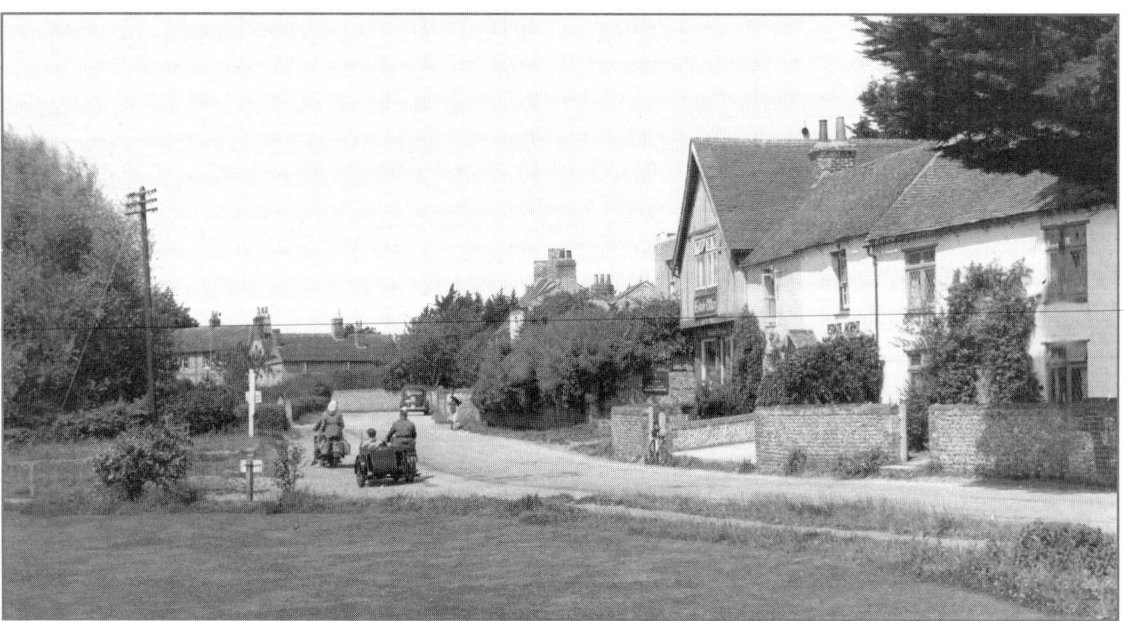

West Wittering, The Village Green c1955 W325008
West Wittering has some larger houses in residential areas that are ever expanding. The 11th-century church of St Peter and St Paul is heavily restored. Cakeham Manor House is a medieval palace of the Bishop of Chichester. The shop is an estate agent's, a sign of the expansion in the housing market at this quiet coastal resort. Old-style motorcyclists wait by the roadside - they are not wearing helmets or other modern safety equipment.

Index

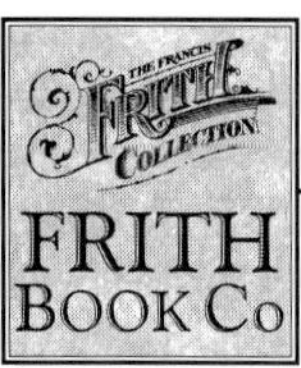

Frith Book Co Titles

www.francisfrith.co.uk

The Frith Book Company publishes over 100 new titles each year. A selection of those currently available are listed below. For latest catalogue please contact Frith Book Co.

Town Books 96pages, approx 100 photos. County and Themed Books 128pages, approx 150 photos (unless specified). All titles hardback laminated case and jacket except those indicated pb (paperback)

Amersham, Chesham & Rickmansworth (pb)	1-85937-340-2	£9.99	Dorset Churches	1-85937-172-8	£17.99
Ancient Monuments & Stone Circles	1-85937-143-4	£17.99	Dorset Coast (pb)	1-85937-299-6	£9.99
Aylesbury (pb)	1-85937-227-9	£9.99	Dorset Living Memories	1-85937-210-4	£14.99
Bakewell	1-85937-113-2	£12.99	Down the Severn	1-85937-118-3	£14.99
Barnstaple (pb)	1-85937-300-3	£9.99	Down the Thames (pb)	1-85937-278-3	£9.99
Bath (pb)	1-85937419-0	£9.99	Down the Trent	1-85937-311-9	£14.99
Bedford (pb)	1-85937-205-8	£9.99	Dublin (pb)	1-85937-231-7	£9.99
Berkshire (pb)	1-85937-191-4	£9.99	East Anglia (pb)	1-85937-265-1	£9.99
Berkshire Churches	1-85937-170-1	£17.99	East London	1-85937-080-2	£14.99
Blackpool (pb)	1-85937-382-8	£9.99	East Sussex	1-85937-130-2	£14.99
Bognor Regis (pb)	1-85937-431-x	£9.99	Eastbourne	1-85937-061-6	£12.99
Bournemouth	1-85937-067-5	£12.99	Edinburgh (pb)	1-85937-193-0	£8.99
Bradford (pb)	1-85937-204-x	£9.99	England in the 1880's	1-85937-331-3	£17.99
Brighton & Hove(pb)	1-85937-192-2	£8.99	English Castles (pb)	1-85937-434-4	£9.99
Bristol (pb)	1-85937-264-3	£9.99	English Country Houses	1-85937-161-2	£17.99
British Life A Century Ago (pb)	1-85937-213-9	£9.99	Essex (pb)	1-85937-270-8	£9.99
Buckinghamshire (pb)	1-85937-200-7	£9.99	Exeter	1-85937-126-4	£12.99
Camberley (pb)	1-85937-222-8	£9.99	Exmoor	1-85937-132-9	£14.99
Cambridge (pb)	1-85937-422-0	£9.99	Falmouth	1-85937-066-7	£12.99
Cambridgeshire (pb)	1-85937-420-4	£9.99	Folkestone (pb)	1-85937-124-8	£9.99
Canals & Waterways (pb)	1-85937-291-0	£9.99	Glasgow (pb)	1-85937-190-6	£9.99
Canterbury Cathedral (pb)	1-85937-179-5	£9.99	Gloucestershire	1-85937-102-7	£14.99
Cardiff (pb)	1-85937-093-4	£9.99	Great Yarmouth (pb)	1-85937-426-3	£9.99
Carmarthenshire	1-85937-216-3	£14.99	Greater Manchester (pb)	1-85937-266-x	£9.99
Chelmsford (pb)	1-85937-310-0	£9.99	Guildford (pb)	1-85937-410-7	£9.99
Cheltenham (pb)	1-85937-095-0	£9.99	Hampshire (pb)	1-85937-279-1	£9.99
Cheshire (pb)	1-85937-271-6	£9.99	Hampshire Churches (pb)	1-85937-207-4	£9.99
Chester	1-85937-090-x	£12.99	Harrogate	1-85937-423-9	£9.99
Chesterfield	1-85937-378-x	£9.99	Hastings & Bexhill (pb)	1-85937-131-0	£9.99
Chichester (pb)	1-85937-228-7	£9.99	Heart of Lancashire (pb)	1-85937-197-3	£9.99
Colchester (pb)	1-85937-188-4	£8.99	Helston (pb)	1-85937-214-7	£9.99
Cornish Coast	1-85937-163-9	£14.99	Hereford (pb)	1-85937-175-2	£9.99
Cornwall (pb)	1-85937-229-5	£9.99	Herefordshire	1-85937-174-4	£14.99
Cornwall Living Memories	1-85937-248-1	£14.99	Hertfordshire (pb)	1-85937-247-3	£9.99
Cotswolds (pb)	1-85937-230-9	£9.99	Horsham (pb)	1-85937-432-8	£9.99
Cotswolds Living Memories	1-85937-255-4	£14.99	Humberside	1-85937-215-5	£14.99
County Durham	1-85937-123-x	£14.99	Hythe, Romney Marsh & Ashford	1-85937-256-2	£9.99
Croydon Living Memories	1-85937-162-0	£9.99	Ipswich (pb)	1-85937-424-7	£9.99
Cumbria	1-85937-101-9	£14.99	Ireland (pb)	1-85937-181-7	£9.99
Dartmoor	1-85937-145-0	£14.99	Isle of Man (pb)	1-85937-268-6	£9.99
Derby (pb)	1-85937-367-4	£9.99	Isles of Scilly	1-85937-136-1	£14.99
Derbyshire (pb)	1-85937-196-5	£9.99	Isle of Wight (pb)	1-85937-429-8	£9.99
Devon (pb)	1-85937-297-x	£9.99	Isle of Wight Living Memories	1-85937-304-6	£14.99
Dorset (pb)	1-85937-269-4	£9.99	Kent (pb)	1-85937-189-2	£9.99

Available from your local bookshop or from the publisher

Title	ISBN	Price	Title	ISBN	Price
Kent Living Memories	1-85937-125-6	£14.99	Shrewsbury (pb)	1-85937-325-9	£9.99
Lake District (pb)	1-85937-275-9	£9.99	Shropshire (pb)	1-85937-326-7	£9.99
Lancaster, Morecambe & Heysham (pb)	1-85937-233-3	£9.99	Somerset	1-85937-153-1	£14.99
Leeds (pb)	1-85937-202-3	£9.99	South Devon Coast	1-85937-107-8	£14.99
Leicester	1-85937-073-x	£12.99	South Devon Living Memories	1-85937-168-x	£14.99
Leicestershire (pb)	1-85937-185-x	£9.99	South Hams	1-85937-220-1	£14.99
Lighthouses	1-85937-257-0	£17.99	Southampton (pb)	1-85937-427-1	£9.99
Lincolnshire (pb)	1-85937-433-6	£9.99	Southport (pb)	1-85937-425-5	£9.99
Liverpool & Merseyside (pb)	1-85937-234-1	£9.99	Staffordshire	1-85937-047-0	£12.99
London (pb)	1-85937-183-3	£9.99	Stratford upon Avon	1-85937-098-5	£12.99
Ludlow (pb)	1-85937-176-0	£9.99	Suffolk (pb)	1-85937-221-x	£9.99
Luton (pb)	1-85937-235-x	£9.99	Suffolk Coast	1-85937-259-7	£14.99
Maidstone	1-85937-056-x	£14.99	Surrey (pb)	1-85937-240-6	£9.99
Manchester (pb)	1-85937-198-1	£9.99	Sussex (pb)	1-85937-184-1	£9.99
Middlesex	1-85937-158-2	£14.99	Swansea (pb)	1-85937-167-1	£9.99
New Forest	1-85937-128-0	£14.99	Tees Valley & Cleveland	1-85937-211-2	£14.99
Newark (pb)	1-85937-366-6	£9.99	Thanet (pb)	1-85937-116-7	£9.99
Newport, Wales (pb)	1-85937-258-9	£9.99	Tiverton (pb)	1-85937-178-7	£9.99
Newquay (pb)	1-85937-421-2	£9.99	Torbay	1-85937-063-2	£12.99
Norfolk (pb)	1-85937-195-7	£9.99	Truro	1-85937-147-7	£12.99
Norfolk Living Memories	1-85937-217-1	£14.99	Victorian and Edwardian Cornwall	1-85937-252-x	£14.99
Northamptonshire	1-85937-150-7	£14.99	Victorian & Edwardian Devon	1-85937-253-8	£14.99
Northumberland Tyne & Wear (pb)	1-85937-281-3	£9.99	Victorian & Edwardian Kent	1-85937-149-3	£14.99
North Devon Coast	1-85937-146-9	£14.99	Vic & Ed Maritime Album	1-85937-144-2	£17.99
North Devon Living Memories	1-85937-261-9	£14.99	Victorian and Edwardian Sussex	1-85937 157 4	£14.99
North London	1-85937-206-6	£14.99	Victorian & Edwardian Yorkshire	1-85937-154-x	£14.99
North Wales (pb)	1-85937-298-8	£9.99	Victorian Seaside	1-85937-159-0	£17.99
North Yorkshire (pb)	1-85937-236-8	£9.99	Villages of Devon (pb)	1-85937-293-7	£9.99
Norwich (pb)	1-85937-194-9	£8.99	Villages of Kent (pb)	1-85937-294-5	£9.99
Nottingham (pb)	1-85937-324-0	£9.99	Villages of Sussex (pb)	1-85937-295-3	£9.99
Nottinghamshire (pb)	1-85937-187-6	£9.99	Warwickshire (pb)	1-85937-203-1	£9.99
Oxford (pb)	1-85937-411-5	£9.99	Welsh Castles (pb)	1-85937-322-4	£9.99
Oxfordshire (pb)	1-85937-430-1	£9.99	West Midlands (pb)	1-85937-289-9	£9.99
Peak District (pb)	1-85937-280-5	£9.99	West Sussex	1-85937-148-5	£14.99
Penzance	1-85937-069-1	£12.99	West Yorkshire (pb)	1-85937-201-5	£9.99
Peterborough (pb)	1-85937-219-8	£9.99	Weymouth (pb)	1-85937-209-0	£9.99
Piers	1-85937-237-6	£17.99	Wiltshire (pb)	1-85937-277-5	£9.99
Plymouth	1-85937-119-1	£12.99	Wiltshire Churches (pb)	1-85937-171-x	£9.99
Poole & Sandbanks (pb)	1-85937-251-1	£9.99	Wiltshire Living Memories	1-85937-245-7	£14.99
Preston (pb)	1-85937-212-0	£9.99	Winchester (pb)	1-85937-428-x	£9.99
Reading (pb)	1-85937-238-4	£9.99	Windmills & Watermills	1-85937-242-2	£17.99
Romford (pb)	1-85937-319-4	£9.99	Worcester (pb)	1-85937-165-5	£9.99
Salisbury (pb)	1-85937-239-2	£9.99	Worcestershire	1-85937-152-3	£14.99
Scarborough (pb)	1-85937-379-8	£9.99	York (pb)	1-85937-199-x	£9.99
St ALbans (pb)	1-85937-341-0	£9.99	Yorkshire (pb)	1-85937-186-8	£9.99
St Ives (pb)	1-85937415-8	£9.99	Yorkshire Living Memories	1-85937-166-3	£14.99
Scotland (pb)	1-85937-182-5	£9.99			
Scottish Castles (pb)	1-85937-323-2	£9.99			
Sevenoaks & Tunbridge	1-85937-057-8	£12.99			
Sheffield, South Yorks (pb)	1-85937-267-8	£9.99			

See Frith books on the internet www.francisfrith.co.uk

FRITH PRODUCTS & SERVICES

Francis Frith would doubtless be pleased to know that the pioneering publishing venture he started in 1860 still continues today. A hundred and forty years later, The Francis Frith Collection continues in the same innovative tradition and is now one of the foremost publishers of vintage photographs in the world. Some of the current activities include:

Interior Decoration

Today Frith's photographs can be seen framed and as giant wall murals in thousands of pubs, restaurants, hotels, banks, retail stores and other public buildings throughout the country. In every case they enhance the unique local atmosphere of the places they depict and provide reminders of gentler days in an increasingly busy and frenetic world.

Product Promotions

Frith products are used by many major companies to promote the sales of their own products or to reinforce their own history and heritage. Frith promotions have been used by Hovis bread, Courage beers, Scots Porage Oats, Colman's mustard, Cadbury's foods, Mellow Birds coffee, Dunhill pipe tobacco, Guinness, and Bulmer's Cider.

Genealogy and Family History

As the interest in family history and roots grows world-wide, more and more people are turning to Frith's photographs of Great Britain for images of the towns, villages and streets where their ancestors lived; and, of course, photographs of the churches and chapels where their ancestors were christened, married and buried are an essential part of every genealogy tree and family album.

Frith Products

All Frith photographs are available Framed or just as Mounted Prints and Posters (size 23 x 16 inches). These may be ordered from the address below. From time to time other products - Address Books, Calendars, Table Mats, etc - are available.

The Internet

Already twenty thousand Frith photographs can be viewed and purchased on the internet through the Frith websites and a myriad of partner sites.

For more detailed information on Frith companies and products, look at these sites:

www.francisfrith.co.uk
www.francisfrith.com
(for North American visitors)

See the complete list of Frith Books at:
www.francisfrith.co.uk
This web site is regularly updated with the latest list of publications from the Frith Book Company. If you wish to buy books relating to another part of the country that your local bookshop does not stock, you may purchase on-line.

For further information, trade, or author enquiries please contact us at the address below:
The Francis Frith Collection, Frith's Barn, Teffont, Salisbury, Wiltshire, England SP3 5QP.
Tel: +44 (0)1722 716 376 Fax: +44 (0)1722 716 881 Email: sales@francisfrith.co.uk

See Frith books on the internet www.francisfrith.co.uk

TO RECEIVE YOUR FREE MOUNTED PRINT

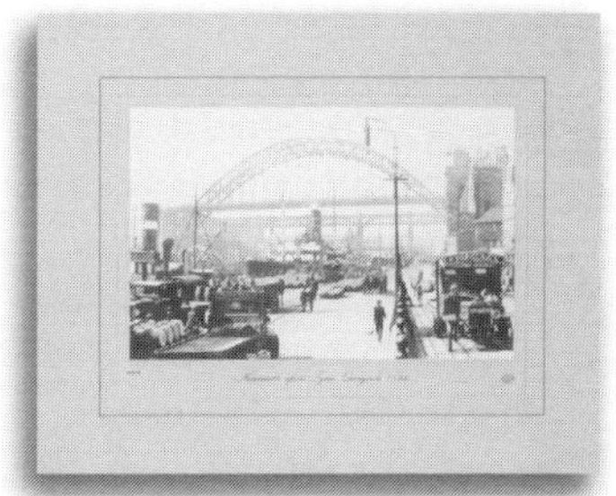

Mounted Print
Overall size 14 x 11 inches

Cut out this Voucher and return it with your remittance for £1.95 to cover postage and handling, to UK addresses. For overseas addresses please include £4.00 post and handling. Choose any photograph included in this book. Your SEPIA print will be A4 in size, and mounted in a cream mount with burgundy rule line, overall size 14 x 11 inches

Order additional Mounted Prints at HALF PRICE (only £7.49 each*)

If there are further pictures you would like to order, possibly as gifts for friends and family, purchase them at half price (no additional postage and handling required).

Have your Mounted Prints framed*

For an additional £14.95 per print you can have your chosen Mounted Print framed in an elegant polished wood and gilt moulding, overall size 16 x 13 inches (no additional postage and handling required).

*** IMPORTANT!**
These special prices are only available if ordered using the original voucher on this page (no copies permitted) and at the same time as your free Mounted Print, for delivery to the same address

---

Frith Collectors' Guild

From time to time we publish a magazine of news and stories about Frith photographs and further special offers of Frith products. If you would like 12 months FREE membership, please return this form.

Send completed forms to:
The Francis Frith Collection, Frith's Barn, Teffont, Salisbury, Wiltshire SP3 5QP

Voucher for **FREE** and Reduced Price Frith Prints

Picture no.	Page number	Qty	Mounted @ £7.49	Framed + £14.95	Total Cost
		1	**Free of charge***	£	£
			£7.49	£	£
			£7.49	£	£
			£7.49	£	£
			£7.49	£	£
			£7.49	£	£

Please allow 28 days for delivery	*** Post & handling**	**£1.95**
Book Title	**Total Order Cost**	**£**

Please do not photocopy this voucher. Only the original is valid, so please cut it out and return it to us.

I enclose a cheque / postal order for £ . . . . made payable to 'The Francis Frith Collection' OR please debit my Mastercard / Visa / Switch / Amex card *(credit cards please on all overseas orders)*

Number . . . .

Issue No (Switch only) . . . . Valid from (Amex/Switch) . . . .

Expires . . . . Signature . . . .

Name Mr/Mrs/Ms . . . .

Address . . . .

. . . .

. . . . Postcode . . . .

Daytime Tel No . . . .   Valid to 31/12/02

The Francis Frith Collectors' Guild

Please enrol me as a member for 12 months free of charge.

Name Mr/Mrs/Ms . . . .

Address . . . .

. . . .

. . . .

. . . . Postcode . . . .

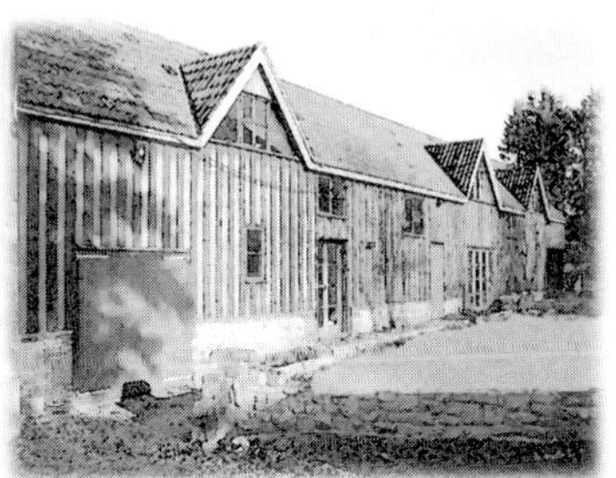

Would you like to find out more about Francis Frith?

We have recently recruited some entertaining speakers who are happy to visit local groups, clubs and societies to give an illustrated talk documenting Frith's travels and photographs. If you are a member of such a group and are interested in hosting a
presentation, we would love to hear from you.

Our speakers bring with them a small selection of our local town and county books, together with sample prints. They are happy to take orders. A small proportion of the order value is donated to the group who have hosted the presentation. The talks are therefore an excellent way of fundraising for small groups and societies.

Can you help us with information about any of the Frith photographs in this book?

We are gradually compiling an historical record for each of the photographs in the Frith archive. It is always fascinating to find out the names of the people shown in the pictures, as well as insights into the shops, buildings and other features depicted.

If you recognize anyone in the photographs in this book, or if you have information not already included in the author's caption, do let us know. We would love to hear from you, and will try to publish it in future books or articles.

Our production team

Frith books are produced by a small dedicated team at offices in the converted Grade II listed 18th-century barn at Teffont near Salisbury, illustrated above. Most have worked with the Frith Collection for many years. All have in common one quality: they have a passion for the Frith Collection. The team is constantly expanding, but currently includes:

Jason Buck, John Buck, Douglas Burns, Heather Crisp, Isobel Hall,
Rob Hames, Hazel Heaton, Peter Horne, James Kinnear, Tina Leary,
Eliza Sackett, Terence Sackett, Sandra Sanger, Shelley Tolcher, Susanna Walker,
Clive Wathen and Jenny Wathen.